Mastering SEO Strategies for the Modern Web

Boost Visibility, Drive Traffic, and Dominate Search Rankings with Proven SEO Strategies to Accelerate Business Growth

Michael Van Den Reym

www.orangeava.com

First Published: December 2024

Published By: Orange Education Pvt Ltd, AVA®

Address: 9, Daryaganj, Delhi, 110002, India

275 New North Road Islington Suite 1314 London,

N1 7AA, United Kingdom

ISBN (PBK): 978-93-48107-97-8

ISBN (E-BOOK): 978-93-48107-92-3

About the Author

Michael Van Den Reym is an SEO-expert with a data-driven approach and a passion for helping businesses grow their online presence.

His journey with the internet began in 2001, when he started building websites, sparking a lasting love for all things digital. This passion led him to pursue a master's degree in applied economics, specializing in marketing and ICT. During his studies, he created an online survey platform, with over 200000 users, mainly driven by SEO traffic. In 2008, he entered the professional world as an SEO specialist, marking the beginning of a career dedicated to digital marketing and analytics. Michael worked as a domain lead in SEO and innovation at iO, the largest digital agency in Belgium.

Michael collaborates with entrepreneurs, startups, and scaleups, offering data-driven SEO services designed to drive impactful results. He is passionate about exploring new technologies and methodologies that can enhance the effectiveness of SEO strategies. This involves staying informed about emerging tools and platforms, as well as embracing creative solutions that help his clients stand out in a competitive market.

Michael focuses on results that directly contribute to clients' business growth. He takes time to understand their unique goals and challenges, then crafts tailored strategies that maximize their online visibility and engagement.

In his free time, Michael enjoys staying active by participating in sports such as cycling and running. He also has a passion for reading, which allows him to continuously learn and explore new ideas.

As a dedicated learner and advocate for the SEO community, Michael draws inspiration from various platforms and conferences. He is actively involved in educating others about the latest trends in digital marketing and analytics. Michael has shared his insights as a speaker at prominent conferences, including SEO Benelux, MeasureCamp, MeasureFest, BrightonSEO, and the International Search Summit.

This book reflects his commitment to knowledge sharing.

About the Technical Reviewer

Kaushal is a seasoned SEO expert with over two decades of experience. He is the founder and CEO of *Infidigit, Inc.*, an AI-enabled digital growth partner for 200+ brands worldwide, and *Infigrowth*, an SEO tool designed to accelerate SEO growth. Combining a data-driven approach with GenAI technologies and innovative solutions, Kaushal and his team of 170 digital marketers have won over 60 awards.

Kaushal has conducted workshops on SEO for over 10,000 people and is a regular columnist at various publications. He has been recognized as one of the top 100 digital influencers by YourStory. A passionate advocate for sustainability, Kaushal has contributed to the organic growth of more than 16000 trees.

Acknowledgements

I would like to take a moment to express my gratitude to a few key people and communities who have supported me throughout the journey of writing this book. First and foremost, I want to thank my parents. Their support and encouragement have been a source of strength for me, inspiring me to pursue my passions with confidence.

I also want to extend my appreciation to my former colleagues at iO. Their insights and collaboration have greatly enriched my understanding of the digital landscape and have played a vital role in shaping my writing. The teamwork we shared provided invaluable perspectives that not only influenced this book but also helped shape me as a person.

Additionally, I am thankful to the entire SEO community, including organizations like SEO Benelux, BrightonSEO, and SEO Mastermind. Their commitment to organizing inspiring events and sharing knowledge has fueled my passion for this field and inspired me for writing this book.

Finally, I want to express my sincere appreciation to the publisher. Their dedication to bringing this book to life has been crucial in helping it reach its fullest potential. Thank you all for your invaluable contributions; this book would not have been possible without your support.

Preface

This book is organized into several chapters, each focusing on an essential aspect of SEO. We will begin with the foundational SEO tasks before moving into three strategic chapters that align SEO with your business strategy. Additionally, we will explore the latest trends and effective reporting techniques.

As you progress through the book, you will gain confidence in implementing SEO correctly. Each chapter provides clear, actionable insights, helping you to understand not only the necessary SEO actions but also how these efforts can significantly impact their business results.

Chapter 1. Introduction to SEO: This chapter introduces the fundamental concepts of SEO and explains its importance for businesses in the digital age. It explores what SEO is, the history of Google and other search engines, and how their evolution impacts search engine optimization. Additionally, it discusses key ranking factors and how effective SEO can deliver significant ROI for businesses.

Chapter 2. Indexation: In this chapter, we will cover how search engines index websites and the essential steps to ensure your site gets indexed. Key topics include crawling, sitemaps, robots.txt, HTTP status codes, and best practices for redirecting and migrating content. Tools such as Google Search Console and XML sitemaps will be highlighted for practical application.

Chapter 3. Keyword Research: This chapter focuses on the critical process of keyword research. You will learn techniques to identify relevant keywords and categorize them effectively

Chapter 4. Copywriting for SEO: In this chapter, you will discover how to create SEO-friendly content. We will discuss the importance of quality content, the role of title tags and meta descriptions, and how to balance keyword density with user intent.

Chapter 5. Links: This chapter teaches you how to build a strong backlink profile, distinguish between good and bad links, forming a link building strategy and optimize internal linking.

Chapter 6. Local SEO: Focusing on local SEO, this chapter outlines how to optimize your Google Business Profile, manage reviews, and target local keywords effectively. You will learn best practices to enhance your visibility in local searches.

Chapter 7. Business Strategy and SEO: This chapter aligns SEO with your business goals. It discusses how to integrate SEO into your overall business strategy and how to work with business stakeholders.

Chapter 8. Content Strategy and SEO: You will learn to create a content strategy that supports SEO in this chapter. Topics include types of content, content audits and effective content planning.

Chapter 9. Technical SEO Strategy: This chapter dives into technical SEO, covering page speed, Core Web Vitals, structured data, and technical SEO audits. We discuss auditing techniques and stakeholder management for technical SEO.

Chapter 10. SEO Trends: Here, we will explore emerging SEO trends, including the role of AI, zero-click results, and how social media and video impact SEO strategies. This chapter will help you stay ahead in the evolving SEO landscape.

Chapter 11. SEO Reporting: In the final chapter, we will discuss measuring and reporting on SEO performance. You will learn about key performance indicators (KPIs), data sources, and how to communicate your SEO results effectively.

Get a Free eBook

We hope you are enjoying your recently purchased book! Your feedback is incredibly valuable to us, and to all other readers looking for great books.

If you found this book helpful or enjoyable, we would truly appreciate it, if you could take a moment to leave a short review with a 5 star rating on Amazon. It helps us grow, and lets other readers discover our books.

As a thank you, we would love to send you a free digital copy of this book, and a **30%** discount code on your next cart value on our official websites:

www.orangeava.com

www.orangeava.in (For Indian Subcontinent)

☑ **Here's how:**

Leave a review for the book on Amazon.

Take a screenshot of your review, and send an email to **info@orangeava.com** (it can be just the confirmation screen).

Once, we receive your screenshot, we will send you the digital file, within 24 hours.

Thank you so much for your support – it means a lot to us!

Colored Images

Please follow the links or scan the QR codes to download the ***Images*** of the book:

You can find code bundles of our books on our official Github Repository. Go to the following link to and QR code to explore the further:

https://github.com/orgs/ava-orange-education/repositories

Please follow the link to download the Colored Images of the book:
https://rebrand.ly/b59530

In case there's an update to the code, it will be updated on the existing GitHub repository.

Errata

We take immense pride in our work at **Orange Education Pvt Ltd,** and follow best practices to ensure the accuracy of our content to provide an indulging reading experience to our subscribers. Our readers are our mirrors, and we use their inputs to reflect and improve upon human errors, if any, that may have occurred during the publishing processes involved. To let us maintain the quality and help us reach out to any readers who might be having difficulties due to any unforeseen errors, please write to us at :

errata@orangeava.com

Your support, suggestions, and feedback are highly appreciated.

DID YOU KNOW

Did you know that Orange Education Pvt Ltd offers eBook versions of every book published, with PDF and ePub files available? You can upgrade to the eBook version at **www.orangeava.com** and as a print book customer, you are entitled to a discount on the eBook copy. Get in touch with us at: **info@orangeava.com** for more details.

At **www.orangeava.com**, you can also read a collection of free technical articles, sign up for a range of free newsletters, and receive exclusive discounts and offers on AVA® Books and eBooks.

PIRACY

If you come across any illegal copies of our works in any form on the internet, we would be grateful if you would provide us with the location address or website name. Please contact us at **info@orangeava.com** with a link to the material.

ARE YOU INTERESTED IN AUTHORING WITH US?

If there is a topic that you have expertise in, and you are interested in either writing or contributing to a book, please write to us at **business@orangeava.com**. We are on a journey to help developers and tech professionals to gain insights on the present technological advancements and innovations happening across the globe and build a community that believes Knowledge is best acquired by sharing and learning with others. Please reach out to us to learn what our audience demands and how you can be part of this educational reform. We also welcome ideas from tech experts and help them build learning and development content for their domains.

REVIEWS

Please leave a review. Once you have read and used this book, why not leave a review on the site that you purchased it from? Potential readers can then see and use your unbiased opinion to make purchase decisions. We at Orange Education would love to know what you think about our products, and our authors can learn from your feedback. Thank you!

For more information about Orange Education, please visit **www.orangeava.com**.

Table of Contents

1. **Introduction to SEO** **1**
Introduction 1
Structure 1
Definition of SEO 1
Importance of SEO 4
History of Google 6
How Google Works - Ranking Factors 9
SEO as an Investment 11
Compounding Returns 12
Calculating SEO ROI 13
Conclusion 15
2. **Indexation** **16**
Introduction 16
Structure 16
Tracking Page Count for Indexing 16
Setting Up Search Console 17
Status Code and Indexation 19
Google Crawling and Indexation Process 20
`Sitemap.xml` File 23
`Robots.txt` File 25
Optimizing Crawl Budget with `Robots.txt` 27
Duplicate Content 28
Metatags for Indexation 30
Advanced Topics 31
Solving the Indexation Puzzle 32
Conclusion 33
3. **Keyword Research** **34**
Introduction 34
Structure 34
Goals of Keyword Research 35

Keyword Types ... 37
Keyword Research Briefing ... 38
Collecting Keywords ... 40
Categorizing Keywords ... 42
SERP Analysis ... 45
Social Media and YouTube Keyword Research ... 46
SEA versus SEO Keyword Research ... 49
B2B Keyword Research ... 51
Conclusion ... 53

4. Copywriting for SEO ... 54

Introduction ... 54
Structure ... 55
Importance of Quality Content ... 55
Metatags Optimization ... 56
Keyword Density versus Keyword Intent ... 58
Topics and Clusters ... 61
Defining Topic Cluster Structure ... 61
Benefits of Topic Cluster Model ... 62
Real-World Example ... 62
Copywriting Techniques for SEO ... 63
Headlines and Subheadings are Very Important ... 63
Bullet Points: Making Information Easy to Read ... 64
Long-Tail Keywords: Be Specific to Attract the Right Audience ... 64
Length of Your Articles ... 64
Understanding the Power of Questions in SEO ... 65
Storytelling for SEO ... 66
E-E-A-T Optimization ... 69
Search Quality Rater Guidelines ... 71
Data-Driven Copywriting ... 71
Using SurferSEO ... 73
Conclusion ... 73

5. Links **75**

Introduction 75

Structure 75

Optimizing Internal Linking 75

Backlink Types 78

Advantages of Backlinks 80

The Importance of Backlink Quality 81

Backlink Audits and Maintenance 83

Link Building Techniques 86

Brand Authority Strategy for Link Building 88

Case Studies on Link Building 91

Link Building Reporting 92

Conclusion 94

6. Local SEO **96**

Introduction 96

Structure 96

Local SEO and the Map Pack 96

Importance of Local SEO 98

Local SEO Keywords and Rankings 99

Local Web Page Optimization 101

Google Business Profile Optimization 102

Attracting Reviews on Google Business Profile 105

Importance of Review Quantity 105

Getting More GBP Reviews 106

Managing Reviews 106

Linkbuilding for Local SEO 108

Other Platforms 109

Optimization 110

Bing Places for Business 110

Monitoring and Reporting Local SEO 111

Conclusion 112

7. Business Strategy and SEO **114**

Introduction 114

Structure ... 114
Introduction to Good Strategy ... 114
Goals Setting ... 117
Market-Adjusted Goals ... 118
Business Strategy Models Applied to SEO ... 119
SWOT Analysis ... 121
Resource-Based and Market Demand Strategy ... 122
Value Disciplines Model and SEO ... 123
Market Analysis and SEO ... 124
The Lean Startup and SEO ... 124
Stakeholder Management ... 125
Conclusion ... 127
8. Content Strategy and SEO ... 128
Introduction ... 128
Structure ... 129
Steps to Form a Content Strategy ... 129
Types of Content ... 132
Content Inventory and Audit ... 135
Competitor Analysis ... 138
Content Planning and Stakeholders ... 140
Conclusion ... 143
9. Technical SEO Strategy ... 144
Introduction ... 144
Structure ... 144
Structured Data ... 144
PageSpeed and Core Web Vitals ... 147
Improving PageSpeed ... 150
Improving Core Web Vitals ... 151
Website Migration ... 152
Website Migration Steps ... 154
Technical SEO Auditing ... 157
Parts of an SEO Audit ... 158

Next Step: Business-Proof SEO Audit 160

Next Step: Technical Savvy SEO Audit 161

Implementation of Technical SEO Proposals 162

The Business Value of Technical SEO 162

The Technical SEO Action Plan 164

Presentation of Technical SEO Findings: The REBUS Framework 165

Conclusion 168

10. SEO Trends 169

Introduction 169

Structure 169

Zero-Click Searches 169

Large Language Models 171

The Evolution of AI and Language Models 171

ChatGPT: AI's iPhone Moment 171

Challenges and Ethical Considerations 172

Future Trends and Conclusion 172

TikTok SEO 173

Summary 174

Bing SEO 174

Local SEO 175

A Smaller Index 175

Keywords and Visitors 176

Advertising Strategy 176

Taking Advantage of The Increase in Search Traffic on Bing 176

Summary 176

Automation, Generative AI, and Your Team 177

Importance of Prompt Engineering Skills 177

Organizational Success Factors and Barriers 178

Evolving Towards Human-AI Collaboration 179

Impact on SEO Strategies and Practices 180

New Coding and Data Analysis Skills for Your SEO Team 180

Summary 181
Real-Life Ranking Signals 181
Website Usage 181
Real-Life Visits 182
YouTube SEO 182
Conclusion 183
11. SEO Reporting 185
Introduction 185
Structure 185
Importance of SEO Reporting 185
Key Metrics for SEO Reporting 187
SEO Reporting Tools: Your Digital Swiss Army Knife 189
Know Your Audience: Tailoring SEO Reports for Maximum Impact 192
The C-Suite: Executive Realness 192
The Marketing Team: Strategy Central 192
The Development Team: Tech Talk 193
The Client: Value Demonstration 193
Data Visualization: Making Stories Out of Data 194
Choose the Right Chart for Your Data 194
Declutter Your Charts 195
Storytelling 195
Make it Interactive (When Appropriate) 196
Design for Your Audience 196
Test Your Visualizations 196
Mastering SEO Report Communication: Action Titles and Pyramid Structure 197
Action Titles: Your Report's Secret Weapon 197
Pyramid Communication: Building Your SEO Story 197
Putting it All Together 199
Conclusion 199
Index 201

Chapter 1
Introduction to SEO

Introduction

SEO is often one of the biggest traffic drivers for websites and is therefore an important marketing channel. In this introductory chapter, we will dive into why SEO is essential for businesses today. We will explore the current state of SEO, how Google ranks sites, and actionable tips to boost your rankings. Additionally, we will discuss how SEO can deliver significant ROI. Let us discover why SEO is an important part of our marketing strategy.

Structure

In this chapter, we will cover the following topics:

- Definition of SEO
- Importance of SEO
- History of Google and Other Search Engines
- How Google works - Ranking Factors Evolution
- How SEO Offers ROI

Definition of SEO

Search Engine Optimization (SEO) refers to the strategies, techniques, and practices used to increase a website or web page's visibility on search engines.

In simpler terms, SEO is the art and science of making your website and other online company assets more discoverable to those searching for the products, services, or information you offer.

When discussing SEO, we primarily refer to **organic** or **natural** search results, which are the non-paid listings that appear when someone enters a query into a search engine.

This differs from pay-per-click (PPC) advertising, which involves paying for higher visibility in search results.

Roughly, SEO is often divided into three fields: technical SEO, content SEO, and authority. To illustrate this, we make an analogy where we think about SEO as a shopping mall. A shopping mall's foundational infrastructure – functioning escalators, proper lighting, and clean pathways – equates to Technical SEO. Without these, shoppers would struggle to find stores or might even avoid the mall altogether.

In our shopping mall, imagine each store as a piece of content. Some stores have bright displays, attentive staff, and products neatly arranged in a logical manner (structured content). The most successful stores also ensure their merchandise (content) is always fresh, relevant to the season (trending topics), and meets the shoppers' desires (user intent). A mall with diverse, quality stores (rich, varied content) will attract a broader range of shoppers and keep them returning.

Think of the shopping mall's reputation (authority) in the broader community. If influential people and publications frequently recommend the mall and discuss its unique stores and services (high-quality references), more people are likely to visit. Similarly, when reputable websites link to yours or mention your brand, it boosts your site's authority in the eyes of search engines.

Just like it takes more than just a building for a shopping mall to be successful, it takes more than just a website to be successful in SEO. SEO requires, like a shopping mall, an interplay between technical, content, and authority factors. In this book, we will delve deeper into these aspects of SEO.

Technical SEO refers to the suite of tactics and strategies used to optimize a website's infrastructure, enabling search engines to crawl, interpret, and index its content efficiently. It lays the foundation for successful SEO and is crucial to ensure that the website's visibility is not hampered by structural or technical issues. Key elements include optimizing site speed, enhancing mobile-friendliness, implementing secure connections (HTTPS), creating XML sitemaps, and managing redirects properly. Technical SEO also involves addressing and fixing crawl errors, ensuring that every page gets indexed well in Google, which will be addressed in the next chapter. You don't want to optimize content just to find out your **`robots.txt`** is blocking Google bot.

However, technical SEO is not only about errors and indexation. Technical optimization, using structured data to facilitate understanding of the content by search engines, optimizing page speed, and ensuring an efficient, logical site structure, will also help your SEO efforts. This will be addressed in *Chapter 9, Technical SEO Strategy*.

Content SEO is centered around optimizing the actual content on the website. This involves the use of relevant, high-quality, and keyword-optimized text, as well as images and multimedia. The aim is to create content that is valuable and engaging to the user but also easily understandable and favorably evaluated by search engine algorithms. Content SEO incorporates strategies like keyword research and implementation, content formatting, and multimedia optimization. The most important strategy, however, is to ensure that the content aligns well with user intent and contributes to a better user experience. Furthermore, creating comprehensive, authoritative, and fresh content helps in establishing the website's credibility and authority on the subject matter.

Off-page SEO involves optimization activities that occur outside the website but have a significant impact on its search engine rankings. It primarily focuses on building the website's authority and reputation through the acquisition of backlinks from other reputable websites. A diverse and high-quality backlink profile is a strong indicator of the website's credibility and relevance, influencing its position in search engine results pages (SERPs). Off-page SEO also encompasses strategies like social media marketing, influencer outreach, and brand building, aimed at increasing the website's visibility and traffic through external platforms. Additionally, local SEO and reputation management are crucial off-page activities, ensuring a positive and consistent brand image across the web.

Between these three properties, there are some synergies. A good technical website architecture provides a place for many content pages, and exceptionally good content may attract backlinks from other websites.

What skills are needed to be a successful SEO?

Since SEO is multifaceted, a top SEO expert should combine skills in different areas too. When reading this book, you will improve your skills in these areas.

Technical proficiency is a crucial skill required to be an SEO expert. This involves a deep understanding of website architecture. For example, as an SEO expert, you must be adept at crafting XML sitemaps to guide search engines through a site's pages, and creating and modifying **`robots.txt`** files to control which pages search engines can access.

A good SEO expert should also have an analytical mind. He should be able to research and select relevant keywords. For instance, an SEO expert working for a bakery might discover that while thousands search for "*best chocolate cake recipe*," a substantial number also query "*how to make a gluten-free chocolate cake*." Such insights drive content strategies. Beyond keywords, data analysis is vital when reporting results and can help drive the correct conclusions for certain data.

In SEO, content is both king and kingdom. Content creation and optimization are about more than just crafting compelling articles. It is about ensuring each piece aligns with both the audience's needs and business goals. Furthermore, link building, UX, and local SEO knowledge will also help SEO performance. Of course, you can start with one skill, but a good SEO expert will combine these different skills.

Lastly, soft skills can help you in a daily job as an SEO expert. Whether it's to communicate ranking drops to a customer or work together with a web development team to solve technical issues, effective communication is crucial.

But now we can ask ourselves the question: What distinguishes an average SEO specialist from an exceptional one? It's not just about mastery over various SEO techniques but also aligning those techniques with core business objectives to drive tangible results.

We provide two examples where the way of working of a good SEO differs from that of a great SEO: one in keyword research and one in reporting. You may see how the great SEO will come up with a better SEO strategy, thanks to applying business thinking to SEO.

For keyword research and selection, a good SEO may suggest targeting high-volume keywords that are somewhat relevant to the business. A great SEO will dive deeper into long-tail keywords and align keywords with customer journeys to ensure the content format aligns with the intent. They may also consider seasonal search volume to determine the most relevant time to create additional content. Additionally, they may analyze competitor rankings to assess feasibility and gain a competitive advantage.

Then there's the matter of reporting. A good SEO typically tracks organic traffic, rankings, and conversions - key performance indicators that are undoubtedly important. Yet, a great SEO goes beyond the conventional. They will set up custom goals aligned with the business's overarching objectives. They will segment data by categories or business units, offering granular insights. Moreover, they will incorporate search and market trends into reports, providing a strategic viewpoint that can guide business decisions. In doing so, great SEO experts will create comprehensive dashboards, a tool that refines their SEO strategy while ensuring alignment across business stakeholders.

In conclusion, while both the good and the great SEO professionals are competent, the latter stands out by consistently including business logic in their SEO approach. SEO strategy is not just about visibility but about driving real business impact.

Importance of SEO

Before diving into SEO techniques, let us explore why SEO is a valuable tool. There are some unique advantages SEO has over other marketing channels, such as:

- **Organic Traffic**: Unlike paid advertising, SEO drives **organic** traffic, meaning users find your site without you having to pay for each click. Once you establish a solid SEO foundation and rank well for your target keywords, you can receive a continuous flow of traffic without additional per-visit costs.

  For instance, when I created my survey website, I managed to get ten times as many SEO visitors as SEA visitors. A large number of visitors led to many new accounts. I could get a lot of traffic and conversions without relying on paid advertising. This is not an exception; many websites tend to have a big share of organic traffic compared to their total website traffic. For example, Amazon.

com has 20% organic search traffic compared to 5% paid search traffic and 3% social media traffic.

- **High Intent**: People who use search engines are often in a state of high intent. They are actively looking for information, products, or services. Take, for example, someone who recently moved and is looking for a dentist in their new location. This person is very likely to type in "*dentist + location*" in Google search. The ideal time to have marketing visibility for the dentist is to appear at that precise moment, which is exactly what a good SEO strategy aims to achieve.

  Therefore, when your website appears in search results for relevant queries, you are connecting with potential customers exactly when they are most interested.

- **Long-Term Results**: While paid advertising campaigns have a limited lifespan (they work as long as you pay), SEO efforts can yield long-term results. A well-optimized site can maintain high rankings for years, provided you keep updating it in response to algorithm changes, search behavior, and user behavior.

- **Credibility and Trust**: Users often trust organic search results more than paid advertisements. Take, for example, a software company. Software companies use a lot of search advertising. However, from the viewpoint of a potential client of a software company, they would want reliable software for their business. The end customer may have more faith in a credible, authoritative long-lasting company rather than a startup that may have paid its way to the top of advertisements. They assume Google's organic results will show a credible market-leading company in the top position.

  So earning a top spot in organic search rankings can enhance the credibility of a business, as it is perceived by many potential clients as a sign that the top spot will also be the authority or market leader in the field.

- **Synergy with Other Marketing Efforts**: SEO works well in tandem with other marketing channels. For instance, content created for SEO can be shared on social media. Similarly, insights from keyword research can inform content strategies for email marketing. This makes SEO a significant part of the marketing mix.

  For example, once a client invested a lot of time in writing an e-book or whitepaper, but used this whitepaper only as an advertisement on a download form. To leverage SEO, new pages were added to their website containing excerpts from the whitepaper, along with a call-to-action to download the full whitepaper. In the end, more whitepaper downloads came from these website pages rather than the campaign.

- **Measurable**: With tools such as Google Analytics and Google Search Console, businesses can closely monitor their SEO performance. They can track metrics such as organic traffic, bounce rate, conversion rate, and the keywords driving traffic. By analyzing the keywords people use to find your website, you could also gain valuable business insight.

  For example, consider an online fashion store that uses Google Analytics and Search Console to track which keywords are driving the most traffic and sales. Now, they discover that "*vegan leather jackets*" is a high-performing SEO keyword for them and decide to expand their product range in this category, further boosting revenue.
- **Enhanced User Experience**: A good SEO strategy often aligns with best practices for user experience (UX). Optimizing for SEO means improving site speed, mobile optimization, and creating high-quality, user-friendly content, all of which will also benefit the visitors of a website. Some people may claim **SEO is dead**, with the recent AI/ChatGPT evolutions. However, the truth is that optimizing your website to contain relevant information, have good page speed, work on mobile, and match the intent of the searcher will never go away.
- **Ever-Evolving Challenge**: SEO is not a static field. As search engine algorithms change and evolve, there is always something new to learn or a new challenge to tackle. This continuous evolution can be seen as an advantage because it allows adaptive businesses to stay ahead of competitors who may be slower to react. There will always be SEO opportunities left to explore.

History of Google

Before the arrival of Google in 1998, the landscape of search engines was varied and dynamic. Altavista, Lycos, Yahoo, and Ask Jeeves were some popular search engines. These pioneering platforms laid the groundwork for many of the features and functionalities we now associate with modern search engines. However, the algorithms of these search engines were mostly based on how many keywords appeared in the website text. In 1998, at Stanford University, Larry Page and Sergey Brin invented the search engine Google.

One thing Google did better than the other search engines was having a simple loading website, which was in contrast with the cluttered pages of the competitors. Google also had a more sophisticated algorithm than the other search engines, thanks to the PageRank algorithm, named after Larry Page.

We can explain Pagerank with a simplified example. Imagine the web consisted of three pages: A, B, and C.

A links to both B and C.

B links only to C.

C links only to A.

Since C is linked from two pages, C would have the highest page rank. And since A got the link from the most important page (page C with the highest page rank), A would have a higher page rank than B.

Over the years, Google has released several significant algorithm updates to ensure relevant, quality content ranked prominently while penalizing low-quality, spammy content. Some notable updates include:

- **Panda (2011)**: Targeted **content farms** and websites with low-quality, thin content.
- **Penguin (2012)**: Penalized sites using manipulative link schemes.
- **Hummingbird (2013)**: Focused on understanding the intent behind users' queries rather than just the individual keywords.
- **Mobilegeddon (2015)**: Prioritized mobile-friendly websites as smartphone usage soared.
- **RankBrain (2015, ongoing)**: Introduced around 2015, RankBrain is a machine learning (ML) artificial intelligence (AI) system used to help process Google search queries. Its main role is to understand the intent behind queries, especially for new, unique, or ambiguous searches that the system might not have seen before. For example, if you search for Giants in New York, you will likely get search results of the NFL team, while in other regions, you might get search results related to very tall people.
- **BERT (2019)**: Used Natural Language Processing and language models to better understand the context of words in search queries.
- **EAT (2022)**: Emphasized the importance of experience, authority, and trust, especially on your money - your life sites (health and finance), to ensure users land on authoritative pages.
- **EEAT and Helpful Content Update (2023-2024)**. As Google is fighting against spammy AI-generated content, real life experience and helpful content gets more important. Think about a blogger sharing his personal experience visiting a city outranking an AI-generated article about travelling to a certain city.

These algorithm updates affect your SEO strategy: Since the black hat strategy gets punished by Google, it is important to practice good SEO. Black hat SEO strategies – tactics that attempt to trick or **game** search engines – are consistently targeted and penalized by Google's algorithm updates. Actions such as keyword stuffing, using hidden text, and building artificial backlinks can lead to severe repercussions, from a drop in rankings to removal from the index altogether. Consider the numerous websites that relied on buying vast numbers of low-quality backlinks; they found themselves penalized after Google's Penguin update in 2012. This made clear the importance of organic link-building rather than trying to manipulate the algorithm.

Since Google added context and intent to their algorithm, it is essential to not only look for matching keywords but also prioritize understanding user intent in your SEO strategy. This shift means content should be created not just around keywords but also around the solutions and answers users genuinely seek. For example, if a user searches for "*how to care for indoor plants*," they are likely seeking a guide or tips rather than just a list of indoor plants. Websites that offer thorough care instructions, watering schedules, and common mistakes to avoid will better match this user intent and, as a result, rank higher.

Besides the algorithm, the Google Search layout has evolved over the last few years. Some new Google search features are included, and for only a very few keywords, the classic 10 blue link result page will be shown by Google.

Here are some of the notable features in Google Search:

- **Featured Snippets**: These are blocks at the top of the search results that provide quick answers to user queries. For instance, if someone searches for "*how to boil an egg*," a featured snippet might display a brief step-by-step guide without the user having to click any particular website.
- **Knowledge Graph**: Introduced in 2012, the Knowledge Graph is a visual box that appears on the right side of the search results (or at the top on mobile), providing a quick overview of a searched topic, such as a brief biography of a famous person or facts about a landmark.
- **Local Pack**: For location-based queries, such as "*coffee shops near me*," the SERPs display a map with the locations of nearby businesses, along with their ratings, hours, and other pertinent information.
- **People Also Ask**: This is a box containing related questions to the initial query. For instance, if someone searches for "*symptoms of the flu*," the "*People Also Ask*" box might show related questions like "*How long does the flu last?*" or "*Flu versus cold symptoms.*"
- **Video and Image Results**: Depending on the nature of the search, Google might display relevant videos or images alongside or in place of text-based links.
- **Ads**: Over time, the display and positioning of ads have evolved. They are seamlessly integrated into the SERPs but are labeled as **Ads** for transparency.

Companies may need to react to these changes by adding structured data, considering video and image SEO, and optimizing their local profile. Additionally, they should review the types of result pages that appear for searches on their keywords.

We will discuss SEO trends in more detail later in *Chapter 10, SEO Trends*.

In general, SEO and content professionals should focus on quality content, user experience, and understanding search intent to score in Google. Businesses and marketers who follow these principles will not only deliver value to the end users but are also more likely to obtain the top position in Google.

How Google Works - Ranking Factors

What are these ranking factors that will determine who will rank first and be the winner in search engines? To gain top rankings, of course, one must have a broad view of ranking factors.

Before delving into Google's ranking criteria, it is essential to address common misconceptions. In the SEO world, many myths surrounding ranking factors continue to live, and it is important to differentiate fact from fiction.

One prevalent myth revolves around social signals – tweets, Facebook likes, and shares – and their influence on Google search rankings. This belief stemmed from an observed correlation between socially popular content and its subsequent search ranking. However, Matt Cutts, Google's former head of web spam, debunked this in 2014, affirming that Google's algorithm doesn't directly consider such social signals.

Moreover, certain meta tags have become obsolete over the years. For instance, the **`meta name="keyword"`** tag lost its relevance in ranking, a fact Google acknowledged years ago. However, it is worth noting also that the **`meta name="description"`** tag does not directly influence the ranking. It is still important to write a meta description though. While it doesn't directly influence rankings, it shapes user perceptions and click-through rates, making it indispensable for SEO. Therefore, stuffing keywords in the meta description is not only unnecessary but counterproductive.

While several factors might seem critical, it is essential to prioritize what truly impacts rankings. For instance, the text-to-code ratio is not a direct ranking factor, as confirmed by Google. Yet, aspects like page speed and the quality of content remain important. Additionally, the rise of mobile internet usage brought innovations like Accelerated Mobile Pages (AMP) to the fore. These pages, designed to enhance mobile user experience, are beneficial, but they are not direct ranking boosters, as confirmed by John Mueller, a search advocate from Google.

Lastly, John Mueller clarified that user engagement metrics such as clicks or bounce rates aren't integral to Google's ranking algorithm. Although this is disputed by some SEO experts.

In the ever-evolving landscape of SEO, it is crucial to know the real ranking factors while avoiding distractions.

Now that we know some factors that don't influence rankings, let us discuss the real Google ranking factors. To make ranking factors very clear, we will only discuss direct ranking factors - factors that we are certain have a significant influence on the search result - rather than indirect ranking factors.

Direct ranking factors have a clear and immediate impact on search engine rankings. When optimized correctly, they can lead to a boost in search position. Google's algorithms take these factors into account when determining the position of a webpage in search results. For example, including a certain keyword in a meta title can directly influence your position in the search result.

Indirect ranking factors may not affect search engine rankings directly, but they can influence direct factors or user behaviors that, in turn, impact rankings. Their effect is often more nuanced and can be longer-term.

For example, having a popular brand will get you more backlinks, indirectly helping SEO, but it won't have a direct impact on your SEO rankings.

Here are the top 10 direct ranking factors that will gain you direct SEO rankings and traffic:

- **High-quality content:** Search engines, especially Google, aim to provide the best answers to users' queries. High-quality content meets users' needs more effectively, ensuring they find what they're looking for. High-quality content is readable, well-written, in-depth, and unique.
- **Backlinks:** We know from the PageRank algorithm that backlinks are part of Google's ranking factors. With backlinks, quality is more important than quantity. To quote John Mueller, "*One good link from a relevant website can be more impactful than millions of low-quality links.*" Focus on acquiring high-quality, relevant links. Natural link-building strategies, such as content marketing, guest blogging, and public relations, are generally more beneficial and less risky than black hat tactics like linking schemes.
- **Internal links:** In addition, internal links on your website will help you rank, by using relevant anchor text within your links.
- **Answers search intent:** Search intent (or user intent) refers to the primary goal a user has when typing a query into a search engine. Essentially, it is the reason behind the query. Common types of search intent include informational, navigational, transactional, and commercial. For example, for the keyword "*banana*", Wikipedia and other informational pages rank first because Google thinks the user intent is searching for information about bananas. However, for "*buy banana*", local search results of stores where you can buy bananas will be shown. So make sure that for every page, you have an idea which search intent you may address and optimize for this intent.
- **Content freshness:** Since Google wants to provide users with current

information, new and updated articles will be ranked higher than old articles for many keywords.

- **On-page SEO optimization:** On-page optimization can be meta titles, keywords in metatags and alt-tags, as well as optimizing content for SEO.
- **Website loading speed:** Google will give the edge on faster-loading websites and will penalize lower-loading websites within the ranking. It introduced core web vitals reports and updates to increase page speed.
- **Expertise, authority, and trust:** Authoritative content written by experts will rank better as it will likely be more trustworthy.
- **Website security:** HTTPS websites will be ranked above HTTP websites. Since 2014, this was confirmed by Google as a ranking factor within the search results.
- **Mobile-friendliness:** An important confirmed direct ranking factor is the mobile-friendliness of your website. Since 50% of searches on Google are from mobile devices, mobile-friendly websites will get an edge on the search results. We had one example of a medical e-commerce website that dropped significantly after it started failing the Google mobile-friendly test, so this is a major one. Even on desktop devices, mobile friendliness is a big ranking factor.

SEO as an Investment

In today's digital age, the significance of SEO often remains under-recognized. SEO expert Itamar Blauer paints a vivid picture of this reality, stating, "*I once conversed with a brand that easily spends a five-figure sum on ads every month without a second thought. Yet, when I proposed an annual SEO investment of the same amount, they balked.*"

This scenario prompts an essential question: Why such disparity in approach?

Certainly, the instant gratification offered by ads is alluring. They provide rapid results, clear metrics, and a sense of predictability that businesses often crave. But, is this short-term allure blinding companies to the long-term, sustainable benefits that SEO offers?

SEO is not merely an expenditure; it is an investment – a commitment to building an online presence that will get you results over time. While the initial costs might be high, the long-term returns, in terms of organic reach and credibility, often surpass that of ad spend. SEO ensures sustainable, lasting benefits from a strategy that is typically more cost-effective in the long run. If you are in for a marathon, you should consider SEO.

It is crucial to emphasize that integrating ads into one's marketing mix is not the issue. The real concern emerges when businesses exclusively rely on them, neglecting the potent value SEO brings to the table.

There's an old saying: "*You don't know what you've got until it's gone.*" This is also true in the world of SEO. The immense value of search engine optimization becomes clear when a minor problem results in a catastrophic drop in your organic search traffic.

Imagine pouring endless hours into crafting content, only to have it disappear from search results due to a seemingly inconsequential tweak. Perhaps a minor change in the **`robots.txt`** file mistakenly blocks search engines, rendering your website virtually invisible. Or in the excitement of launching a new website, SEO considerations fall by the wayside, leading to a plummet in rankings and traffic.

Such blunders underscore the delicate nature of SEO. It is a field where attention to detail matters immensely. Small problems can result in disproportionate consequences, turning thriving websites into unfindable ghost pages overnight. When this happens, the value of SEO becomes very clear.

These kinds of setbacks can also serve as invaluable lessons. By understanding these missteps, you not only recover lost traffic but also cement best practices for the future.

Compounding Returns

Another aspect of measuring ROI for SEO is thinking about compounding returns. As you invest in SEO, the efforts compound over time. Quality content, for example, does not just attract traffic when it is published; it can continue to draw in visitors months or even years later. The more quality content and backlinks you accumulate, the stronger your domain authority becomes, making it easier to rank for more and more keywords. Because of these compounding returns, it is better to start now than later with SEO.

Imagine your website's domain authority (DA) starts at a base value of 10 (on a scale of 0 to 100, though this is just a hypothetical example, and actual domain authority (DA) can vary).

Starting now:

Year 1: 10 (initial DA) + 20% = 12

Year 2: 12 + 20% = 14.4

Year 3: 14.4 + 20% = 17.28

By the end of three years, if you start SEO now, your DA will be approximately 17.28.

Waiting 2 years:

Year 1 and 2: No change (because you did not do SEO) = 10

Year 3: 10 + 20% = 12

If you waited for two years to begin your SEO efforts, by the end of the third year, your DA would only be 12.

The difference in domain authority by the end of Year 3 would be 17.28 vs. 12, which is significant. This gap only widens as time goes on. The hypothetical scenario illustrates the power of compounding in SEO. Each year you are not only building on the previous year's foundation but also benefiting from the accumulated trust, backlinks, and content.

Moreover, while you are postponing your SEO efforts, competitors who recognize the value of SEO are likely forging ahead, making it even more challenging for you to catch up later. It must be painful watching your competitors reaping the benefits of compounding returns while you lag. In the constantly evolving landscape of search engines, standing still essentially means moving backward as others progress.

Thus, the old Chinese proverb holds in the context of SEO: "*The best time to plant a tree was 20 years ago. The second-best time is now.*" The earlier you start with SEO, not only will you reap its benefits sooner, but all of your future SEO will be brighter. Of course, the time to get SEO results will depend on market size, competition and the products and services you provide.

Calculating SEO ROI

You may calculate the ROI of SEO directly by just looking at your leads generated from organic traffic and comparing it to the SEO costs.

This approach may be an underestimation for the following reasons:

- **Lifetime Value of a Customer (LTV)**: Instead of considering just the immediate sale, think about the estimated revenue a customer will bring over the lifetime of their relationship with your business.
- **Attribution Models**: Since SEO can play both a direct and assistive role in conversions, consider using attribution models that give credit to all touchpoints a customer interacts with before conversion.
- **Non-Monetary Metrics**: While ROI deals with financial returns, it also considers other metrics like increased organic traffic, improved keyword rankings, and enhanced domain authority. These factors can provide value in the long run and may eventually translate to financial gains.
- **Time**: SEO often requires patience. Immediate results are rare, and it is common for campaigns to start showing a significant ROI only after several months. So looking at historical data will not give you the total return on SEO. This is different from spending money on advertising.
- **Competitive Landscape**: If you are operating in a highly competitive niche, your initial SEO costs might be higher to break through the competition.

However, once you start ranking and building authority, the ROI might significantly improve.

- **Brand Awareness**: When your site ranks highly on search engines, more people see your brand's name and associate it with the keywords they are searching for. This increased visibility can improve brand recall and authority over time.
- **Trust and Credibility**: High rankings in organic search results often signal to users that your site is a trusted source of information or services. This can lead to a perception of credibility, which, while not immediately monetizable, can have long-term benefits.
- **Improved User Experience**: Many SEO optimizations, such as improving site speed, ensuring mobile responsiveness, and having a well-structured website, enhance the overall user experience, leading to lower bounce rates and longer session durations.
- **Higher Engagement on Your Website**: By optimizing web pages for quality and relevance, your engagement metrics may improve. While engagement metrics such as time on site, pages per session, and bounce rate may not immediately translate into revenue, they indicate that users find your content valuable, which can lead to increased trust and potential conversions in the future.
- **Increased Referral Traffic**: A good SEO strategy often involves securing backlinks from reputable websites. These backlinks not only boost your SEO but can also drive referral traffic.
- **Feedback and Insights**: From doing keyword research, competitive analysis, or Google reviews, you can gain useful feedback and insights.
- **Synergy with Other Marketing Efforts**: SEO can support and be supported by other marketing channels. For example, content created for SEO can be shared on social media, driving additional traffic and social signals that further benefit SEO.
- **Long-Term Audience Growth**: While PPC (Pay-per-click) campaigns can drive immediate traffic, they stop the moment you stop funding them. In contrast, SEO efforts can continue to bring in organic traffic over time, even if you reduce investments in the future. So when calculating ROI, you should not look only in the past but also in the future.
- **Improved Operations:** If your website has an extensive FAQ or support that is optimized for SEO, then customers may be less likely to contact the helpdesk, which will make your company work more effectively.

You see, there are many aspects to consider when you want to determine the ROI of SEO.

Conclusion

In this introductory chapter, we have gained an understanding of SEO, including its importance and the necessary skills for an SEO expert. We have also learned about the real ranking factors and the potential returns of SEO.

Before we proceed with trying to rank our web pages on Google, it is important to ensure that our web pages will be properly indexed by Google. This will be the focus of the next chapter in the book.

CHAPTER 2
Indexation

Introduction

In this chapter, you will learn how search engines, such as Google, crawl, understand, and ultimately index websites and web pages. This process is the foundation of any effective SEO strategy, and understanding it is vital for anyone looking to boost their online presence.

We will start from the basics of crawling and sitemaps to the more advanced concepts like handling HTTP status codes and the role of **`robots.txt`** files. We will look at common pitfalls and challenges businesses face in the digital world and offer practical solutions to navigate these complexities.

Indexation can be tricky. For instance, a real estate website had an outdated sitemap that missed new listings. It also had many 404 errors because old listings were not correctly redirected. Additionally, it lacked proper URLs with canonical tags for different cities, affecting its search rankings for terms such as *'real estate in [city]'*. Fixing these issues led to more pages being indexed and an increase in website traffic.

Structure

In this chapter, the following topics will be covered:

- Tracking Page Count for Indexing
- Status Code and Indexation
- Sitemaps
- Robots.txt
- HTTP Status Codes
- Redirecting and Migration

Tracking Page Count for Indexing

How many pages are indexed? Keeping track of this is important for SEO. If a page is not indexed, it won't show up in search results, no matter how well it is optimized. Always check if your pages are indexed before you start optimizing them

Checking which pages are indexed can reveal technical issues on your website. For example, during a technical SEO audit, compare the number of pages you expect to be indexed against the actual number. Poor indexation often points to technical problems. Understanding these issues can help you make better technical SEO improvements

The last part is content strategy, if you find for example valuable optimized pages that are not indexed, it might be time to consider their place on your website. Restructure to increase internal linking on these pages.

In this chapter, we will use Google Search Console (GSC), a free tool from Google. GSC helps you monitor and fix issues related to your website's visibility in Google Search results. It allows you to see your site as Google does, find potential problems affecting its appearance in search results, and learn how to enhance visibility and user experience.

Google Search Console (GSC) is essential for SEO. If a website does not use it, set it up immediately. GSC offers valuable data on your site's performance in Google searches, including how often it appears, the queries that bring it up, and user click-throughs. It is also great for content optimization. You can use GSC to see which content is most popular, how often it is viewed, and clicked.

Setting Up Search Console

Setting up GSC is to create direct line of communication with Google about your website. Begin by navigating to Google Search Console and signing in with your Google account. If you are new to the platform, you will be prompted to '`Add Property`'. This property is your website, and you can define it either by its domain or by a specific URL prefix.

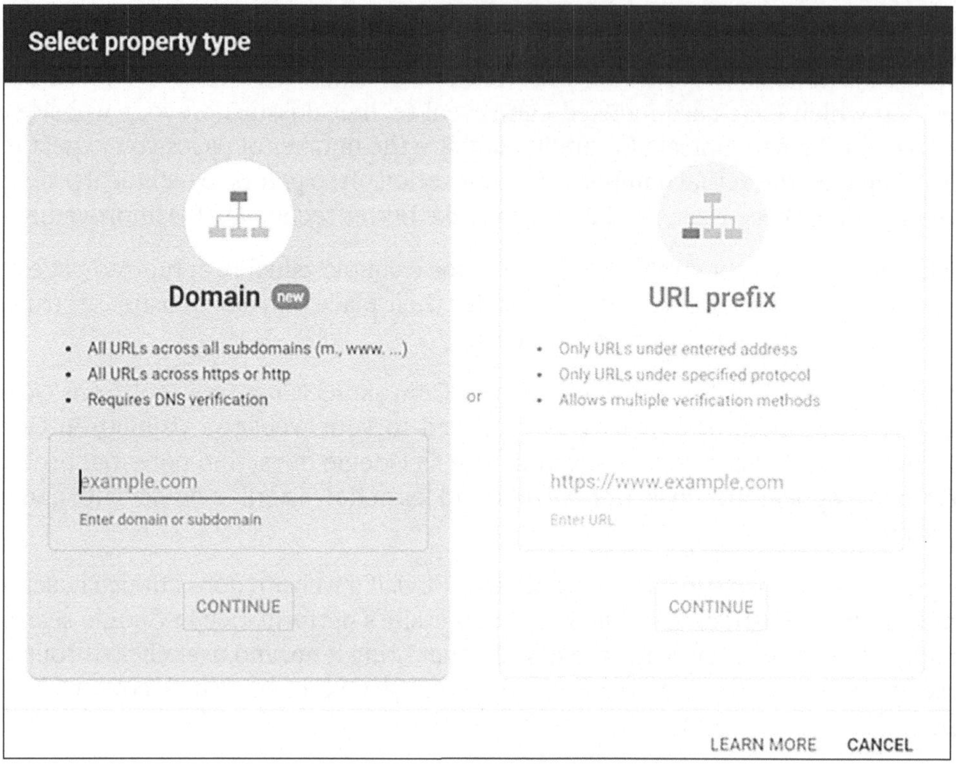

***Figure 2.1**: Google Search Console: New property*

Once you enter your website details, Google will request verification to ensure you own the property you are trying to manage. This is a security check. There are multiple ways to verify your ownership: uploading a specific HTML file, adding a meta tag to your website, or even going through your domain provider. Choose the most convenient for you (or your developer).

Note: *DNS record verification gathers data from all subdomains at once.*

So, if you have subdomains like jobs.domain.com and a www.domain.com, DNS verification will combine them, while for the other verification methods you need to add both subdomains to the Google search console.

To submit a sitemap to Google, navigate to the **`'Sitemaps'`** section in Google Search Console. Enter the URL of your sitemap, usually something like https://www.yourwebsite.com/sitemap.xml, and click **`'Submit'`**. This acts like a map for Google, helping it understand and navigate your site more effectively.

This chapter will focus on the indexation report within Google Search Console.

Determining Indexed URLs

While total website size offers some insight into indexation, a more granular approach is often better. You can check for specific URLs or lists of URLs to analyze indexation issues. Here, you can also use the site search operator: **`site:urlofthepage`** command (for example, site:example.com/example.html)

In Google Search console, you can find the reason why a certain page is not indexed.

Once you are in, there is a tool called "URL *inspection*". Enter your web page's address and check if Google knows about it. And if you would like to check out a whole group of pages, there is a spot called the "*Coverage*" report. It will show you all the pages Google knows and even tell you if it is having trouble with some.

Status Code and Indexation

Think of web servers like shop doors that send simple messages to Google: **`'Open'`**, **`'Closed'`**, or '**`Move to a new location`**'. These are called '*status codes*'. Knowing these codes is crucial for SEO because they tell Google about the status of your website pages.

Status codes are three-digit numbers that servers send when a webpage is requested. They are like the web's answers: **`'Yes'`**, **`'No'`**, or **`'Maybe'`**. These codes inform search engines about a page's status. For example, codes starting with '**2**' mean things are fine, but codes starting with '**4**' indicate a problem.

Key Status Codes and Their SEO Implications

- **200 OK:** This is the virtual equivalent of a warm welcome. It means everything is running smoothly, and the page has loaded correctly. For Google, this indicates that the page is good for indexing.

  Example: When you visit your homepage and everything loads as it should, the server returns a 200 status code.

- **301 Moved Permanently:** Sometimes, pages need to move, just like businesses might relocate. A 301 status tells search engines that the page has permanently moved to a new address and any SEO value from the old page should be transferred to the new one.

  Example: If you rebrand and change your website's domain, use a 301 redirect to send visitors from the old site to the new one.

- **404 Not Found:** This is the digital version of a dead-end street. It tells visitors and search engines that the page they are looking for doesn't exist. While occasional 404s are natural, too many can be a red flag for Google, indicating a poorly maintained site.

  Example: If someone tries to visit a page on your site that has been deleted or never existed, they would encounter a 404 error.

- **503 Service Unavailable:** This suggests the server is not ready to handle the request. It could be due to maintenance, or server overload. Google understands that websites occasionally need downtime, but extended periods might affect indexation.

  Example: If your website is undergoing maintenance and is temporarily offline, visitors might see a 503 status.

Google's primary goal is to provide users with relevant and accessible content. When Google's robots, often referred to as *'crawlers'* or *'spiders'*, visit a website, they use status codes to determine the health and structure of that site. A site with mostly **'200 OK'** statuses suggests it is well-maintained and user-friendly, making it a prime candidate for good rankings.

Conversely, a site riddled with '**404 Not Found**' errors can be viewed as unreliable, leading Google to think twice before showcasing it in top search results. Moreover, good use of '**301 Moved Permanently**' can ensure that any earned SEO value is not lost during transitions or rebrands. When a page has a status code starting with a 3 or a 4, this page will likely be removed from Google.

Google Crawling and Indexation Process

To understand why a webpage is not indexed, it is helpful to know Google's four-step crawling and indexing process:

1. **Google Discovers Your Site**: Google finds your site's URL, because it was shared on another site or because you submitted your sitemap. The URL is added to Google's list of pages to visit.
2. **Google's First Visit:** Google sends a request to your website, similar to making a phone call using a number from a business card. Your site responds with its HTML content and a status code. A 200 status code means *'all good'*, while a 404 means *'page not found'*. If your website is down or slow, this could affect your visibility in search results.
3. **Google's Second Visit**: Rendering and Understanding. Imagine Google as a customer entering your store to browse. Googlebot reads your site's content and runs any JavaScript. This process helps Google understand what your site offers.
4. Finally, Google evaluates if your webpage is of good quality. Just as customers might leave reviews, Google determines if your website is valuable enough to show to others who are searching.

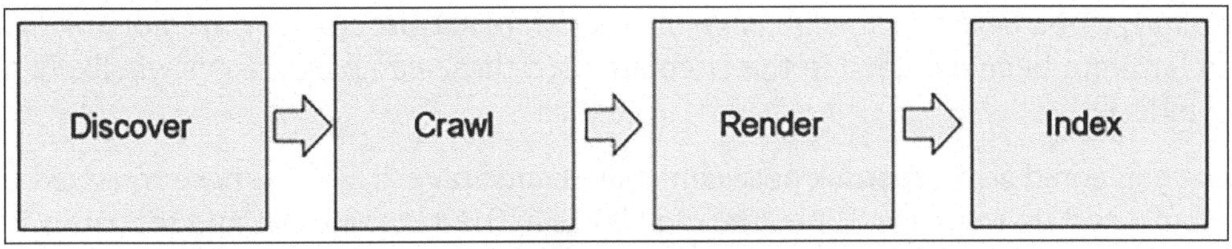

***Figure 2.2**: Google crawling process*

We might make an analogy with Google bot deciding to buy a product in a shop. Imagine your website is a newly opened shop in a bustling market, and Google is a potential customer.

- **Window Shopping (Discovered - Currently Not Indexed):** The customer (Google) has heard about your shop either through a market map (your sitemap) or word of mouth (a referring page). However, they have just glanced at it from a distance and have not decided to step in yet. At this stage, your shop has caught their eye, but they have not experienced it firsthand.
- **Locked Doors and No Entry (HTTP Status Codes):** Now, let us say the customer decides to enter your shop. But they find the door locked (404 - Page Not Found) or see a sign that says the shop is temporarily closed for repairs (5xx - Server Errors). Sometimes, they might find that the entry leads them elsewhere (redirect). All these scenarios prevent the customer from exploring your shop further. Similarly, if you have put up a "`No Entry`" sign (blocked by `robots.txt`), Google respects that and does not venture in.
- **Inside, But Just Browsing (Crawled - Currently Not Indexed):** Here, the customer has entered the shop and is merely looking around. In web terms, Google has made its initial visit, taken in the surroundings, but has not deeply engaged with the contents or the products yet.
- **Choosing Not to Buy (Noindex or Duplicate Content)**: At times, a customer might explore a shop, appreciate everything, but then decide not to make a purchase. Similarly, after rendering your webpage, Google might opt not to "`buy`" (`index`) it. Reasons could be a sign been placed saying "`Not For Sale`" (`noindex` tag) or perhaps Google noticed that the same product (content) is available in another shop (`duplicate` page). In these scenarios, even after going through the first three stages, Google decides not to finalize the deal in the fourth.

To ensure a flourishing business (a well-indexed site), it is essential to understand the journey of the customer (Google) and address any roadblocks they might face. This way, the doors to your shop are always open, inviting both customers and opportunities.

Now when you understand this pattern, it is easier to tackle indexation issues by knowing in which stage the indexation issue arises. A page that has no referral links and no sitemap.xml will be undiscovered for Google, so it won't even make stage 1. For example, if you have a campaign page on a separate subsite that you are not linking to and have not been included in the sitemap, then these campaign pages will likely not get indexed.

Now, you could also get stuck between stage 1 and stage 2, say you have renamed the URL of a certain webpage. When the old URL is in the **`sitemap.xml`** and returns a 404, Google will likely not index the URL. If you are stuck between stage 3 and stage 4, this means Google will have crawled and rendered your webpage already, you may need to improve the content on this page.

Now, we can also connect the search console indexation issue report with the steps of indexing by Google.

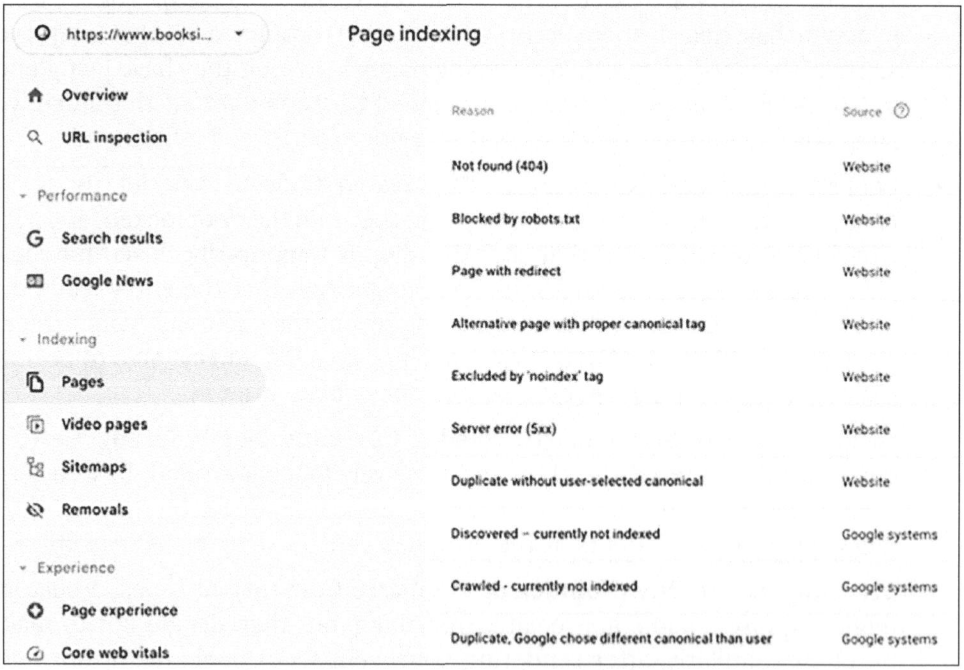

***Figure 2.3**: Google Search Console Page Indexation Status*

- **Discovered - Currently Not Indexed:** At this phase, Google has acknowledged the URL, most likely through the sitemap or a referring page. However, it has not made any requests to the page. It is in its initial phase of recognition.
- **Handling HTTP Status Codes:** If Google encounters status codes such as 404, 5xx, or even a redirect, the page won't be indexed since it is not readily accessible. In this scenario, Googlebot has carried out its initial checks, but it won't continue with the indexation process. Additionally, if pages are intentionally off-limits to Google, you will encounter the "**`Blocked by robots.txt`**" status.
- **Crawled - Currently Not Indexed**: This status means that Google has made its

first visit to the page, retrieving basic information. But, it hasn't rendered or deeply processed the page content yet.

- **Indexation Decision Post-Rendering:** After Google has rendered the page, it may still decide against indexing it. This could be because of a **`noindex`** tag set by the website owner or Google identifying the content as potentially duplicates. At this juncture, the first three steps have been completed, but in the final step, the decision to index might not materialize.

`Sitemap.xml` File

In the landscape of the web, the **`sitemap.xml`** file ensures search engines, such as Google, to efficiently crawl, understand, and index a website's content. While a sitemap.xml file may look rather simple, still some issues may arise. A sitemap is not a one-time setup tool. As your website grows and evolves, so should your sitemap. Regularly updating the sitemap ensures that new pages are indexed, and outdated ones are recognized.

We once had a customer where half of the vacancies on the website were not findable in Google because the sitemap was last updated 4 years ago and the vacancies in this sitemap were the ones from 4 years ago. After updating the sitemap, the new vacancies did get indexed well.

Now how to make a sitemap? A sitemap is simply a list of URLs of your website with for each URL certain attributes. There are some attributes like **`<url>`** **`<loc>`** that are required, as these contain the URL of the pages to be indexed, while **`<lastmod>`** attribute is really recommended to Google to let you know when the last changes. Google claims in their documentation on sitemap the **`<changefreq>`** and **`<priority>`** tags have no use at all. A sitemap should look like this:

```
<?xml version="1.0" encoding="UTF-8"?>
<urlset xmlns="http://www.sitemaps.org/schemas/sitemap/0.9">
   <url>
      <loc>https://www.example.com/</loc>
      <lastmod>2023-10-10T18:23:17+00:00</lastmod>
   </url>
   <url>
      <loc>https://www.example.com/about</loc>
      <lastmod>2023-08-15T14:25:15+00:00</lastmod>
   </url>
</urlset>
```

There are some technical limitations on the sitemap.xml size. A blog with thousands of articles uses a single sitemap.xml file. As their content grew, they may approach the 50,000 URL limit for a single sitemap. Google may began missing out on their latest articles if they reach this limit. Splitting the sitemap into multiple smaller sitemaps can resolve this issue. So whenever you hit the 50,000 URL limit, you should create a sitemap index.xml file. Hereby, we will show you an example of the structure of the sitemap:

```
<?xml version="1.0" encoding="UTF-8"?>
<sitemapindex xmlns="http://www.sitemaps.org/schemas/sitemap/0.9">
   <sitemap>
      <loc>https://www.example.com/sitemap1.xml</loc>
      <lastmod>2023-10-10T18:23:17+00:00</lastmod>
   </sitemap>
   <sitemap>
      <loc>https://www.example.com/sitemap2.xml</loc>
      <lastmod>2023-08-15T14:25:15+00:00</lastmod>
   </sitemap>
</sitemapindex>
```

When you split the XML file, it may be worthwhile to split by page type (for example, separate sitemaps for blog pages and product pages) so you can easily retrieve indexation status for these pages. Also, don't forget to submit the **`sitemap_index.xml`** file to Google Search Console.

Then, when examining a sitemap, it is also worth checking if the pages in the sitemap have a 200 status code. It does not make any sense to include pages with a 404 status code or pages that get redirected into the sitemap. Also, there are cases where the URLs in the **`sitemap.xml`** files do not contain the domain name, make sure that the URLs listed always contain the correct domain name. In some cases, we even found the sitemap.xml file containing URLs of the development server, so always double-check.

Finally, there is the question of how complete the sitemap.xml file should be. Some URLs tend to be forgotten in **`sitemap.xml`** files, such as PDF files. If you use parameters in the URL and want to index them separately, be sure to include these URLs in the sitemap. We recommend using Google Search Console's indexation report to identify which unsubmitted pages are indexed and whether these types of pages are worthwhile to include in the sitemap.

If your website heavily relies on visual content, such as photography portfolios, e-commerce sites with product images, art galleries, or any site where image search traffic is of significant value, then we also recommend the use of an image sitemap. In this more detailed sitemap, you can also add captions and license information for the image.

In case your website has a lot of original video content, like tutorial videos, product demos, or any other type of videos that you believe would be beneficial for your target audience to find via search engines, then we also recommend you use a video sitemap. These image and video sitemaps can also be added to the Google Search Console sitemap section.

Robots.txt File

Imagine having a storefront and a sign by the entrance that instructs visitors about which areas they can or cannot access. In the digital realm, the **`Robots.txt`** file plays a similar role. It is a simple text file residing in the root directory of your website, serving as a guideline for search engines on which parts of your site they can or cannot crawl and index.

For instance, if you run an e-commerce business and have a checkout page, you probably don't want this checkout page showing up in search results. The **`Robots.txt`** file can instruct search engines to skip this particular page. It ensures that search engines spend their time efficiently, crawling and indexing the right parts of your website.

Imagine you are launching a new product line but want to keep it a secret until the official reveal. If search engines were to access and index this information prematurely, the surprise will be ruined. **`Robots.txt`** helps prevent such mishaps.

The **`Robots.txt`** file is structured with simplicity, yet it is effective. We will list the content of the robots.txt file here:

- **User-Agent Declaration**: This is like addressing a specific group of visitors. For example, "**`Hey Google`**" or "**`Attention Bing`**."
- **Allow and Disallow Directives:** These are the essential commands. It is like saying, "*You can enter the living room, but please stay out of the bedroom.*" For a business, it could be, "*Please index our product pages, but stay away from our internal team pages.*"
- **Sitemap Reference**: A sitemap is like the blueprint of your website. By referencing it in the **`Robots.txt`**, you are essentially providing a map to search engines, guiding them to the most critical parts of your site. For businesses, this ensures that your key service pages or product listings are easily discoverable.

For example, in the following **`robots.txt`** example, you will find that all user agents (so all crawlers) will be disallowed to visit the private and temp folders on your website.

```
User-agent: *
Disallow: /private/
Disallow: /temp/

Sitemap: https://www.example.com/sitemap.xml
```

The **`robots.txt`** file looks simple, but small mistakes can have big consequences. For example, you should never block images, CSS, or JavaScript files in it. If these are blocked, Google can't display your pages properly. We had a client who blocked all URLs with parameters in **`robots.txt`**, which accidentally included CSS files. This made Google think their site was not mobile-friendly, resulting in an 80% drop in their SEO traffic

Another example was an architecture client who was not showing up in Google Image Search because their site's **`robots.txt`** file blocked all images. This was a problem since Google often shows images at the top of search results for architecture-related queries. When we allowed Google to index the images by updating the **`robots.txt`** file, their images began appearing in search results, which was great for the visibility of their projects within Google.

Before launching a new site or implementing changes, test the **`Robots.txt`** file. Websites like online fashion stores should ensure that seasonal collections are not mistakenly blocked from search engines, as this could lead to lost sales during peak seasons. When launching a new website, typically on the staging server, **`robots.txt`** blocks the crawlers. However, once the website is live, one should not forget to check whether crawlers have access to the website.

Then, you may encounter some issues with the order of lines in the **`robots.txt file`**. The order in which you place your "**`Allow`**" and "**`Disallow`**" directives can determine which parts of your website search engines can explore and display in their search results. Search engines, when they visit your website, will read the **`Robots.txt`** from top to bottom. Once they find a directive that matches a specific URL or path, they typically stop and follow that instruction.

Imagine you are in charge of the SEO of a prominent city hospital. Your hospital's website houses a plethora of resources: patient guides, physician directories, service details, and an archive for internal training documents. Some of these resources, such as the internal archive, are not meant for public viewing due to their sensitive nature. Now suppose you therefore created the following **`robots.txt`** file:

```
User-agent: *
Disallow: /internal-archive/
Allow: /resources/
```

The intention is straightforward: allow everyone to access the general resources but restrict the internal archive. However, if the internal archive is nested within the "/ resources/" directory (example, on directory /resources/internal-archive/), search engines might still index it, thanks to the "**`Allow`**" directive that follows the "**`Disallow`**".

When you reverse the order, the internal archive in the folder resources will be blocked.

```
User-agent: *
Allow: /resources/
Disallow: /internal-archive/
```

It must be noted that while **`Robots.txt`** can instruct search engines not to crawl specific pages, it does not hide those pages from the public. Suppose an online retailer has a confidential pricing page meant only for vendors. If they only rely on **`Robots.txt`** to hide this page, a competitor might still access it directly using the URL. For complete privacy, businesses should implement password protection or other security measures.

Then, a commonly misunderstood concept in **`robots.txt`** is the specificity of user agents. Many website owners mistakenly believe that there is an inherent inheritance mechanism in the **`robots.txt`** file. In simpler terms, they believe that if they set general rules under User-agent: * (which means rules that apply to all bots), they can then specify more particular rules for specific bots such as Googlebot or BingBot underneath, and that the specific bot would obey both the general and the specific rules.

However, that's not how it works. If you specify rules for a particular bot, like User-agent: Googlebot, then that bot will only follow the rules listed under its specific section. It will ignore the general rules set for User-agent: *. This behavior might not align with what some website administrators expect, leading to potential SEO and crawling issues.

TikTok provides a revealing illustration of this misunderstanding. TikTok's **`robots.txt`** file, at a certain point in time, had a general section of rules under User-agent: *. Later, they decided to block BingBot from accessing their /discover folder, so they added a specific rule under User-agent: BingBot. The unintended consequence of this was that all the general rules they had set under User-agent: * were now being ignored by BingBot, allowing it to crawl paths TikTok might not have intended.

In essence, TikTok thought they were adding just one more rule for BingBot, but in reality, they unintentionally changed the entire set of rules that applied to BingBot. This could have serious implications for their crawl budget, as Bing might now start accessing parts of the site they previously couldn't, using up more of TikTok's server resources.

You can see there are many possible issues with **`robots.txt`** files. Now the question is how to spot these issues. There are different tools and ways of working to check your **`robots.txt`** file. First, you can check the already mentioned indexation report in Google Search Console. Second, you can use online **`robots.txt`** validators to check if a URL is blocked by **`robots.txt`** or not, an example is https://technicalseo.com/tools/robots-txt/. Then, it is always a good idea to run the Google mobile-friendly tool and click the link "**`View tested page`**" to make sure all stylesheets were loaded. If you see a non-responsive website without design elements, then mobile CSS may be blocked.

Optimizing Crawl Budget with `Robots.txt`

`Robots.txt` can also be a tool to guide the crawler away from pages. Since Google has a limited crawl budget for each website, when a lot of pages are discovered but not indexed, it may be worthwhile to check how to optimize the crawl budget so these pages will get indexed. With the launch of new a website containing at least 100000 webpages that were not indexed smoothly, we decided to look at how to index this more efficiently.

The objective is to have content indexed efficiently by search engines. However, upon inspecting Google Search Console crawl statistics, they discovered a problem: search engine crawlers, such as Googlebot, were spending about 90% of their time accessing JSON files on the site. These JSON files, while important for the site's internal operations, are not crucial for indexing purposes. You won't like to land your visitors on JSON code anyway. The result? Essential HTML pages are being ignored or are taking longer to be indexed because the majority of the crawl budget was being exhausted on these JSON files.

Using **`robots.txt`**, the website can optimize its crawl budget by directing search engine bots away from the less important JSON files and toward the crucial HTML content. This was accomplished by adding the line Disallow: **`/*.json$`** at the end of the **`robots.txt`** file.

Duplicate Content

Search engines aim to deliver the best and most relevant content to users. When faced with multiple identical pieces, they are left to decide which version is most relevant, which can lead to less optimal ranking results.

Think of a library with five identical copies of the same book. A librarian would not recommend all five to a reader. Similarly, a search engine won't rank identical content from multiple sources equally.

There are two types of duplicate content:

- **Internal Duplicate Content:** Arises within the same website.

  For example, you have got a mobile version and a desktop version of your site where mobile has a separate subdomain but contains the same content as the desktop set. If not set up correctly, search engines might treat these as duplicate versions.

- **External Duplicate Content**: Occurs across different domains.

  You distribute a standard product description to multiple retailers. Each retailer's website now has the same content.

  Some issues could arise with duplicate content: when multiple versions of content exist, the inbound links get split among these versions.

Imagine two pages on your website: Page A and Page B. Both have identical content. A popular blog links to Page A, while a forum post links to Page B. Instead of consolidating this link value, it is divided, weakening the potential ranking power.

Having duplicate content on your site can waste your '*crawl budget*' - the time Google spends on your site. Think of your website as a big house and Google as a visitor. If you have duplicate content, it is like showing the same room to your guest over and over, instead of showing all the different rooms you have.

Then, another problem could be that search engines might not display your preferred version, leading to a loss in conversions.

You have an outdated page with old pricing and a new updated page. Due to duplicate content, the outdated page ranks higher. Potential customers see the old prices, leading to confusion and lost sales.

You might think duplicate content would not appear on your website, as it does not make sense to host multiple copies of the same content on separate URLs. However, there are some cases where unintentionally duplicate content issues arise. Consider the following problems with duplicate content:

- Sometimes, websites can be accessed both with and without the "`www`" prefix or through both "`http`" and "`https`". If not configured correctly, this can be treated as duplicate content. The same happens when URLs with trailing slash will have the same content as the URLs without trailing slash.
- Parameters can lead to multiple URLs serving identical or very similar content.

  Example: Different sorting orders for products might generate different URLs but display the same products:

  www.electronicsstore.com/products?category=laptops&sort=price

  www.electronicsstore.com/products?category=laptops&sort=date
- Also duplicate content may exist because of UTM-campaign-parameters in URL, for example, campaign tags like `?utm_campaign= or <`
- E-commerce sites sometimes create separate pages for minor product variations such as color or size, leading to substantially similar content across different URLs. Think about selling a shoe in ten different sizes.
- Finally, duplicate content may arise is in the indexation of dev and staging servers. Search engines encountering identical content on the main site and staging/dev servers will consider this as duplication, diluting the ranking power of the original content. A bigger problem could be that users will access the staging server instead of the live server. What would happen if they find a non-compete or vulnerable website and start placing orders on the dev website rather than the live website?

Now, we know the issue of duplicate problems, let us solve duplicate content problems.

To solve duplicate content problems, Google launched in 2009 Canonical tags. A canonical tag, denoted as `rel="canonical"`, is a snippet of HTML code that directs search engines to the primary version of a page when multiple pages with duplicate or similar content exists. This helps in tackling duplicate content issues which can adversely affect a website's ranking.

Consider an e-commerce website that sells a variety of shoes. Each shoe model has its own page, accessible through various URLs based on selection criteria such as color, size, or brand. Without canonical tags, search engines might index these as separate pages with duplicate content, diluting the site's SEO performance. For example, a shoe model available in sizes 12 and 13 could have a product page at https://example.com/shoe-model, and two parameterized URL's with preselected sizes:

- https://example.com/shoe-model?size=12
- https://example.com/shoe-model?size=13

Here is how a canonical tag is implemented. On all three URL's, you would place a canonical tag that will refer to the main product page https://example.com/shoe-model:

```
<head>
   <link rel="canonical" href="https://example.com/shoe-model/" />
</head>
```

In this code snippet, irrespective of how users navigate to a particular shoe model, search engines will be directed to the main page (https://example.com/shoe-model/). Thanks to the canonical tag, all SEO equity is consolidated to this primary page.

Metatags for Indexation

Sometimes, the goal isn't to be seen–it's to stay hidden. Enter the "**`noindex`**" and "**`nofollow`**" metatags.

Metatags are snippets of code that reside in the background of a webpage, and though you cannot see them, search engines like Google certainly can. They give search engines clues about what a page is all about. The most important ones are the meta title and meta description, which we will explore in the next chapter. Here, we will discuss the metatags that will impact indexation.

Now, let us talk about the "**`noindex`**" metatag. Imagine you have written a personal letter and you do not want anyone else to read it. In the digital world, if you want to keep a web page away from prying eyes, use the "**`noindex`**" tag. This tag politely asks search engines to look the other way and not list the page in their search results. You might do this for pages that are still being polished, have sensitive information, or may have content too similar to something else on your website.

On the other hand, we have the "**`nofollow`**" metatag. Think of it as a signpost on a trail that says, "**`Don't go this way`**." When you use this tag, you are telling search engines to ignore the links on a page. This is handy when you don't trust the links, like when they come from someone else's comments on your blog. Or maybe you have been paid to put a link on your site and you want to play by the rules, ensuring search engines don't get the wrong idea about your intentions.

Putting these metatags to work is not a hard job. Just insert them into the `<head>` section of your webpage's HTML. For keeping a page out of search results, add `<meta name="robots" content="noindex">`. And if you want search engines to ignore links, go with `<meta name="robots" content="nofollow">`. But if you find a page containing the `noindex` tag, Screaming Frog is a useful tool for listing pages containing `noindex` tags and `nofollow` tags in bulk.

Advanced Topics

We will cover three advanced topics: website structure for indexation (especially for e-commerce websites), log file analysis, and indexing API.

When discussing website structure for indexation, especially for webshops, URL structuring, and canonical tag usage are crucial. Consider a webshop with the URL www.example.com/shop. For each product category, such as food, a common approach is using a URL like www.example.com/shop?category=food. However, this approach involves a critical SEO consideration: filter parameters.

If you use a canonical tag pointing back to www.example.com/shop for filtered URLs, it can prevent specific categories like food from being indexed. To address this, it is recommended to create separate pages for each category, subcategory, or filter, each with its canonical tag. This ensures that each category is properly indexed and visible to search engines.

However, there is a balancing act required here. Allowing the indexing of every possible filter combination can overwhelm Google by creating millions of page combinations (for example, by combining all possible color, size, category, subcategory) filter combinations), leading to inefficiencies. The key is finding the right trade-off, ensuring a comprehensive yet efficient indexing strategy that enhances your webshop's SEO performance.

When there is an indexation problem, it can pay off to use more advanced techniques to solve this issue. Two such techniques are log file analysis and the Google Indexing API, which offer deeper insights into how search engines interact with your website and how you can optimize this interaction for better visibility and ranking.

Log file analysis is a more advanced topic within indexation. A log file is like a diary for your website, recording every request made to the server. Analyzing these files can unveil how search engine crawlers, such as Googlebot, interact with your site. This analysis can reveal critical information such as the most frequently crawled pages, crawl errors, and the time spent on different sections of your site. Of course, you need to get the log files from the server, something a developer may assist with.

For instance, let us consider an e-commerce platform, "`E-Shop`," which used log file analysis to identify that their most important product pages were not being crawled frequently. By reorganizing its site structure and improving internal linking, E-Shop ensured these pages were crawled more often, leading to improved indexing and higher search rankings.

In Google Search Console, you can also find the "`crawl stats`" reports, which are linked from the settings. Here, you can also see an overview about with which pages GoogleBot is interacting with and it is a bit less technical than log files.

A more proactive tool to increase indexing speed in the SEO arsenal is the Google Indexation API. Traditionally, site owners had to wait for search engines to discover and index their new or updated content. The Google Indexing API changes this by allowing webmasters to directly notify Google when content is added, updated, or deleted, speeding up the indexing process.

Consider "`Daily News`," an online news portal that publishes timely articles. By integrating the Google Indexing API, they ensured that their latest articles were quickly indexed and appeared in search results, giving them an edge over competitors in delivering breaking news.

The real magic happens when you use log file analysis and the Google Indexing API together. By analyzing log files, businesses can identify which important pages are not being indexed promptly and then use the Google Indexing API to expedite the process.

For example, a real estate website, "`HomeFinder`," noticed through log file analysis that their new property listings were taking days to get indexed. By utilizing the Google Indexing API, they could significantly reduce this time, leading to quicker visibility for their listings and an improved user experience. Combining these two approaches with the help of a developer may improve your website indexation considerably.

Solving the Indexation Puzzle

Navigating the world of SEO indexation is solving a complex puzzle. Each piece - from understanding the basics of crawling and sitemaps to optimizing Googlebot behavior - plays a crucial role in the overall picture. This chapter not only describes these individual components but also shows how they fit together to improve a website's visibility within Google.

Conclusion

Now you have gained a good understanding of the indexation process, you are equipped to tackle common challenges and implement effective strategies. Whether it involves optimizing your website's structure, leveraging tools such as Google Search Console, or understanding the impact of log file analysis and the Google Indexing API, this chapter demonstrates how these tools can work together to enhance the indexation process. In the next chapter, let us begin researching keywords to optimize your indexed webpages.

CHAPTER 3
Keyword Research

Introduction

Welcome to the crucial chapter on keyword research, a key skill for optimizing your SEO strategy. This chapter will guide you through the process of conducting keyword research, including collection, categorization, and effective application of keywords.

In this chapter, we will learn the vital role of keywords in engaging your audience and how to apply this knowledge across various business contexts. We will delve deeper than just using traditional keyword planner tools. By examining your business strategy, analyzing search engine results, understanding user language, and considering social media trends, you will be equipped to master keyword research.

By the end of this chapter, you will have a comprehensive understanding of keyword research. You will understand how to find and use the right keywords to improve your visibility online and connect more effectively with your target audience. This knowledge is crucial for anyone looking to enhance their online marketing skills and grow their business in the digital space.

Let us get started on this journey to mastering keyword research, a key component in the success of your online presence.

Structure

In this chapter, we will cover the following topics:

- Goals of Keyword Research
- Different Keyword Types
- Keyword Research for Various Business Models
- Collecting and Categorizing Keywords
- SERP Analysis
- Social Media and YouTube Keyword Research

Goals of Keyword Research

Keyword research is a fundamental component of SEO, serving as the initial step to ensure that your website and content reach the intended audience. Let us explore how keyword research integrates into the broader SEO process:

- **Understanding what people search for:** SEO is all about being visible on search engines such as Google. Keyword research helps you understand the exact words and phrases people use when they search for something related to your business. This means you can tailor your website's content to match these searches.
- **Enhancing website visibility in search engines:** Search engines prioritize websites that closely align with user searches. Integrating the right keywords into your website's titles, headings, content, and meta descriptions boosts your site's relevance, elevating its position in search results.
- **Creating relevant content:** Knowing the popular keywords in your industry helps you create content that your audience is interested in. For example, if you run a fitness blog and find that many people search for "*home workouts*," you can write articles or make videos about this topic. This not only attracts more visitors but also keeps them engaged.
- **Reporting:** One of the most direct ways to measure SEO success is by tracking the rankings of your targeted keywords. Keyword research helps identify which keywords are most relevant and valuable to your business. By monitoring how these keywords perform over time in search engine result pages, you can measure the effectiveness of your SEO strategies.

Keyword research transcends being a mere step in SEO; it is a significant component of your online strategy. It tells you what people are actively searching for, enabling you to tailor your website and content to be more useful and accessible. This is not just good for SEO, but it also helps your writing, understanding your competition, and making your website better for your visitors.

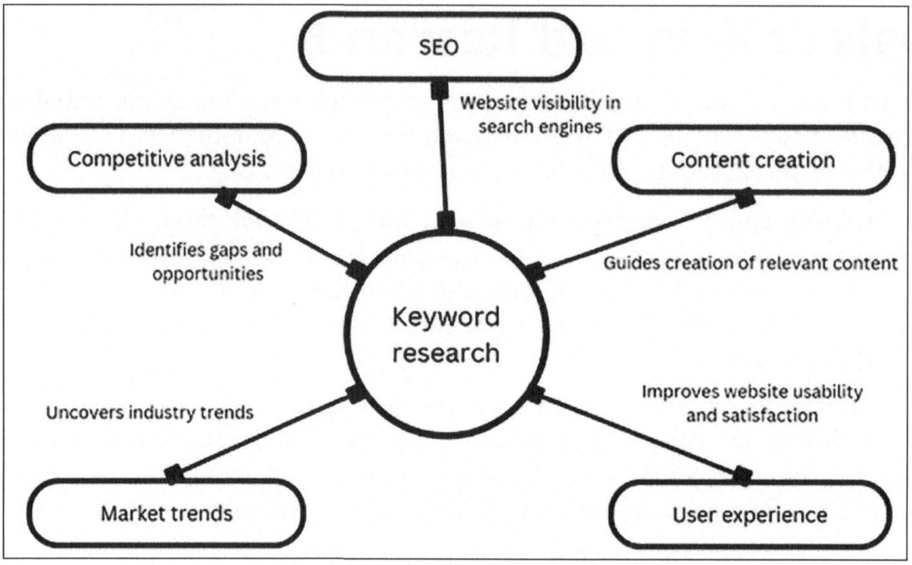

Figure 3.1: *Keyword research*

By researching keywords, you learn the language your customers use and the problems they are trying to solve. For example, if you run a gardening supply store and find that many people are searching for "*organic pest control*," this is a signal. It tells you that your customers are interested in eco-friendly gardening solutions. Armed with this insight, you can stock more organic pest control products, write blog posts about eco-friendly gardening, and even host workshops on the same topic.

Employing appropriate keywords out of your keyword research enhances your website's user-friendliness, enabling visitors to find what they need swiftly, thereby improving satisfaction and encouraging return visits. Knowledge of the right keywords also leads to content improvement, resulting in articles and web pages that are more engaging and beneficial for your audience.

Keyword research is instrumental in uncovering market trends. For instance, a surge in searches for "*smart home gardening systems*" could signal an increasing demand for tech-based gardening solutions. Recognizing such trends promptly allows you to adapt your business strategy, potentially incorporating smart gardening products to establish your brand as a trailblazer in the industry.

Knowing what keywords your competitors rank for, can uncover gaps in their offerings. For instance, if you notice none of your competitors are focusing on "*budget-friendly garden tools*," but there is a decent search volume for this term, you have found a potential niche. You can then offer products or content that fills this gap, attracting customers who are being overlooked by others. But when you notice your competitors ranking for "*buy garden tools*", while you are not, this can signify an opportunity to also optimize your content for this keyword.

Let us say you own a local bakery. Through keyword research, you discover a high number of searches for "*gluten-free baked goods*" in your area. This insight can lead you to introduce a new line of gluten-free products. By advertising these products using the same keywords your customers are searching for, you draw in a new customer base. Over time, you become known as the go-to bakery for gluten-free treats, expanding your market reach and boosting sales.

In essence, effective keyword research is a way to align your business with customer needs, staying ahead of market shifts, and finding unique opportunities to stand out in a crowded market. When used properly, it can be a strategic asset that goes beyond SEO, influencing the direction and success of your business.

Keyword Types

In keyword research, knowing the different types of keywords is like knowing your customers. Each type of keywords brings different people to your site. Let us look at these keyword types. Every type of keywords has its advantages and its disadvantages. Imagine you have an online shoe shop and are looking for relevant keywords.

- **Short-Tail Keywords:** These are short, general words like "*shoes*" or "*running shoes*." They are broad and can bring a lot of people to your site. The problem is that they are too general. If someone searches for "*shoes*," they could mean any kind of shoe. Plus, lots of other shoe sites are trying to use these same keywords, making it very hard to rank on these terms.
- **Long-Tail Keywords:** These are more like phrases, such as "*women's waterproof hiking shoes*" or "*best shoes for marathon training*." They are more specific, so they bring in people who are looking for exactly that. The good part is there is less competition for these phrases, and they often bring in people ready to buy. We see a trend of increasing in long term search, with now 70% of searches using long tail keywords.
- **Informational Keywords:** When people just start looking for shoes, they might use terms like "*how to choose running shoes*" or "*what are the best shoes for flat feet*." These keywords are great for writing articles or blog posts that help people. But the people using these keywords are usually just looking for information and might not buy anything right away.
- **Transactional Keywords:** These are for when someone wants to buy something. They include words like "*buy women's hiking shoes online*" or "*best deals on men's basketball shoes*." They are great because they bring people who want to buy right now. But lots of other shoe sites are trying to use these keywords too, so it can be tough to stand out.
- **Navigational Keywords:** These keywords contain a brand or a specific website. Like "*Nike women's running shoes*" means someone already knows they want

Nike shoes. If you sell Nike shoes, that's great. But if you don't, these keywords won't help much.

- **Geographically Targeted Keywords:** If you have a shoe store in a certain place, these are key. "*Shoe stores in Amsterdam*" targets people in Amsterdam. They are perfect for bringing in local customers. But if your store is not in Amsterdam, these keywords won't be much use.

In short, picking the right keywords is like picking the right shoes for a run. You need a mix to fit different needs. For your shoe store, using different types of keywords helps you reach everyone, from people just looking around to people ready to buy. Knowing what each type does helps you make a better plan for your website and get the right visitors.

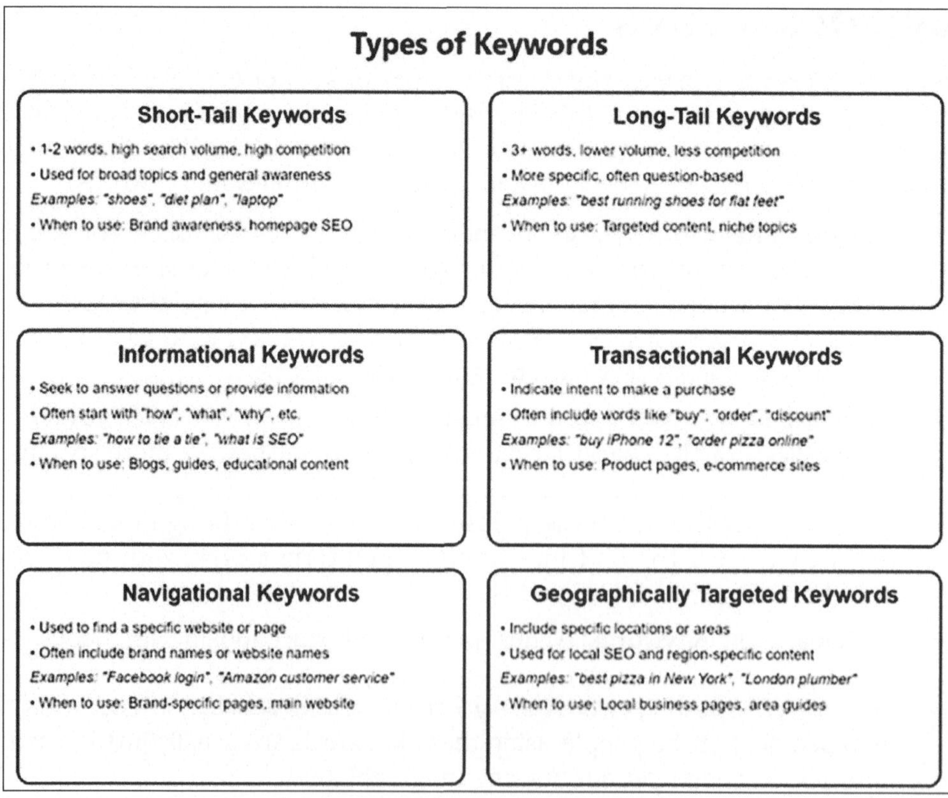

***Figure 3.2**: Types of keywords*

Keyword Research Briefing

Effective keyword research, such as devising a strategy for an online shoe store, hinges on acquiring detailed information about the overarching business strategy. A deeper understanding of this strategy enables more precise alignment with the business's needs.

- **Knowing the Client**: It is important to start with a clear picture of who the client is. Just like knowing whether a shoe store specializes in sports footwear or high-end fashion shoes, understanding the client's identity helps shape your keyword research. If the store focuses on professional and high-end running shoes, your keywords should reflect more athletic themes than if the shop would specialize in basic cheap running shoes.
- **Client's Products or Services**: Delving into the specific products or services offered guides the direction of your keyword research. If the store offers a wide range of children's shoes, your keyword strategy should include terms that parents are likely to search for.
- **Existing SEO Tools and Access:** Access to tools such as Google Search Console can provide valuable insights into past performance. For instance, if certain types of shoe styles have historically driven traffic to the site, they might be good candidates for continued focus.
- **Unique Selling Propositions (USPs)**: Identifying the client's USPs helps to distinguish them from competitors. If a shoe store is known for custom-made shoes, keywords should highlight customization and personalized services.
- **Industry and Field of Operation:** Understanding the sector helps in using industry-specific terms. For a sports shoe store, keywords related to sports, fitness, and athletic performance would be relevant.
- **Target Persona and Audience:** Knowing the client's target audience ensures that the keywords are tailored to their specific needs. If the store's primary customers are professional athletes, keywords should cater to high-performance and professional sports.
- **Business Model: B2B or B2C**: This determines the nature of keywords. B2B keywords for a shoe wholesaler would differ significantly from B2C keywords for a retail shoe store.
- **Purpose of the Keyword Research:** The objective of the research, whether for a new website or improving an existing one, influences the keyword strategy. A new site might require broader, more general keywords to establish its presence, while an existing site might focus on more specific, niche keywords to attract a targeted audience.

Having access to this detailed information ensures that the keyword research is not only comprehensive but also customized to align with the specific characteristics and goals of your manager's client. It is a crucial step in developing a strategy that effectively drives traffic and engagement for the client's website.

Collecting Keywords

Having gathered all the necessary information, we can now advance to the next phase of keyword research - identifying keywords. A thorough keyword research project typically encompasses a range from a few hundred to several thousand keywords. This extensive range aims to capture the varied ways potential customers might think about and search for your products. The specific number of keywords depends on various factors, including your business's size and nature, your product range's diversity, and the depth of your online content. For a comprehensive strategy, it is better to start with a larger list and then prioritize based on relevance, search volume, and competition later on.

Conducting keyword research for an online shoe store involves understanding the myriad ways customers might search for your products. It is about delving into the mindset of potential visitors to your site. Here are several strategies to effectively identify keywords for your business:

- **Drilling Down:** Begin with broad categories such as '*men's shoes*' and '*women's shoes*,' then narrow down to specific types and brands. The aim is not merely to compile an extensive list of keywords but to curate a list that captures the diverse search queries of your customers.
- **Start with What You Have:** First, check out your own website. If you are selling running shoes, use Google Search Console to see what is already bringing people to your site. You might find terms such as "*running shoes sale*" or "*sports shoes for men*" that work well.
- **Look at Competitors**: Do not forget to look at your competition. Tools such as SEMrush can show you the keywords that your competitors are using. If they are getting a lot of traffic for "*lightweight running shoes*," that is a sign of a popular search term.
- **Use Google Keyword Planner:** Google Keyword Planner is great for finding keywords based on how many people are searching for them. It might suggest "*durable running shoes*" as a popular search. Also, check out Google's related searches at the bottom of their search results pages. You could find long-tail keywords, such as "*running shoes with ankle support*." An advantage of using the Google keyword planner is that it immediately shows the search volume for a certain keyword. To access Google keyword planner, you need to have access to a paid Google Ads account.
- **Check out Google Trends:** Google Trends can be really helpful too. It shows you what is popular right now. If you see a spike in searches for "*summer running shoes*," it could be a seasonal trend worth targeting. So enter your main keywords within Google Trends to find related and trending searches. Trends and seasons can affect search behavior. Including seasonal keywords

such as "*winter running shoes*" or trending terms such as "*latest running shoe technology*" can help capture timely traffic.

- **Explore Other Keyword Tools:** Use tools such as `Ubersuggest` and `AnswerThePublic` to get a broader look. `Ubersuggest` gets all Google suggestions. For example, when you enter "`best running shoes`" on ubersuggest.com, `Ubersuggest` might show you phrases such as "*best running shoes for women,*" as these keywords are listed within the Google suggestion. `AnswerThePublic` can reveal what questions people have, such as "*what are the best running shoes for daily use?*".
- **Social Media and Online Forums:** Look at social media and forums. People might talk about what they want in running shoes, using terms you had not thought of. Popular general online forums to look for keyword ideas are Reddit and Quora.
- **Listen to Your Team or Client:** Gaining insights from your team or clients is invaluable. Inquire with your sales or customer service departments about common queries from clients. For example, if there is a focus on specific products such as "*customizable running shoes,*" ensure these are included in your research. Such keywords, while possibly having lower search volumes, are highly relevant and could be easier to rank for.
- **Buyer Journey Stages and Intention:** Customers are at different stages in their buying journey. Some might be in the early stages, using broad searches such as "*running shoes,*" while others might be closer to a purchase, searching for specific types such as "*Nike Air Zoom running shoes.*" Having a mix of broad and specific keywords helps you reach customers at each stage. Thus, search intentions can vary from informational (learning about running shoes to transactional (ready to buy running shoes). Including keywords that cater to different intentions ensures you attract a wider audience.
- **Geographical Variations:** If your store serves different regions, including location-specific keywords is important. Terms such as "*running shoes in New York*" can help attract local customers.
- **Mix and Match Keywords:** Think about combining different types of keywords. For example, pair actions with products – such as "*buy running shoes*" or "*order sports shoes online.*" This helps in targeting people who are ready to make a purchase. So think about combining "*verbs*" and "*nouns*" to quickly come to a huge list.
- **Finalizing Your Keyword List**: Now, once you used all of these approaches, have a look at the website and the keyword research briefing to double-check you did not forget to include any possible important keywords.

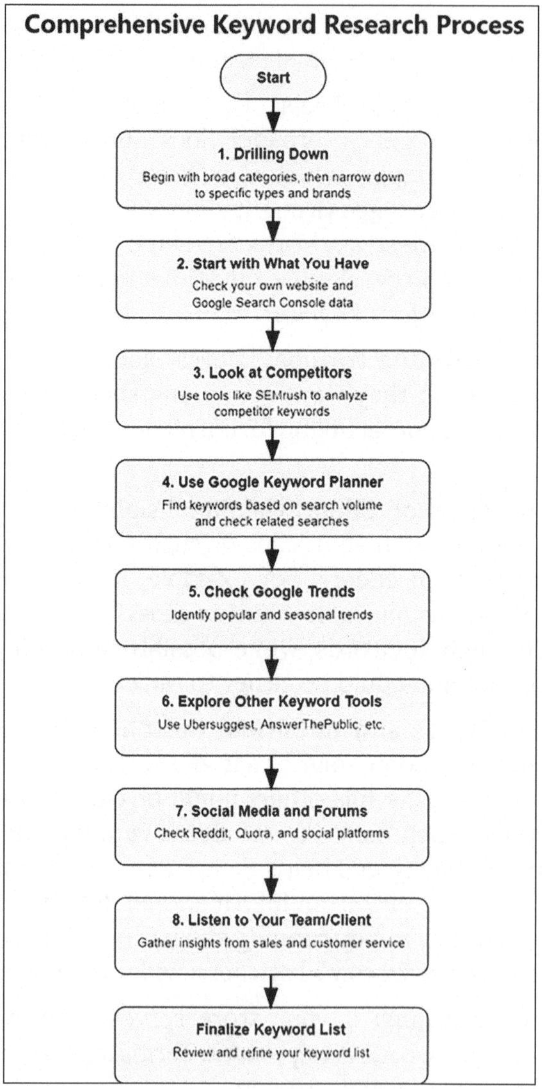

Figure 3.3: *Comprehensive research keyword process*

Categorizing Keywords

In keyword research, categorizing and grouping keywords is key. It is about putting your keywords into categories that make sense for your business and for your website's structure. This step is vital because it helps you to be strategic about where and how you use these keywords on your site.

Because of the big strategic importance, we recommend using three levels for keyword categorization. Example: Category, Subcategory and Search Intent. This will make it easier to group and process keywords than just using one main category.

When you are diving into keyword research for an online shoe store, imagine how each keyword is a puzzle piece fitting into the larger picture of your website. This process is not just about collecting terms; it is about weaving them into the fabric of your site's structure, whether that involves aligning with the current layout or proposing a new, more effective structure.

Start by Exploring Your Current Website

Take a good look at how your website is currently set up. It is such as doing a walkthrough of a shoe store and noticing how the aisles and shelves are arranged. Does your site have distinct sections for '*Men's Running Shoes*', '*Women's Casual Shoes*', or '*Children's Sports Shoes*'? Use these existing categories as your initial guide for grouping keywords. Place relevant keywords under each category; for example, '*Men's Running Shoes*' can include terms such as "*lightweight men's running shoes*" or "*affordable men's jogging shoes*". This alignment ensures that your keyword strategy enhances what is already there, making each section of your website more robust and search-friendly.

Consider a New Structure When Needed

Sometimes, your research might point you towards a different path. If you find that a lot of people are searching for something specific, such as '*Eco-Friendly Running Shoes*', but you do not have a dedicated space for this on your site, it is such as realizing you need a new display in your store. This is where you can propose creating new sections on the website. Group all the relevant '*Eco-Friendly*' keywords together and suggest adding a category for them. This approach is not just about SEO; it is about evolving your website to better serve what your customers are actively looking for.

The Art of Grouping Keywords

Think of grouping keywords as crafting a story for each part of your website. Your broad categories are the chapters, like '*Women's Running Shoes*', '*Running accessories*', and so on. Within these chapters, the sub-categories add depth and detail. Under '*Running Shoes*', there could be sections for different types – perhaps one for '*Trail Running*' and another for '*Competition Shoes*'. These categories can be based on different aspects like product types, customer intentions, shoe features, and so on. Within these categories, you can further group keywords based on more specific criteria. For instance, under '*Women's Running Shoes*', you might have sub-groups like '*Lightweight Women's Running Shoes*', '*Affordable Women's Running Shoes*', or '*High-Performance Women's Running Shoes*'.

Now, refine these groups further based on the intent behind the searches. Some people might be looking to buy, while others might be seeking advice or reviews. This distinction helps you tailor the content for each group more precisely.

Categorizing and grouping keywords will help you later on in your content strategy, as it enables you to enhance data analysis on keyword groups. By monitoring the performance of specific keyword groups, you can gain insights into customer preferences and trends. This structured approach to keyword categorization makes reporting more efficient, whether it is for a client or an in-house manager. You can provide clear, segmented data that demonstrates the impact of your SEO strategies on different parts of the business, like increased traffic to a particular shoe category or higher engagement with a specific type of content.

Grouping keywords will also help you to create targeted content that specifically addresses the searches people are making. Imagine your keyword research reveals a high search volume for "*women's trail running shoes.*" You could create a blog post titled "*Top 10 Trail Running Shoes for Women in 2024,*" which directly addresses this search query - and you could optimize this for the all the keywords within your keyword group "*Trail running shoes for women*", which you can now find easily, thanks to the structure within your keyword research. By including all keywords within the group, your content will attract visitors who are specifically looking for women's trail running shoes using different search keywords.

Categorizing keywords may later be used to also categorize and organize your website more effectively, so it is easier for both users and search engines to find relevant content. Let us say your categories include '*Eco-Friendly Running Shoes*', '*Men's Running Shoes*', and '*Running Shoe Accessories*'. You can structure your website with separate pages or sections for each of these categories. This way, when someone searches for "*eco-friendly running shoes,*" they are directly led to a page that lists all the eco-friendly options you offer, making the user experience smoother and helping search engines index your site more effectively.

Keyword grouping assists in identifying content or product gaps that require attention. For instance, if you notice a significant interest in "*running shoes for flat feet*" during your keyword grouping, this is an area to focus on. By adding keyword position data for this group, you might find that none of the keywords in this group are ranking well. This indicates a gap in your inventory or content, suggesting a need for a range of running shoes designed for flat feet. Creating content such as "*Choosing the Right Running Shoes for Flat Feet,*" optimized for keywords in this group, can help attract and inform customers seeking this specific solution. You have to consider adding a range of running shoes designed for flat feet to your product line and create content like "*Choosing the Right Running Shoes for Flat Feet*" to attract and inform customers who are searching for this specific solution - also by optimizing for the keywords within this keyword group.

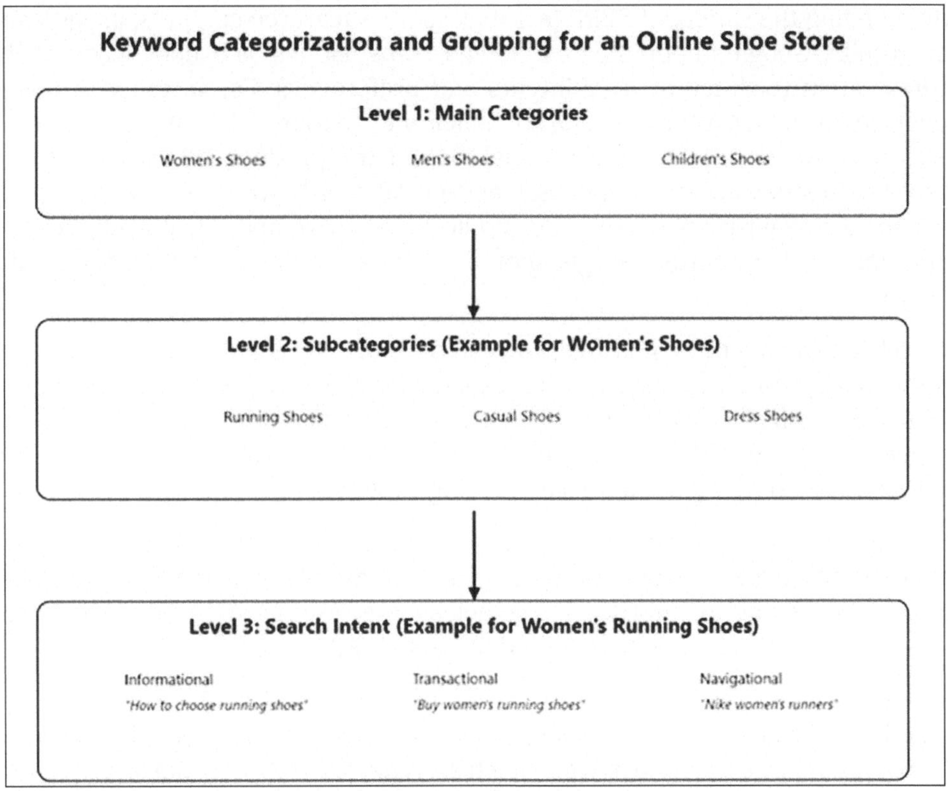

Figure 3.4: *Keyword categorization and grouping for an online shoe store*

The table in *Figure* 3.4 helps you visualize how to organize your keywords. When creating content or optimizing product pages, you can later on refer to these categories. Make sure each page or piece of content focuses on keywords from one category or sub-category. This will help to ensure that your content is targeted and relevant.

In conclusion, categorizing and grouping keywords in your keyword research is like organizing a store into clear, easy-to-navigate sections. It makes it simpler for your customers (and search engines) to find exactly what they are looking for, and it ensures that your content strategy is as effective and targeted as possible.

SERP Analysis

Enhance your keyword research by analyzing Google's search results pages for your targeted keywords. These pages vary significantly, featuring elements like featured snippets, videos, or local results. Integrating an analysis of these SERP (Search Engine Results Page) features into your research can substantially refine your SEO strategy. When you analyze the types of results that appear for queries like "*best running shoes for marathons*," you gain invaluable insights into what potential customers are looking for and how they want to receive that information.

Understanding the variety of SERP features, such as featured snippets, image results, video results, Google Shopping, and Google Maps listings, is crucial. Each of these features caters to different user intents and preferences. For instance, a featured snippet might attract users looking for quick information, while image results may appeal more to those who want a visual idea of the product. So by looking at the featured snippets Google provides for certain keywords, you know what the main intent for a certain keyword may be. While featured snippets will likely be shown on informational keywords, Google shopping results will be shown on transactional keywords.

By closely examining these features, you can develop a targeted content strategy that aligns with what users are most likely to engage with. For example, optimizing for image results involves high-quality, keyword-rich images that could entice visually driven customers. Similarly, video content might be the key to engaging users interested in detailed reviews or demonstrations of running shoes.

Additionally, this analysis offers a competitive edge. By understanding which features your competitors are utilizing effectively, you can identify gaps in your own strategy and areas where you can improve. It also helps in fine-tuning your approach to match the specific user needs to be highlighted by each SERP feature.

It is suggested to create SERP Feature columns as part of your keyword research. This additional columns to your table would categorize your keywords by the types of SERP features they commonly trigger, such as '*Featured Snippet*', '*Image Result*', '*Video Result*', and more. Such a table would not only streamline your SEO efforts but also provide a clear visual guide on how to tailor your content and optimization strategies for each keyword based on the dominant SERP features.

This holistic approach to keyword research, considering the diverse range of SERP features, ensures that your SEO strategy is comprehensive and aligned with the actual user experience and preferences on search engines - and will also match the search intent.

Social Media and YouTube Keyword Research

Keyword research for social media and YouTube presents unique challenges and opportunities, differing significantly from traditional Google keyword research.

- **Platform-Specific Trends and Language:** Social media often has a more conversational and trend-driven nature. Hashtags, for example, play a significant role in social media but are irrelevant for Google. Social media also tends to have more real-time and seasonal trends compared to Google.
- **Type of Keywords Used:** Google keyword research often focuses on longer,

more specific queries (long-tail keywords), such as "*lightweight running shoes for long-distance*." On social media, shorter, more general keywords or hashtags like **#RunningShoes** or **#MarathonTraining** are more common.

- **Intent Behind Searches:** Searches on Google often have a direct intent, like seeking information or making a purchase. Social media, on the other hand, often involves keywords that align with lifestyle, engagement, and community building, reflecting a more social and interactive intent.

So the keyword research for social media like YouTube, Instagram or TikTok may look a bit different than doing keyword research for Google. Here you can find a strategy for social media keyword research:

1. **Analyzing Your Own Content for Trends**: Start by diving into your existing social media content. If you are running a shoe store, look at your posts and identify which ones have garnered the most attention. For instance, if a post about "*best shoes for trail running*" received high engagement, this indicates an area worth exploring further. Analyze the language used in these posts and the questions your audience asks in the comments to identify potential keywords.

2. **Conducting Competitor Analysis**: Keeping a close eye on competitors is essential. Utilize tools like SEMrush to analyze the keywords they are targeting in their social media campaigns. If a competitor is successfully engaging an audience with hashtags like **#UltraMarathonShoes**, consider how you can incorporate similar or related keywords into your content strategy.

3. **Utilizing Social Media Tools for Trending Topics**: Platforms like BuzzSumo can be invaluable for discovering trending topics related to running shoes. These tools provide insights into the most popular and talked-about content in your industry, revealing potential keywords that resonate with your target audience.

4. **Using Engagement Metrics to Guide Keyword Choices:** Pay attention to the likes, shares, and comments your posts receive. High engagement indicates that your audience finds the content valuable, making the keywords used in these posts potential candidates for future content.

5. **Implementing Hashtag Research to Find Relevant Keywords:** Hashtags are crucial for visibility on social media. Use tools like **Hashtagify** to identify popular and relevant hashtags in the running shoe niche. For example, if **#MarathonTraining** is trending, incorporating it into relevant posts could increase your visibility to runners training for marathons.

6. **Leveraging Built-in Search Functions for Keyword Discovery**: Social media platforms often have robust search functionalities. Typing in a term like "*running shoes*" in the search bar can not only show you the number of posts

with that hashtag but also suggest related hashtags, expanding your keyword possibilities.

7. **Monitoring Trending Hashtags for Real-Time Insights:** Regularly check the trending sections on social media platforms. Look for hashtags that align with running shoes and athletic gear, and consider how these trends can be incorporated into your social media strategy.
8. **Observing Influencers for Industry-specific Keywords:** Influencers in the running and fitness industry often use optimized and trending hashtags. Monitoring their posts can provide insights into effective hashtags that could be relevant to your store.
9. **Analyzing Hashtag Performance for Strategic Use**: It is important to choose hashtags that have a good balance of popularity and relevance. On Instagram, for example, you can see how many posts are using a specific hashtag, helping you decide whether it is too broad or niche for your content.
10. **Studying Competitors' Hashtags for Insights:** Examine the hashtags your competitors use regularly. This can provide clues into what is working for them and might offer opportunities for your strategy.
11. **Engaging with Your Audience for Organic Keyword Discovery:** Your followers can be a great source of keyword ideas. Pay attention to the hashtags and keywords they use in their posts and comments.
12. **Applying Cross-Platform Hashtag Strategies**: Some hashtags that are popular on one platform can be effective on another. A hashtag trending on Twitter, for instance, might be worth experimenting with on Instagram.

In summary, the strategies for social media keyword research involve a mix of internal content analysis, competitor monitoring, and leveraging various social media tools and trends. Deepening this research through detailed hashtag analysis and audience engagement can provide more nuanced insights and drive a more targeted social media marketing strategy.

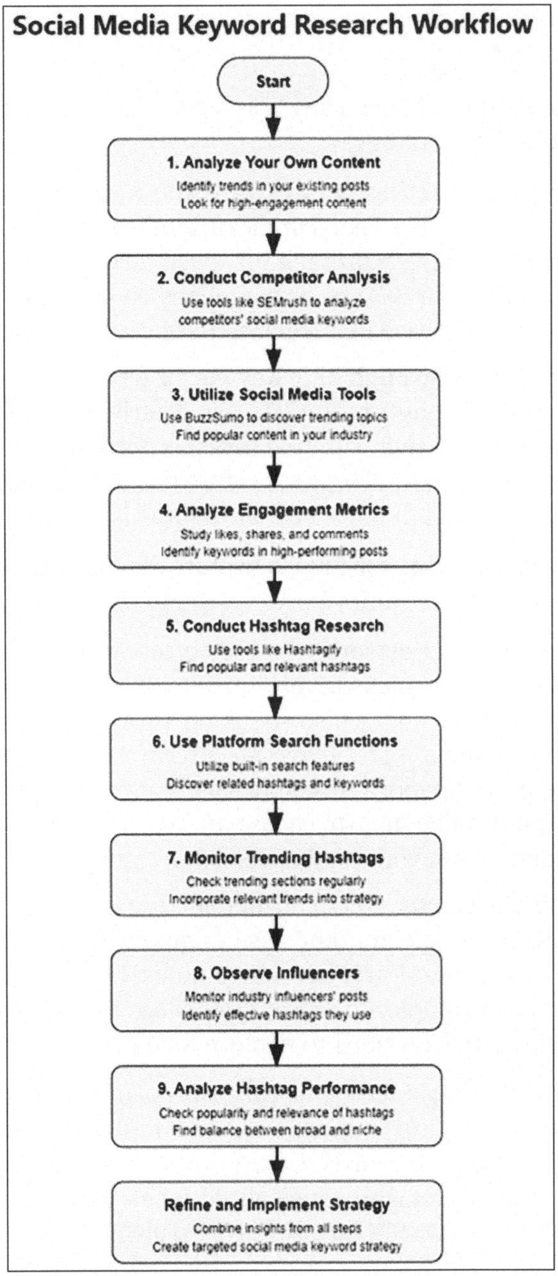

Figure 3.5: *Social media keyword research workflow*

SEA versus SEO Keyword Research

For enhancing your website's SEO, consider leveraging insights from your Search Engine Advertising (SEA) campaigns, as these can offer valuable cues for effective keyword selection. Let us explore how you can use insights from SEA to enhance your SEO keyword research.

SEA gives you a clear picture of which keywords get clicks and lead to sales, which can be a goldmine for your SEO strategy:

- **Focus on High-Converting Keywords:** If you notice that certain keywords in your SEA campaigns, like "*waterproof running shoes*," are consistently leading to sales, it means people searching for these terms are likely to buy. Including these keywords in your SEO research means you are targeting terms that you already know are effective in attracting potential customers.
- **Look for High Click-Through Rate Keywords:** Keywords in your SEA campaigns with a high click-through rate (CTR) are clearly catching people's attention. For instance, if "*lightweight running shoes*" is getting a lot of clicks in your ads, it is worth researching similar phrases for your SEO. These could be variations like "*best lightweight running shoes*" or "*lightweight running shoes for women*."

  While using SEA insights for SEO is useful, it is important to understand how the use of keywords can differ between the two:

  - **Keyword Intent:** Keywords in SEA often target immediate purchases, so they are more sales-driven. In SEO, while you still want sales, your keyword strategy might also focus on providing information, answering questions, or solving problems. So, a term like "*buy running shoes online*" might be great for both SEA and SEO. But for SEO you may also want to rank on queries like "*how to choose the right running shoes*." which may not be included within your paid advertising campaign.
  - **Long-Tail Keywords:** SEO can benefit greatly from long-tail keywords, which are more specific and less competitive. These might not be the focus in SEA due to lower search volumes, but they can be very effective for SEO. For example, "*best running shoes for flat feet 2023*" could be a valuable long-tail keyword to explore for SEO.

By tapping into the insights gained from your SEA campaigns, you can enrich your SEO keyword research, making it more targeted and effective. Remember, while there are differences in how keywords are used in SEA and SEO, the data from your SEA campaigns can provide valuable clues about what your potential customers are looking for, helping you craft an SEO strategy that truly resonates with your audience.

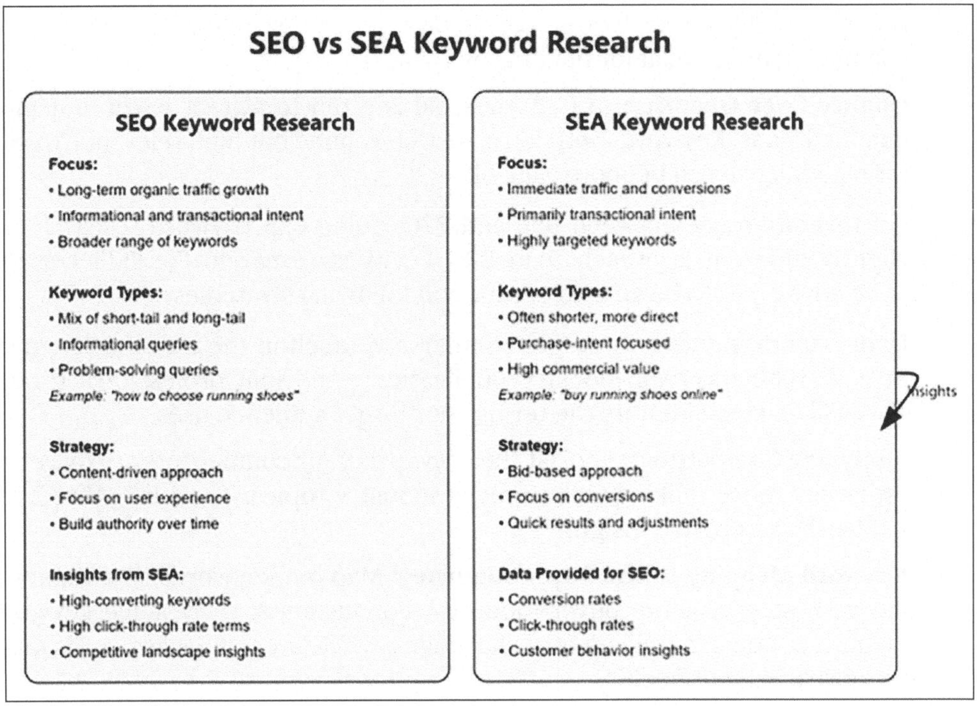

***Figure* 3.6**: *SEO versus SEA keyword research*

B2B Keyword Research

Keyword research for B2B (Business to Business) markets requires a unique approach compared to B2C (Business to Consumer). B2B decision-making processes are often longer, more complex, and involve multiple stakeholders. Thus, the focus in B2B keyword research extends beyond mere search volume to understanding the specific needs and language of a professional audience.

Some of the specific thing you need to be aware when conducting keyword research for B2B are the following:

- **Niche Targeting:** B2B businesses often operate in niche markets with specific jargon and needs. High search volume keywords may not effectively capture the specialized nature of these markets. Often high search volume keywords may be used for a more general audience and may be less relevant to a business audience.
- **Decision-Maker Search Habits:** B2B decision-makers often search for detailed, technical, and industry-specific information. They may use specific phrases that have lower search volumes but are highly relevant.
- **The Buyer's Journey**: In B2B, the buyer's journey is typically longer and more complex. It involves awareness, consideration, and decision stages, each

requiring different keywords. Early-stage keywords might have less search volume but are crucial for building awareness.

- **Quality Over Quantity:** In B2B, the goal is often to attract fewer, but more qualified leads. Keywords with lower search volume but high relevance to your target audience can be more valuable.

Because of this difference between B2B and B2C, doing B2B keyword research may have a slightly different approach than B2C keyword research. For B2B keyword research, we advise you to be sure to execute on following strategies:

- **Understanding Industry Jargon:** Immerse yourself in the industry language. Attend webinars, read industry publications, and join professional groups. This will help you identify the terms your target audience uses.
- **Analyzing Competitors:** Look at the keywords your competitors are targeting, especially those ranking well in niche industry topics. Tools like Ahrefs and SEMrush can provide insights.
- **Keyword Mapping to the Buyer's Journey:** Map out keywords that align with different stages of the buyer's journey. For instance, early-stage keywords might focus on general industry challenges, while later-stage keywords might be more product-specific.
- **Utilizing Long-Tail Keywords:** Incorporate long-tail keywords that reflect the specific queries of B2B decision-makers. These keywords may have lower search volume but can drive highly targeted traffic.
- **Leveraging LinkedIn for Keyword Ideas**: LinkedIn is a goldmine for B2B keyword research. Look at the language used in industry groups, discussions, and by thought leaders.
- **Focus on Problem-Solving Keywords:** B2B buyers often search for solutions to specific problems. Keywords that address these pain points can be more effective than generic industry terms.
- **Case Example**: A B2B Running Shoe Manufacturer Imagine a business that manufactures running shoes specifically for retail businesses. Their keyword research might focus on terms like "*wholesale athletic footwear suppliers*" or "*bulk running shoe orders*." These terms likely have lower search volumes but are highly relevant to the business's target audience of retail buyers and procurement managers.

In B2B keyword research, the key is to deeply understand your audience and their unique language and needs. It is not about attracting the most traffic, but about attracting the right traffic that will convert into meaningful business relationships. This approach ensures that your online presence is tailored to engage and convert your specific B2B audience effectively.

Conclusion

As we end this chapter, let us remember a wise thought from Nelson Mandela: "*Speak to a man in a language he understands, that goes to his head. Speak to him in his language, and that goes to his heart.*" This idea is at the core of what we have explored together. Keyword research is not just about search engines; it is about really connecting with people.

In this chapter, we have covered a lot, from the basics of SEO keyword research to the specific needs of different businesses like a local bakery, an online shoe store or a B2B running shoe manufacturer. We learned about the different keyword types. From short-tail keywords that capture broad topics to long-tail keywords that cater to specific queries and user intentions, we have seen how each plays a unique role in bridging the gap between your content and your audience. We have looked at how to collect the right keywords from both Google and social media, and discussed the unique ways keyword research works for B2B and B2C companies.

As you move forward, keep in mind that the real goal of keyword research is to understand and speak the language of your audience. This way, you are not just getting better rankings; you are building a stronger, more meaningful relationship with your customers. By using what you have learned here, you can make your online presence more effective and help your business grow.

In the next chapter, you will learn how to write optimized content to rank for the keywords you found within the keyword research.

Chapter 4
Copywriting for SEO

Introduction

In this chapter, we will explore some key topics that are essential for anyone looking to write content on your website that is noticed by both people and search engines.

First, we will discuss why it is so important to have good content. Just like a great story keeps you turning the pages of a book, great content on a website attracts visitors, keeps them interested and brings them back for more.

Next, we will dive into the world of title tags and meta descriptions. These are like the headline and summary of your website's story. They appear in search results and can significantly influence whether someone clicks on your website.

Then, we are going to explore optimizing for keywords – but with a twist. Instead of just stuffing your page full of keywords, we will learn about focusing on what your audience is actually trying to find. By writing content that addresses your audience's needs, you will be more likely to be found.

We will also discuss topics and clusters. This is a way of organizing your website so that it is super easy for search engines to understand what you are all about. It is like having a well-organized bookshelf where everything is easy to find.

Of course, we cannot forget about some practical writing techniques specifically for SEO. These are tips and tricks to make your writing not only interesting for readers but also tasty for search engines.

We will look at something called E-E-A-T and search quality guidelines. This is all about showing that you are an expert in what you are writing about, that you are trustworthy, and that your website is a place people should feel confident visiting. These criteria are getting more and more attention from Google. Finally, we are going to explore the possibilities of using SEO data to improve copywriting.

Structure

In this chapter, we will cover the following topics:

- Importance of Quality Content
- Metatags
- Keyword Density versus Keyword Intent
- Topic and Cluster Model
- Copywriting Techniques for SEO
- EEAT and Search Quality Guidelines
- Adjust Copywriting Based on Data

Importance of Quality Content

High-quality content does more than just sound good; it is a strategic asset that enhances SEO. For instance, well-researched articles with in-depth information are more likely to rank well in search engines. By providing detailed, accurate, and useful content, your website becomes a hub for relevant information, enhancing its authority and search engine rankings. Combining content quantity with content quality is the key to success in Google.

Over the past few years, Google used a team of search quality raters, professionals tasked with evaluating the quality of content appearing in search results. These raters play a crucial role in shaping and refining Google's search algorithms, although they do not directly influence individual rankings.

- **Role of Search Quality Raters:** Search quality raters are provided with specific guidelines to assess the relevance, credibility, and quality of content in search results. Their evaluations are used to gauge the effectiveness of Google's algorithm and identify areas for improvement. This feedback loop helps Google continuously refine its algorithms to better understand and categorize web content.
- **Influence on Algorithm Development:** While raters do not directly impact the ranking of a specific website or page, their collective assessments provide invaluable data to Google. This data informs algorithm updates and changes. For instance, if raters consistently mark certain types of content as low quality, Google's algorithm may be adjusted to reduce the visibility of similar content in search results.
- **Focus on E-E-A-T (Experience, Expertise, Authoritativeness, Trustworthiness):** Google's search quality raters are particularly focused on evaluating E-E-A-T. High E-E-A-T ratings, based on raters' feedback, help ensure that the most reliable and accurate information ranks higher, which is especially critical for queries that could significantly impact users' health, finances, or safety.

- **Impact on Content Creators and SEO Strategies:** The work of search quality raters underscores the importance for content creators and SEO professionals to focus on producing high-quality, authoritative content. Understanding the factors raters are instructed to look for, such as clear sourcing of information, author qualifications, and content accuracy, can help copywriters craft content that aligns with what Google's algorithms are programmed to prioritize.

  Consistently delivering authoritative content establishes your brand as an industry leader. This credibility is not only important for attracting and retaining customers but also influences how search engines rank your website. For example, a series of insightful industry reports or thought leadership articles can enhance your site's perceived topical authority, a ranking factor in Google's ranking algorithm.

Metatags Optimization

In this section, we will explore title tags and meta descriptions, two key elements that greatly affect a business's online visibility and search engine success.

- **Importance of Title Tags and Meta Description Tags Within Google:** Title tags and meta descriptions are essential components of HTML code that provide a snapshot of your webpage's content. The title tag, seen as the clickable headline in search results, plays a major role in whether users decide to click through. The meta description, a brief summary of the page's content, further influences the likelihood of a click. They are super important because they're often the first thing people see before they decide to click on your website. Your title tag should be like a catchy headline - clear and engaging, telling people what they will get from your page. And your meta description? That's like a mini-ad for your page. It should make people want to read more. Keep your titles under 65 characters and descriptions under 155 characters to ensure they show up right in search results.

  Using the title tag and meta description tag carefully can positively influence both rankings and appearance of your website within Google.

- **Make Titles Long and Specific Enough:** Meta titles can be up to 65 characters long. The key is to make the most of them by trying to enhance this meta title to this length. This way, you not only take up more display space within Google but can also optimize for additional keywords.

  A local bakery will benefit more from a specific title tag like '**`Cakes and Pastries | Springfield Bakery`**' than a vague one like '**`Springfield Bakery`**'. This specific and descriptive title not only informs potential customers about the bakery's offerings but also incorporates keywords that improve its visibility for relevant searches.

Using generic meta titles like `'Services'` or `'Products'` fails to highlight the unique aspects of what you offer. A more specific title connects directly with your target audience's needs and interests. For a photography studio, a title like "`Wedding Photography Services | Memories Studio`" is far more descriptive and relevant than a vague "`Our Services | Memories Studio`".

- **Length of Meta Descriptions:** Meta descriptions, with a 155-character limit, should effectively communicate your webpage's value. Utilize this space to highlight unique selling points or special offers. For instance, a bookshop could use: "*Explore our curated collection of bestsellers and rare finds. Special discounts for first-time visitors. Dive into your next great read at Book Haven!*"
- **Use Data to Put the Right Keywords in Your Title Tag:** One method to identify the right keywords is through keyword research. When you already have your page written, it can be worthwhile to check in your Google Search Console account which user search queries on that specific page have the highest clicks and impressions. You can optimize your title tag and description tags so these tags would include exactly the keywords people use to find the webpages. With this technique, you will improve rankings and click-through rate in Google.
- **Make Title and Descriptions Unique for Each Page:** Use distinct titles and descriptions for each webpage to prevent issues of content duplication. For a multi-category online retailer, separate tags for "*Men's Athletic Wear*" and "*Women's Fashion Accessories*" cater to specific searches and interests. Each webpage should have a unique title tag and meta description, tailored to the specific content and offerings.
- **Include a Call-To-Action in Your Meta Description:** A compelling meta description can significantly improve click-through rates. For example, a home renovation company might use: "*Transform your home with our expert renovation services. Custom designs, quality materials, and exceptional craftsmanship. Get a free quote today!*" This description clearly communicates the business's value proposition and includes a call-to-action, encouraging potential customers to engage.
- **OG-Tags:** Open Graph (OG) tags play a vital role in determining how your content is displayed on social networks like Facebook and LinkedIn. These HTML snippets dictate how the title, description, image, and URL of your webpage appear when shared. By customizing OG tags, you can ensure that your content is not only more clickable but also accurately represented on social networks.
    - **OG Title:** This title shows up when someone shares your content on social media. It should be attention-grabbing and reflective of the content.
    - **OG Description:** A brief summary of your page, enticing enough to encourage clicks.

- **OG Image**: The image that will be displayed alongside your shared content. This should be visually appealing and relevant to the topic.

  A captivating title, a clear description, and a striking image can make your content much more appealing on social media.

- **Meta Keywords Tag:** The Meta Keywords tag, once a cornerstone of SEO, has become less relevant in modern SEO practices. Historically, this tag was used to tell search engines what keywords the webpage was targeting. Due to its frequent misuse, search engines like Google now state that meta keywords tags don't affect search rankings.

Keyword Density versus Keyword Intent

Keywords are the words people use when they search for something on Google. While keywords remain an area of focus in SEO copywriting, it is not only about frequently using these words in your writing. This is a practice known as '*keyword density*', which used to be common. But now, it is more about why people are using those words. Are they looking to buy something, learn something, or find a website? For example, if someone searches "*buy waterproof camera*," they are probably looking to buy. But if they search "*best waterproof cameras 2023*," they might be looking to learn about the best cameras before they buy. Your writing should meet their needs depending on why they are searching (keyword intent).

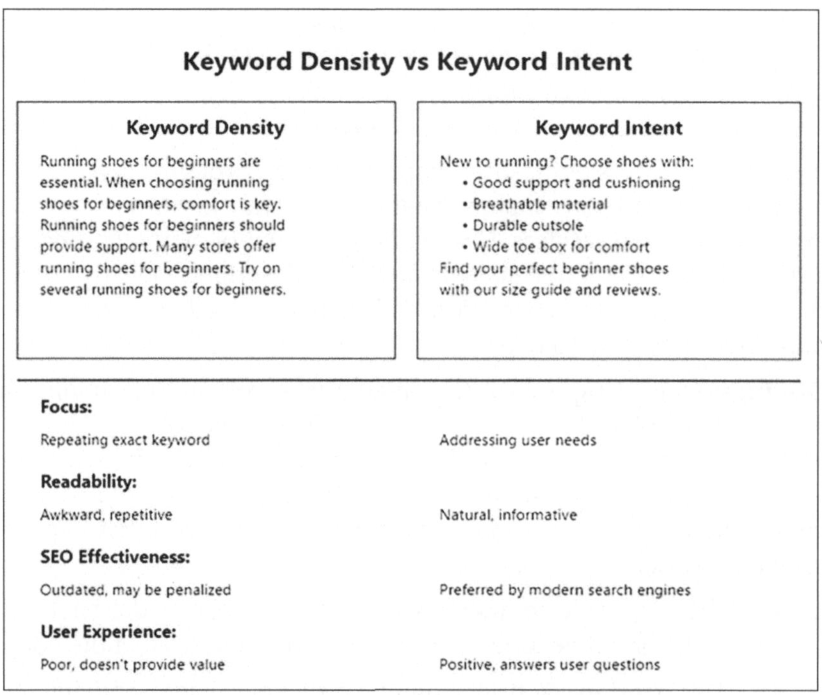

***Figure 4.1**: Keyword density versus keyword intent*

We will illustrate these concepts with detailed examples to show how they work in real situations.

- **Understanding Keyword Density:** Keyword density refers to how often a keyword appears in your content. In the past, a high keyword density was often equated with better search rankings. However, this practice led to poor content quality. For instance, a travel agency repeatedly using the phrase "*cheap flights to Hawaii*" in every other sentence creates awkward and unengaging content. Using the keyword phrase *balancedly*, like in the introduction, middle, and conclusion, would be more effective and pleasant for readers.
- **The Evolution to Keyword Intent:** The focus in SEO has shifted from mere keyword repetition to understanding the user's intent behind searches. This means categorizing keywords into types: those for buying (transactional), learning (informational), or finding a website (navigational). An online electronics store, for instance, might target "*buy wireless headphones online*" for transactional intent and "*best wireless headphones* 2023" for informational intent.
- **Utilizing Long-Tail Keywords for Precision**: Long-tail keywords are longer, more specific phrases with a clear purpose. A small business specializing in eco-friendly office supplies could target long-tail keywords like "*biodegradable office stationery supplier*" instead of the more generic "*office supplies*". This specificity attracts a more targeted audience, increasing the chances of meeting user needs and conversion rates.
- **Practical Examples of How Keyword Intent Works:** Consider a home decor business. For transactional intent, they might focus on keywords like "*buy vintage bedroom decor online*", creating content that guides users towards making a purchase. For informational intent, they might use "*how to style vintage decor in modern homes*", offering valuable advice and establishing authority in their niche. For a local intent, they may optimize the webpage with local contact details for "*home decor New York*".

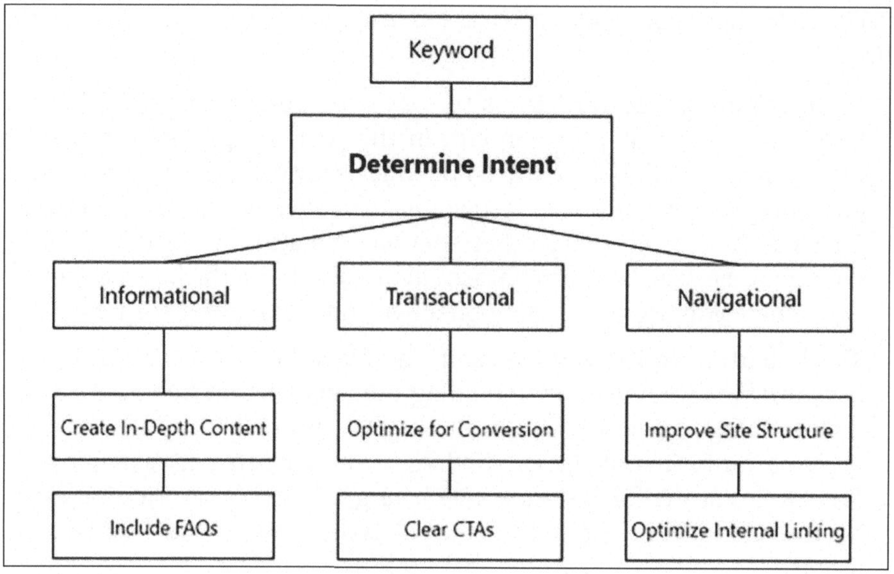

***Figure* 4.2**: *Keyword Intent*

- **Balancing Keyword Density:** Achieving the right keyword density is about natural inclusion. A landscaping company's blog post might naturally include "*sustainable landscaping solutions*" several times throughout an informative article. The key is to ensure the term fits organically within the content, enhancing rather than detracting from the overall quality and readability.
- **Incorporating Semantic Keywords:** Using semantically related keywords can deepen content relevance. A financial consultancy firm could integrate terms like "*wealth management*", "*asset allocation*", and "*retirement planning*" alongside "*investment advisory services*". This approach not only enriches the content but also helps search engines understand the context better, improving SEO.
- **Ongoing Analysis and Adaptation:** Continuous monitoring of keyword performance is vital. For instance, a gourmet coffee shop might initially target "*artisanal coffee beans*" but find through analytics that "*single-origin coffee beans*" drives more traffic. Adapting content to include and focus on the latter term could yield better SEO results.

In summary, the strategic use of keyword density and intent is foundational for businesses aiming to craft content that resonates with both search engines and users. By focusing on the reasons behind searches and embedding keywords in a natural, contextually relevant manner, businesses can not only improve their search engine rankings but also enhance user engagement and satisfaction. So don't just think about optimizing a text by stuffing it with as much keywords as possible, focus on understanding what the user is trying to achieve when typing in a certain keyword, and help the user achieve this.

Topics and Clusters

When conducting keyword research, it may be tempting to go for high-volume short-tail search keywords first, but it is more effective to think about a comprehensive strategy that can help you improve positions for both long-tail and short-tail keywords.

The topic cluster is a sophisticated SEO strategy that organizes content thematically to enhance search engine visibility for a range of keyword types, including short, medium, and long-tail keywords.

Imagine your website is like a big tree. The main topic you are talking about is the trunk of the tree – strong and central. This is your '*pillar page*'. It gives a big overview of a broad subject. Now, the branches growing out from this trunk are like your 'cluster pages'. Each branch (or cluster page) explores a specific part of the big topic in more detail.

Just like a tree's branches are connected to its trunk, your cluster pages link back to the pillar page. This setup makes it easy for your visitors (and Google) to see how everything is connected and related. It is a natural, organized way to explore a topic – start at the trunk (the main idea) and then explore the branches (specific details) as you like.

Through practical examples, we will illustrate how this approach can elevate a business's online presence.

Defining Topic Cluster Structure

So, a topic cluster structure involves creating a "*pillar*" page that provides a comprehensive overview of a broad topic, linked to "*cluster*" pages that delve into specific subtopics. This interlinked structure not only helps users navigate your content more effectively but also enables search engines to recognize your site as a thematic authority. For instance, a health and wellness website might have a pillar page on "*Nutrition and Diet*" with cluster pages covering "*Vegan Diets*," "*Keto Recipes*," and "*Gluten-Free Living*."

Short-tail keywords are broad and highly competitive. The pillar page in a topic cluster targets these keywords. By providing in-depth, authoritative content on a broad subject, the pillar page signals to search engines the site's relevancy in that domain. For a digital marketing agency, a pillar page focusing on "*Digital Marketing Strategies*" can effectively target the short-tail keyword "*digital marketing*."

Medium-tail keywords are more specific than short-tail keywords but less specific than long-tail keywords. Cluster pages are ideal for targeting these. They focus on subtopics, providing detailed content that is still broad enough to attract a wider audience. For example, a cluster page under the "*Digital Marketing Strategies*" pillar might focus on "*Social Media Marketing for Small Businesses*," a perfect fit for medium-tail keyword targeting.

Long-tail keywords are highly specific and often less competitive. Cluster pages can delve into niche topics under the broader umbrella of the pillar content, making them ideal for targeting these keywords. A cluster page in our digital marketing example might cover "*Instagram Marketing Tips for Independent Retailers*," targeting a long-tail keyword like "*Instagram marketing for retailers*."

Benefits of Topic Cluster Model

Topic cluster model offers benefits for ranking across different types of keywords. For short-tail keywords, it establishes domain authority; for medium-tail keywords, it provides depth and specificity; and for long-tail keywords, it addresses niche queries with precision. This comprehensive coverage enhances the website's overall SEO performance, making it more likely to rank for a diverse range of searches.

Besides SEO benefits, topic clusters improve site structure and user experience. This organized approach helps users find information more easily and encourages them to explore related topics, increasing on-site engagement, a positive signal to search engines.

Real-World Example

Consider a home improvement business. A pillar page (topic page) could be "*Home Renovation Guide*," with cluster pages like "*Kitchen Remodeling Ideas*," "*Budget-Friendly Renovation Tips*," and "*Modern Bathroom Designs*." This structure targets a spectrum of keywords, from the broad "*home renovation*" to more specific "*budget-friendly kitchen*".

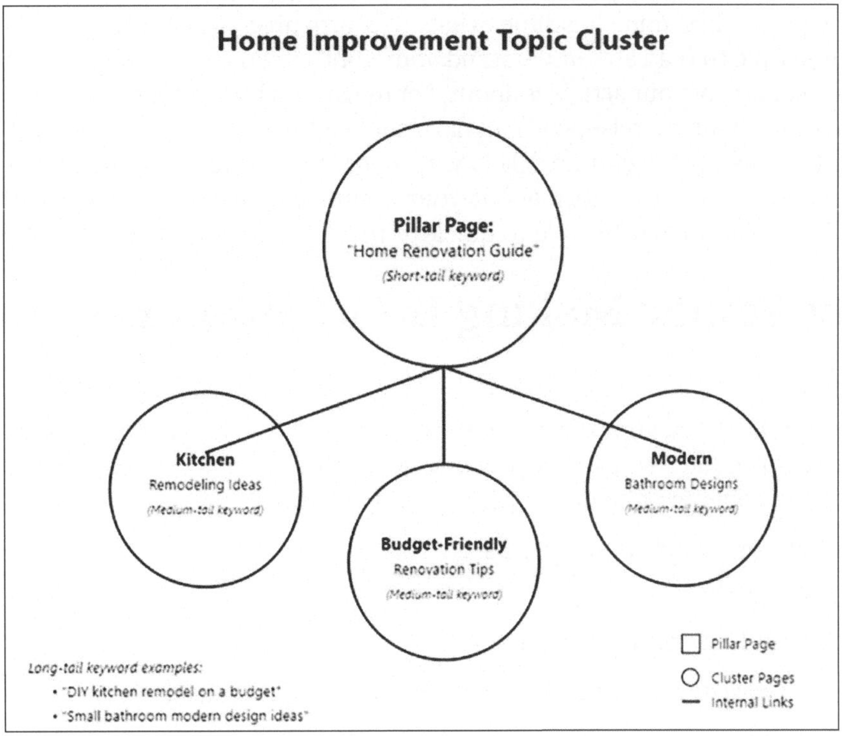

Figure 4.3: *Topic Cluster*

You see, the home improvement business will improve website organization and user experience but also enhances its ability to rank for a wide range of keywords, thanks to this topic cluster model. By thoughtfully developing pillar and cluster pages, businesses can effectively target short, medium, and long-tail keywords, boosting their online visibility and authority.

Copywriting Techniques for SEO

When writing a webpage for SEO, there are some techniques you can use to optimize your text for optimal Google rankings. Here, we list some known techniques that may improve your rankings:

Headlines and Subheadings are Very Important

Headlines are the first thing people see and decide if they want to read more. Think of headlines like the title of a book or the name of a movie. They should make people curious and show what your article or page is about. For example, a garden shop might use a headline like "*Grow a Beautiful Garden in 3 Easy Steps*" instead of just "*Gardening Tips.*" This is more interesting and tells readers exactly what they will learn. So take care of your H1-tag, which is also a ranking factor within Google.

Subheadings are like mini-headlines that help organize your writing. They make it easier for people to read and understand your content. For search engines, they show what each section of your article is about. Let us say you have a fitness website. Instead of just writing about exercise, you can have subheadings like "*Best Morning Workouts*" or "*Easy Exercises for Beginners*." This way, people can find what they need quickly, and search engines know more about your content. By using keywords within your subheadings, visitors may be able to quickly browse to a relevant section on the page.

Bullet Points: Making Information Easy to Read

Bullet points help list important points in a clear way. They are great for showing features of a product, steps in a process, or any key points. For example, a bakery might list the benefits of its new healthy bread like this:

- Made with 100% whole grains
- No added sugar
- Perfect for healthy sandwiches

This makes it easy for customers to see why the bread is special.

Also, these bullet points tend to have an increased chance to get displayed as a featured snippet within Google.

Long-Tail Keywords: Be Specific to Attract the Right Audience

Long-tail keywords are like specific clues that help people find exactly what they are looking for. Instead of using broad, general words, use specific phrases. For example, a small online clothing store might use "*affordable summer dresses for teens*" instead of just "*summer dresses*." This helps the store attract people who are looking for exactly what it offers.

Length of Your Articles

When you are writing for your website, it is important to think about how long your articles or pages should be. While generally, thin content pages with low word count should be avoided, there is no general rule about content length for SEO. Still, content length can really affect how well the webpage is scoring in Google searches. Defining content length is no easy answer because it depends on what people are looking for when they search.

People search online for lots of different reasons. Some want to learn something new, some want to buy something, and some are just trying to find a specific website. Your writing should match what they want.

- **If Someone is Looking to Learn (Informational intent)**: For instance, finding out how to bake a cake, they usually like longer articles with lots of details. These could be around 1,000 to 2,000 words. But remember, every word should be useful – no filling up space with unnecessary stuff!
- **When People Want to Buy (Transactional Intent)**: Now, if someone wants to buy something, like a specific camera, they might not want to read a lot. They are more interested in the camera details, prices, and maybe some reviews. Here, a product page will outrank a very long article.

No matter how long your content is, it needs to be good. Writing just to hit a word count won't help. People (and Google) can tell if you are just adding words without adding value. Always focus on writing something helpful.

A smart trick to find out how many words should be on your webpage is to see how long the articles or pages that show up at the top of Google searches are. This can give you a good idea of what Google and people looking for your topic expect.

Understanding the Power of Questions in SEO

Search engines, especially Google, are increasingly focusing on understanding and answering user queries directly. This trend is evident in features like the "`People Also Ask`" section, where Google displays questions related to the user's original search query along with concise answers. By including relevant questions and their answers in your content, you can increase the chances of appearing in these sections, thereby gaining more visibility.

Incorporate questions and answers naturally into your content. They can be part of your main text or included in a dedicated FAQ section. For instance, a blog post about healthy eating might have a section with a question like "`What are easy healthy meals for busy people?`" followed by a concise list of suggestions.

The answers should be informative, accurate, and to the point. For a question about trends in digital marketing article, you might include an answer like, "*The latest digital marketing trends include the use of artificial intelligence, increased focus on video content, and personalized email marketing strategies.*"

Your answers should be structured in a way that makes them eligible for featured snippets – the highlighted boxes that appear at the top of Google search results. Keep your answers brief (40-50 words), use bullet points or numbered lists where appropriate, and structure them in a clear, logical manner.

Including questions and answers is not just good for SEO; it also improves the user experience. It makes your content more engaging and helpful, as you are directly addressing the concerns or curiosities of your audience. This approach can establish your site as a go-to resource, building trust, and credibility.

The number-1 mindset

To excel in the competitive landscape of SEO, it is essential to embrace the "*Number 1 Mindset.*" This approach goes beyond basic optimization techniques like keyword stuffing. It is about aspiring to be the best possible answer to a user's query, so much so that if Google didn't rank your content at the top, it would seem like an oversight on their part.

Imagine you are writing about "*natural remedies for migraines.*" The Number 1 Mindset begins with researching the current top-ranking pages for this query. This involves studying not just what content ranks at the top but also analyzing why it is there. What makes these pages so effective? Is it their depth of information, the clarity of their advice, the user experience they offer, or their authoritative backlinks?

Next, turn a critical eye to your own content. Ask yourself, "*What can I offer that is even better?*" It is not just about matching the top results but surpassing them. This could involve more comprehensive information, easier-to-understand explanations, more engaging presentation, or newer, more relevant research.

Remember, achieving the number 1 spot on Google can dramatically increase your click-through rate (CTR), often giving you 10 times more clicks and visitors than a number 5 position. This is not just about visibility; it is about being the go-to source for your audience's needs.

Let us say your research shows that the top articles on "*natural remedies for migraines*" are comprehensive but somewhat technical and hard to understand. Your opportunity lies in creating content that is not only thorough but also more accessible and engaging for the average reader. Incorporating infographics, user testimonials, and easy-to-follow advice could be the edge you need.

Storytelling for SEO

People love stories. They can make your business more relatable and interesting. Telling stories about your products or services can help people understand and remember them better. For instance, a local coffee shop might share a story about how they find and choose their coffee beans. This story can make customers feel more connected to the coffee and the shop. We can use the powerful weapon of Storytelling also for SEO purposes.

Storytelling allows for the seamless integration of keywords in a natural, unforced manner. When you tell a story, you are more likely to use a conversational tone, which naturally incorporates long-tail keywords and phrases that people use in everyday language. This organic approach to keyword inclusion is favored by search engines, as it adds keywords in the language of the user, but then also it avoids keyword stuffing. Storytelling makes the content more reader-friendly - and as Google like authentic and original content, storytelling may be the approach to just do that.

Engaging stories are more likely to be shared across social media and other platforms, leading to increased visibility and backlinks. These backlinks are a vital component of SEO, as they signal to search engines that other websites consider your content valuable and trustworthy. A compelling story can turn a regular piece of content into share-worthy material, garnering attention and links from various sources.

Let us understand the different steps of storytelling and SEO with the example of a SAAS project management tool.

- **Understanding the Audience:** The target audience of the project management tool is entrepreneurs who are constantly grappling with meeting deadlines in their startups. These individuals seek effective strategies and tools to manage time and resources efficiently to meet their business goals.
- **Tailoring the Story:** The blog centers on "*Alex*," a driven entrepreneur whose startup is growing rapidly. Despite her passion and dedication, she faces significant challenges in meeting project deadlines. The story begins with a critical project at Alex's startup falling behind schedule, leading to client dissatisfaction and team stress.
- **Seamlessly Integrating Keywords:** Throughout Alex's story, integrate keywords such as "*meeting business deadlines*," and "*deadline management in startups*". Use these phrases naturally as Alex searches for a solution to her deadline woes.
- **Crafting an SEO-Friendly Structure:** Title the blog "*Deadline Challenges in startups: Alex's Success Story*". Use subheadings like "*The Deadline Dilemma in Startups*," "*Solutions for Deadline Management*," and "*Turning the Tide on Startup Project Deadlines Forever*" to guide readers through Alex's journey.
- **Emphasizing Emotional and Relatable Elements:** Detail Alex's initial despair over missed deadlines and the negative impact on her business. Then, pivot to her discovery of your SaaS tool and the subsequent transformation in her approach to deadline management. Highlight the relief and confidence she gains as her team starts to efficiently meet deadlines, thanks to the tool's features.
- **Directing Readers with a Clear Call-to-Action:** End with a call-to-action that encourages readers to explore your tool, offering them a pathway to overcome their deadline challenges. This could be through a trial offer, a webinar on time management, or direct access to your tool's features.
- **Ensuring Readability and Engagement:** Present the story with engaging visuals, like timelines showing Alex's progress, or graphical representations of improved project turnaround times. Keep the narrative concise with short

paragraphs, and use infographics or bulleted lists to emphasize how your tool addresses specific deadline-related challenges.

- **The Story Format:** Stories tend to follow a well-structured format throughout the ages.

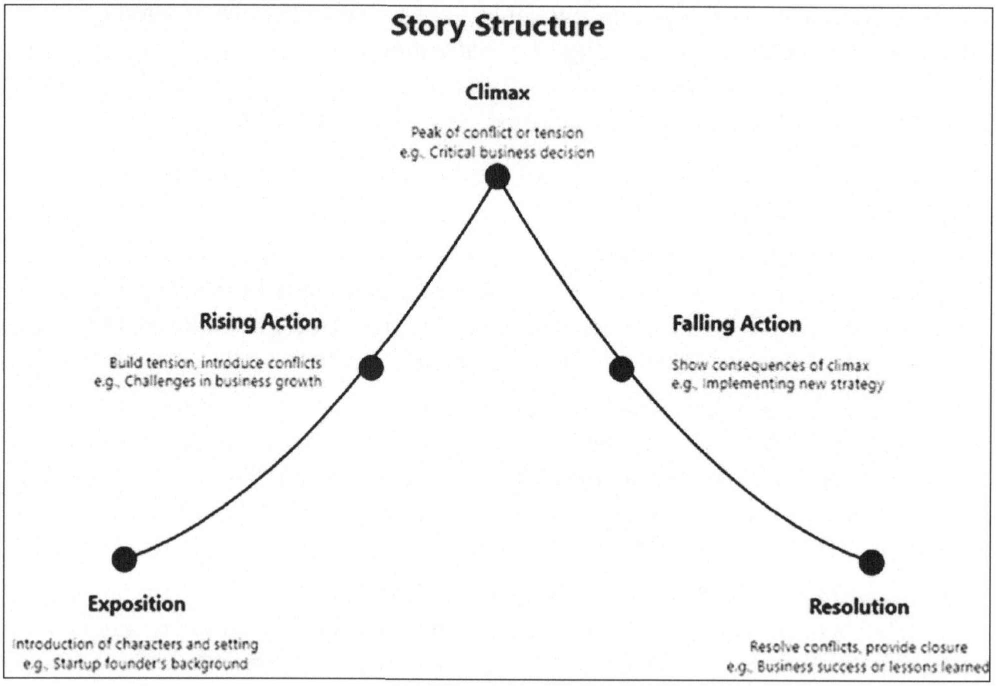

Figure 4.4: *Story Structure*

The different parts of a story are:

- **Exposition**
  This is the introduction of the story where the characters, setting, and initial situation are established. It sets the scene and provides the necessary background information.
  In a business context, this could be the introduction of a startup founder and the initial challenges faced in establishing their business.

- **Rising Action**
  This part of the story builds upon the initial setup, introducing the main conflict or problem. It creates tension and develops the narrative by adding complications or challenges.

- **Climax**
  The climax is the turning point of the story and the moment of greatest tension. It is the point where the main conflict reaches its peak and demands resolution.

- **Falling Action**
  After the climax, the story moves towards resolving the conflict. It shows the consequences of the climax and begins to untangle the story's complexities.
- **Resolution (or Denouement)**
  This final stage resolves the story's conflicts and questions, leading to a conclusion. It provides closure to the narrative, resolving character arcs and tying up loose ends.

E-E-A-T Optimization

When you write for your website, it is important to show that you really know what you are talking about. This is what Google calls E-E-A-T: Experience, Expertise, Authoritativeness, and Trustworthiness. Think of it like this: if you are giving advice on health, you want a doctor or a health expert to write it. This shows Google and your readers that you can be trusted and that you know your stuff. It is like having a seal of approval on your website's information.

Google's search algorithm has evolved to prioritize the trustworthiness and value to users. E-E-A-T is the framework used by Google to assess the quality of content, particularly in financial and health topics (also called YMYL or Your Money or Your Life), which require a high level of accuracy and reliability.

Understanding and applying E-E-A-T principles can significantly enhance your content's standing in Google's eyes. Let us take the example of a page around pain medication. How can it demonstrate the different aspects of E-E-A-T within the content?

- **Experience: Demonstrating Real-World Knowledge**
  Experience is about showing hands-on familiarity with your topic. For a piece on pain medication, this could involve detailing personal experiences in managing pain or case studies from real patients. This firsthand perspective adds a layer of relatability and depth to your content, signaling to Google that you have practical insight into the subject.
- **Expertise: Showcasing Specialized Knowledge**
  Expertise is crucial, particularly in fields that impact health and wellbeing. In content about pain medication, highlighting the author's medical qualifications, such as a degree in pharmacology or experience in pain management, can significantly bolster the content's credibility. Expertise assures readers (and Google) that the information is not only accurate but also comes from a knowledgeable source.
- **Authoritativeness: Establishing Your Authority**
  Authoritativeness involves being recognized as a leading source of information. For content on pain medication, this could be achieved by having the content

featured or referenced in notable medical journals or websites. Being cited by authoritative sources in the medical field demonstrates to Google that your content is not only trustworthy but also respected by peers in the same domain.

- **Trustworthiness: Ensuring Accuracy and Security**
  Trustworthiness is about creating a secure environment for your audience and providing factually correct information. For a website providing information on pain medication, implementing HTTPS to secure user data, citing reputable sources for medical claims, and providing clear, transparent contact information can all contribute to enhancing trustworthiness. This aspect reassures both users and Google that your site and its content are reliable and safe.

To fully leverage E-E-A-T in your writing, focus on creating content that is not just informative but also demonstrates your competence and reliability in the subject matter. This involves creating research-backed information. Use statistics, studies, and credible sources to back your claims. For a tech blog, referencing recent studies or technological breakthroughs can add depth to your content.

Figure 4.5: E-E-A-T

For example, if you were to write an article about effective IT project management, make clear who wrote the article, include quotes of experts within the article and link to an academic study.

Search Quality Rater Guidelines

Google has a team of people (search quality raters) who check if websites are good. They don't decide if your site will be number one on Google, but they help make Google's search better. They look at things like whether your website has good information and if it is trustworthy, with criteria specified in the search quality rater guidelines. For example, if you write about health tips, quality raters check if your tips are safe and if you have the right knowledge about health. Making sure your website follows these guidelines can help your site be seen as a good, trustworthy source. That is why copywriters should be aware of the search quality rater guidelines in order to make future-proof SEO content.

Search quality raters are mainly evaluating webpages on following five points:

- **E-E-A-T**, which is explained in the section before.
- **High Quality Main Content**
  It should provide valuable information that is accurate, comprehensive, and well-presented. This includes text, images, videos, and other types of content that directly help the page achieve its purpose.
- **Purpose of the Page**
  Every page should have a clear and beneficial purpose, whether it is to inform, entertain, sell a product/service, or something else. Quality raters assess if a page fulfills its intended purpose effectively.
- **Website Information and Content Creator Information**
  For certain types of content, raters look for information about the website and the content creator. This is particularly important for "*Your Money or Your Life*" (YMYL) pages. Transparency about who is responsible for the website and who created the content can enhance trustworthiness.
- **Website and Content Maintenance**
  Regular updates and maintenance of the website and its content are seen as indicators of a site's commitment to providing current and relevant information. Outdated, broken, or neglected sites might be viewed as lower quality.

By aligning your website and its content with these principles, you can work towards improving its perceived quality in the eyes of both Google's algorithms and human raters.

Data-Driven Copywriting

When you are writing for your business, knowing what your customers like is super important. Data gives you hints about what they enjoy and what they are looking for.

Google Analytics is a tool that basically tells how much people like your content. It has something called an engagement rate. If the engagement rate is high on a piece of your content, like an article about "*easy cooking recipes*," it means people really like it. This tells you that writing more about cooking could be a good idea. But if you notice a page with low engagement rate but high SEO visits, it means you may still optimize this page even though it is ranking well within Google.

In Google Search Console, you can find the Click-Through Rate (CTR%). This is the percentage of people who see your website in search results and then actually click on it. If you notice pages with a low CTR%, you can ask yourself what you can do to improve the CTR%.

Once you have written and published your content, always go back and look at these numbers. They tell you what is working well and what is not. This helps you know what to write more about and what to change.

Using data from tools like Google Analytics and Google Search Console makes your writing better because it is based on what your customers really want to read. This way, you are not just guessing what they like; you are using facts to make your writing more interesting for them.

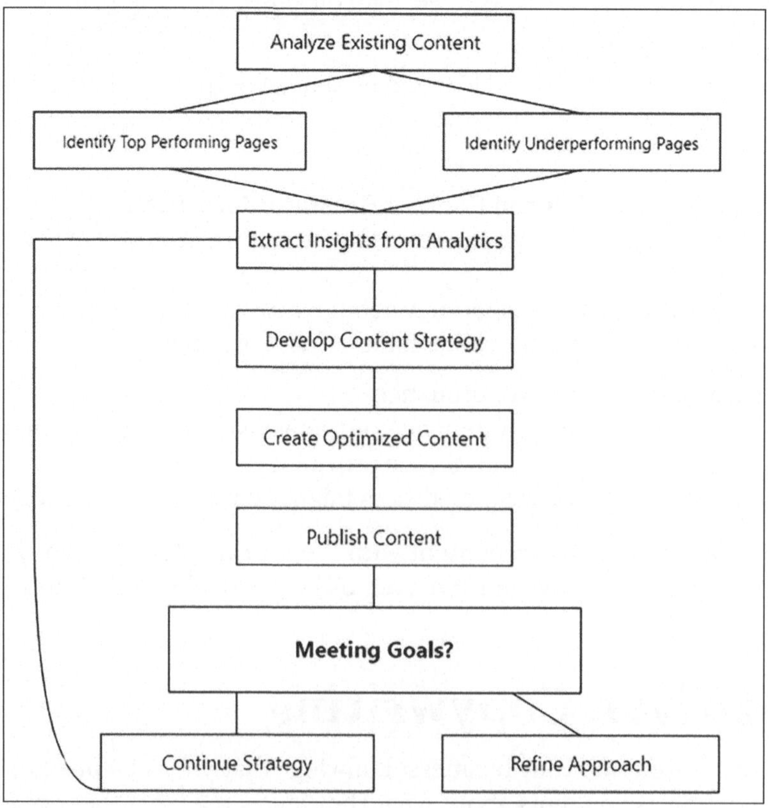

Figure 4.6: *Data-driven copywriting*

Using SurferSEO

If you have a budget for tools, SurferSEO is like a helpful friend for your website. It gives you advice on what words to use and how to arrange your articles. It is like having someone who knows a lot about SEO checking your work and telling you how to make it better. For example, it can suggest how often you should use certain words or how long your article should be. And it can even show you what other websites are doing well so you can learn from them. This tool is great for making sure your writing is just what Google likes. Some key features are:

- **Finding the Best Keywords**: SurferSEO helps you figure out which words you should use in your writing to show up in Google searches. It tells you how often to use these words so your article is just right - not too much, not too little.
- **Help with Headings and Length**: It also gives advice on how to organize your article, like how many headings to use and how long it should be, based on what is working well for other websites that are doing good on Google.
- **Learning from Competitors:** With SurferSEO, you can look at what other websites that sell the same things or talk about the same topics are doing. By understanding their best tricks, you can write your articles in a way that is just as good or even better.
- **Checking What's on Google's First Page:** This tool shows you what kind of articles or pages are getting to the top of Google for the things you want to write about. You will see what these top pages have in common, so you can write your articles in a similar style or format.
- **Writing with SEO Tips:** While you are writing, SurferSEO gives you hints and scores your article to make sure it is friendly for Google. This means you can make your article better for SEO as you write it, without having to make lots of changes later.

Conclusion

As we finish this chapter, we have learned a lot about writing for SEO – how to make your website and articles show up higher in Google searches and really connect with your readers.

An important factor in copywriting is "*the Number 1 Mindset*". This means not just trying to be good, but aiming to be the best. When you write something, you want to make it so good that Google would want to put it at the top of search results. Using the right keywords and optimizing metatags is a part of your SEO strategy, but should not be the only one.

We discussed E-E-A-T, which is all about showing you know what you are talking about, especially on important topics. We also understood how to use data from tools like Google Analytics and Google Search Console. These tools tell you what your readers like and what gets them to click on your site.

We also explored how telling stories can make your writing more interesting and shareable. This is not just about telling any story. It is about using stories to make your writing more enjoyable and to naturally include important words and phrases that people search for.

Lastly, we dived into using technology like SurferSEO to make your writing even better for SEO. These tools help you find the right words to use and see how you can make your articles better than others on the internet.

In short, this chapter gave you the tools and ideas to write in a way that is great for SEO. By using these tips, you can create articles and web pages that will rank well on Google. But, maybe even more important, by optimizing your copywriting, your content will also really speak to and help your readers. In the next chapter, we will cover the topic of links, which will enable you to further optimize your rankings and attract readers.

CHAPTER 5
Links

Introduction

Backlinks, also known as "*inbound links*" or "*external links*," are links from one website to a page on another website. These links are crucial in SEO, signaling to search engines that your content is valued by others. When numerous websites link to the same webpage or website, search engines can infer that the content is worth linking to, and thus also worthy of a good position within the Google rankings. Essentially, backlinks are like votes from other websites, indicating the quality and relevance of your content. They help you to build authority, the third pillar of SEO next to technical and content.

In this chapter, we will learn all about the backlinks, but we also take a look how you can optimize your current internal link strategy for SEO benefits - and how you make your brand an authority.

Structure

In this chapter, we will cover the following topics:

- Optimizing Internal Linking
- Backlink Types
- Advantages of Backlinks
- The Importance of Backlink Quality
- Backlink Audits and Maintenance
- Link Building Techniques
- Brand Authority Strategy for Link Building
- Case Studies on Link Building
- Link Building Reporting

Optimizing Internal Linking

Internal linking is frequently viewed as an accessible and impactful strategy for SEO optimization. In contrast to external backlinks which will be discussed later on this chapter, internal links fall entirely under your domain. You have complete control over how pages within your site are interconnected. This control allows for strategic link placement, enhancing user navigation and reinforcing your site's SEO structure without relying on external partners.

Backlinks are not merely navigational aids but important elements in SEO, contributing to how search engines perceive and rank your website. Apart from SEO benefits, a well-structured internal linking strategy can lead potential customers to enhance the overall browsing experience, encouraging customers to explore and discover the depth and variety of your product range.

Let us discuss some internal linking strategies and how to execute them, with the specific example of a running shoes webshop.

- **Utilizing Descriptive Anchor Text**
  Rather than vague prompts like **`"click here`**," use specific and engaging anchor texts. For instance, a blog post about marathon training could include a phrase like "*Discover our ergonomic marathon running shoes*," linking to a relevant product page. This strategy benefits SEO by aligning the link with the content's context and enhances the user's website experience by offering direct, relevant links. Website visitors tend to scan texts and by renaming your anchor text with descriptive text, you will enhance the scanability of your website.

- **Prioritizing High-Priority Pages**
  Identify and promote the pages that are most crucial to your business goals. For example, if your running shoes web shop is launching a new line of eco-friendly sneakers, ensure these pages are interlinked with related content across your site, such as blog posts about eco-friendly running practices or a dedicated section on your homepage.

  Another way to find high-priority pages to link to is to find those pages within Google Search Console that are currently underlinked but still have a lot of impressions.

- **Creating a Logical Site Structure**
  Organize your website logically, grouping products and content in a way that makes sense. If your store offers various types of running shoes, categorize them under '*Trail Running Shoes*', '*Road Running Shoes*', and '*Track Running Shoes*'. This structure not only helps customers find what they are looking for more easily but also allows search engines to better understand and index your site's content.

- **Balancing Link Quantity**
  While internal links are beneficial, overstuffing a page with links can be detrimental. On your **`'About Us'`** page, for instance, it is more effective to

strategically link to a few key product categories or best-sellers rather than every single product you offer. This approach prevents overwhelming your visitors and dilutes the SEO value of each link. Indeed, both for internal and external links, a general rule is that the more links that appear on a page, the less authority and link value every link will receive.

- **Maintaining and Updating Internal Links**
  Regularly check and update your internal links to ensure they remain relevant and functional. If a particular model of running shoe is discontinued, update links directing to that product, redirecting them to a similar or newer model. This practice keeps your site's content fresh and relevant, improving both user experience and SEO. You can easily check the broken links within a SEO tool like Screaming Frog.
- **Implementing Content Silos**
  Content silos involve grouping related content and products to build topic authority. For your running shoes webshop, you might have a silo dedicated to '*Professional Running Gear*', which interlinks all products, blogs, and guides related to professional running shoes and accessories. This technique boosts the relevance and authority of your pages for specific keywords.
- **Optimizing Link Value**
  Assess the link value of your pages and strategically link higher-value pages, like your homepage or popular category pages, to those that need an SEO boost. For example, you might link a popular blog post on '*Choosing the Right Running Shoes*' to a lesser-known but high-margin product page for specialized running shoes.
- **Incorporating Breadcrumb Navigation**
  Breadcrumbs are navigational aids that show users their current location on your site. On a product page for '`Women's Trail Running Shoes`,' breadcrumbs might look like: `Home` > `Women's Shoes` > `Trail Running Shoes`. This feature not only enhances user experience but also reinforces the site structure for search engines.

The following table summarizes the internal linking strategies and their impact:

Strategy	**Description**	**Impact**
Descriptive Anchor Text	Using clear and relevant text for links	Improves user understanding and SEO relevance
Linking High-Priority Pages	Frequently linking to important pages	Boosts visibility and authority of key pages
Logical Site Structure	Structuring your site and links logically	Enhances navigability and SEO efficiency

Balanced Link Quantity	Avoiding too many links on one page	Prevents dilution of link value and user confusion
Regular Link Maintenance	Checking and updating internal links	Ensures link functionality and content relevance
Content Silos	Grouping related content together	Strengthens topic relevance and authority
Link Value Optimization	Strategically linking based on page value	Distributes authority to improve overall site SEO
Breadcrumb Navigation	Implementing a breadcrumb trail	Improves user experience and site structure

Table 5.1: *Internal link types*

Backlink Types

Backlinks come in a variety of shapes and sizes, each with its own significance. We can distinguish following types of links:

- **Natural Links:** These are spontaneous endorsements from one webpage to another. For instance, a culinary blogger links to your specialty spice shop within their recipe post, unprompted. These links are treasures, earned purely because of the intrinsic value or uniqueness of your content.
- **Links via Outreach:** These are links you garner through deliberate outreach efforts. For instance, you might ask a technology influencer to review your latest gadget, or write a guest post for a notable industry website, embedding a link back to your site. This method focuses on building relationships and actively promoting your content.
- **Self-Created Links:** These are links you place on other websites by yourself, such as in blog comment sections, online forums, or business directories. While they are part of your link-building strategy, they should be used cautiously. Search engines may devalue these if they appear forced or spam-like.
- **Editorial Links:** When your content is so compelling or resourceful that it earns a link from a news site, magazine, or authoritative blog without any direct effort on your part, these are editorial links. For example, a major news outlet citing your research study or report.
- **Backlinks from Partnerships:** Sometimes, you may form partnerships or collaborations with other businesses or organizations, leading to links from their websites. Such links can arise from joint marketing ventures, sponsorships, or collaborations.
- **Social Media Links:** Links that come from your content being shared or mentioned on social media platforms. While their SEO impact is either non-

existent or very low, they are valuable for driving traffic and increasing online visibility.

- **Forum and Comment Links:** Similar to self-created links but more specific, these are links you might add in discussions on forums or in the comments of relevant blog posts. They can be valuable if done tastefully and contextually.
- **Links from Directories and Resource Lists:** Being listed in a carefully curated directory or as part of a resource list on a credible site can be advantageous, especially for local SEO.

In the following table, we provided a list of link types with their characteristics.

Type of Backlink	**Description**	**SEO Value**	**Notes**
Natural Links	Unprompted links from other sites	High	Best type of link, but hard to control
Outreach Links	Links obtained through outreach and collaborations	High	Requires effort but highly effective
Self-Created Links	Links added by yourself on other sites	Low	Can be seen as spammy if overdone
Editorial Links	Links from media or high-authority sites without direct outreach	Very High	Excellent for credibility but hard to achieve
Backlinks from Partnerships	Links arising from collaborations or partnerships	Medium to High	Depends on the partner's website authority
Social Media Links	Links from social media platforms	Low	More valuable for traffic rather than SEO
Forum and Comment Links	Links in forums or blog comments	Low	Can be valuable if relevant and not spammy
Directory/ Resource List Links	Links from directories or resource lists	Medium	Especially good for local SEO

***Table 5.2**: Backlink types*

The following figure illustrates the SEO value scale:

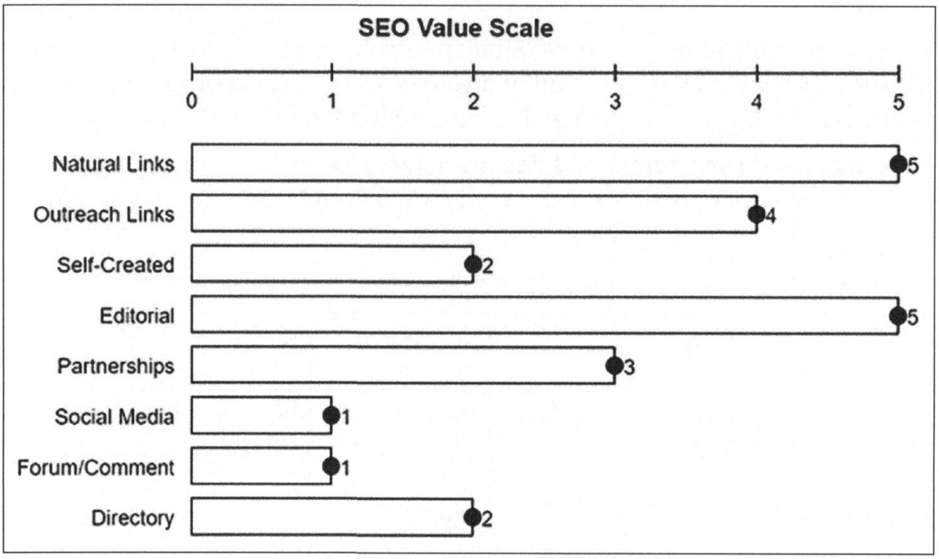

Figure 5.1: *Backlink types*

Advantages of Backlinks

Backlinks are far more than just tools for boosting a website's search engine rankings; they play a critical and multifaceted role in the broader scope of search engine optimization (SEO) and online marketing. Let us have a look at all the benefits backlinks can provide you.

- **Boosting Search Engine Rankings:** Backlinks can significantly elevate a website's position on search engine results pages (SERPs). For instance, imagine a starting tech blog that begins to receive backlinks from industry leaders like Wired or TechCrunch. Such high-caliber endorsements not only validate the blog's content but also improve its visibility and ranking within search engines, making it more likely to be discovered by a broader audience.
- **Aiding in Discoverability:** Search engines utilize backlinks as a means to discover and index new content. A strategically placed link on a high-traffic website will guide search engines to your content, thereby speeding up the indexing process.
- **Driving Referral Traffic:** High-profile backlinks can be substantial sources of referral traffic. A feature or mention on a popular site like BuzzFeed can channel a significant number of visitors to your site. This influx of traffic is not only beneficial for immediate visibility but can also lead to increased engagement and conversions, depending on the nature of your website.
- **Establishing Authority and Credibility:** Acquiring backlinks from reputable

and relevant sources bolsters your site's perceived authority and credibility. For example, a new health blog that secures links from established medical journals or health institutions gains a stamp of legitimacy, which can be invaluable in building trust with not only Google but also your potential audience.

- **Networking and Relationship Building:** The process of acquiring backlinks often involves reaching out and collaborating with other websites and industry figures. This aspect of link building transcends SEO. It will foster a network of relationships and mutual support that can yield long-term benefits beyond mere search rankings.

In the following table, you can find an overview of how backlinks can improve your online marketing:

Aspect of SEO	Impact of Backlinks	Example
Search Engine Rankings	Increases visibility and ranking on SERPs	Tech blog receiving links from Wired
Discoverability	Helps search engines find and index content	New website linked by a high-traffic blog
Referral Traffic	Drives visitors from other websites	Feature on BuzzFeed leading to increased site visits
Authority and Credibility	Enhances the website's trustworthiness	Health blog linked by established medical journals
Networking and Relationships	Builds connections within the industry	Collaborations resulting from outreach for backlinks

***Table 5.3**: Backlink advantages*

In summary, backlinks offer benefits that extend beyond the search rankings. They are important in enhancing a website's discoverability, authority, and network within the whole digital ecosystem. The following sections will delve deeper into strategies for building a strong backlink profile. But first, we will have a look at how to optimize internal linking on your own website to maximize your website's SEO potential.

The Importance of Backlink Quality

The quality of the links pointing to your website can have a significant impact on your site's search engine rankings. John Mueller, search advocate at Google, has consistently advised that artificially building links, such as buying links or dropping links on other sites, is against Google's webmaster guidelines. He notes that Google takes both algorithmic and manual actions against such practices, which can include demoting the site or simply ignoring those links. This highlights that engaging in manipulative link-building practices can lead to negative consequences for a website's search rankings

Recognizing this, it is essential to understand what constitutes high-quality links and how they differ from low-quality counterparts.

The quality of a backlink is determined by several key factors:

- **Relevance:** The most effective backlinks come from websites that are relevant to your site's content. For instance, a link from a leading technology blog is more valuable for a tech startup than a link from a site about gardening.
- **Authority of the Linking Site:** Links from websites that are recognized as authoritative in their field carry more weight. A backlink from a reputable news outlet or an established industry leader can significantly boost your website's perceived authority.
- **Link Placement and Context:** The placement of a link on a webpage matters. A link that is embedded within the main content of a page and surrounded by relevant text is typically more powerful than a link placed in the footer or sidebar. The context surrounding the link also plays a critical role. A link that fits naturally within the content and adds value to the reader is seen as higher quality.

Understanding the difference between high-quality and low-quality links is crucial. High-quality links are typically from reputable, relevant sources and are placed contextually within the content. They are earned based on the merit of your content and are not manipulative in nature. On the other hand, low-quality links often come from spammy, irrelevant sites, are placed in non-contextual locations, or are obtained through manipulative tactics. These can include paid links, link exchanges, or links embedded in low-quality or plagiarized content.

Bad links, typically low-quality or spammy links, can negatively impact your SEO efforts. Search engines like Google use sophisticated algorithms to identify and penalize websites that attempt to manipulate rankings through low-quality link-building practices. This can result in lower rankings or even a manual penalty, which can be challenging to recover from. Therefore, it is imperative to focus on building a healthy backlink profile with high-quality, relevant links. Don't panic if there is a bad link pointing to your website, as long as you have a balanced link profile you likely won't be penalized for Google

Identifying spammy toxic links is a crucial step in cleaning your backlink profile. Luckily, many SEO tools have the option to analyze backlink quality. Tools like SEMrush, Ahrefs, and Google's Search Console will help you in identifying potentially harmful links. These tools highlight the quality of linking domains, anchor text diversity, and flag sites that are known for spammy practices.

Keep a regular check on your backlink profile. An unexpected spike in backlinks, especially from low-quality sites, can be a red flag.

Once you have identified toxic links, the next step is to prepare a file for use in Google's

Disavow Tool. This tool allows you to tell Google which links to ignore when evaluating your site. It is important to use this tool cautiously, as incorrect usage can harm your site's performance.

The disavow file you have to upload in the Google disavow tool is essentially a text file (.txt) that lists the URLs or domains of the toxic links you want to disavow. Here's an example of how to structure a **`disavow`** file:

```
# Disavow Links File
# Date: 2024-01-01
# This file contains links we want Google to ignore due to their low
quality or spammy nature.

# Individual page links
http://spammysite1.com/bad-link-page1.html
http://spammysite2.com/another-bad-link.html

# Disavowing entire domains
domain:spammysite3.com
domain:bad-link-example.com

# Additional links identified on 2024-01-15
http://example-of-bad-link.com/page.html
domain:anotherexample.com
```

Let us explain the lines in the files.

Lines beginning with # are comments, they are just used to keep notes and organize the file for your reference and don't have any effect.

Individual URLs are listed to disavow specific pages.

The domain: prefix is used to disavow all links from an entire domain.

Backlink Audits and Maintenance

To conduct a backlink audit, you should focus on a detailed and systematic approach that complements the points already discussed. Here is a guide on how to perform a backlink audit and explain this with a pet food webshop example.

- **Gather Comprehensive Backlink Data:** Start by collecting complete backlink data for your pet food webshop using multiple tools. While tools like Ahrefs, SEMrush, or Moz are great, also consider using Google Search Console for additional insights. This will provide a comprehensive view of your backlink profile.
- **Categorize Backlinks:** Organize the backlinks into categories. For instance, categorize them by website type (pet blogs, pet adoption centers, pet wellness

forums), link type (editorial, guest post, forum link), and quality (high, medium, low). This categorization helps in analyzing the backlink profile more effectively.

- **Analyze Anchor Text:** Examine the anchor texts used in your backlinks. Are they varied and relevant? For a pet food webshop, anchor texts like "*best dog food*", "*healthy cat treats*", or "*nutritional pet snacks*" are desirable. Over-optimization or irrelevance in anchor texts can signal spammy practices to search engines.
- **Assess the ratio of '*follow*' to '*nofollow*' links.** While '*nofollow*' links don't directly contribute to SEO, they can drive traffic and indicate a natural link profile. An imbalance heavily skewed towards either could be a red flag.
- **Evaluate the Geographical Relevance:** For a webshop serving a specific region or country, it's important to have backlinks from geographically relevant domains. If your pet food webshop targets the US market, links from US-based pet care blogs and forums are more beneficial than those from unrelated geographical locations.
- **Identify and Assess Referral Traffic:** Use analytics tools to see which backlinks bring in the most referral traffic. High referral traffic from a backlink is a good indicator of its quality and relevance to your audience.
- **Analysis of Backlinks Per Page:** Evaluate the distribution of backlinks across different pages of your pet food webshop. Identify which pages are attracting the most links and analyze why. For instance, if a particular product page or a blog post about pet nutrition is garnering more backlinks, understand the factors contributing to this, such as the quality of content, the relevance to the audience, or external factors like social media shares.

Also, assess pages that are underperforming in terms of backlinks, when you take into account page importance, SEO clicks for the page.

- **Analyzing Keyword Rankings in Relation to Backlinks:** Investigate how your current backlinks are affecting your keyword rankings. Identify if the pages with the most backlinks are ranking higher for targeted keywords. For example, if your page about "*organic dog food*" is ranking well for related keywords, see if the backlinks to this page are a contributing factor.
- **Analyze Opportunities Where Additional Backlinks could Improve Keyword Rankings**: if a certain page of your webshop is ranking on the second page of search engine results for a valuable keyword, acquiring more high-quality backlinks to this page could potentially improve its ranking and click-through rate (CTR%). For instance, if your "*grain-free cat food*" page is ranking at position 12 for relevant keywords, additional relevant backlinks might push it onto the first page of search results.
- **Competitor Benchmark:** To effectively analyze your competitors' online presence, employ tools such as Semrush or Ahrefs. These platforms offer

comprehensive insights into where your competitors are obtaining their backlinks. By understanding these sources, you can identify potential opportunities for your own link-building strategy. Begin by compiling a list of your main competitors. Then, use these tools to track down the websites linking to them. Pay attention to the quality and relevance of these linking sites, and consider how you can replicate or surpass their backlink profile. Also have a look at websites that link to at least two of your competitors but not to you, they may be an easy target.

Keep a record of all findings and plan your actions accordingly. For instance, if you find a significant number of low-quality links, consider a strategy to disavow them. If there are opportunities for gaining more high-quality backlinks, list the potential sites for outreach.

Now we made our backlink audit, we can start thinking about some actions that can be taken out of the audit insights.

- **Competitor Links Using SEO Tools (example: Semrush, Ahref):** You can act on the insights of your link benchmark. For instance, if `'PetLoversBlog.com'` links to several similar stores but not yours, it is a potential opportunity. This insight helps in crafting a targeted outreach strategy to get featured on '*PetLoversBlog.com*', enhancing your webshop's visibility among pet enthusiasts.
- **Evaluating the Relevance of Backlinks:** Assess the relevance of each backlink. For the pet food webshop, a link from a general shopping directory might not be as valuable as a link from a dedicated pet care blog.
- **Targeting Specific Types of Sites for Backlinks:** Identify the common types of sites linking to your webshop. If pet adoption centers frequently link to your content on '*Best Pet Foods for Newly Adopted Pets*', consider reaching out to more of these centers or similar organizations for backlinks, thereby reinforcing your presence in this niche.
- **Learning from Broken Links on Competitor Sites:** Look for broken links on competitor sites. If a popular pet website had a link to an outdated article on a competitor's site, you could reach out to the webmaster and provide a link to your updated and relevant article, like '2024's Top Nutritional Trends in Pet Food'.
- **Improving Visibility of Existing Backlinks:** If your pet food webshop has a backlink from a less-visited page on a pet wellness site, negotiate with the site owner to move your link to a more prominent place, like their homepage or a popular article on pet nutrition. It may be easier to target an existing website with already one link to you to get more links rather than getting a link from a website that does not have any link to you yet.
- **Engaging with Sites for Updated Backlinks:** For sites that previously linked

to your pet food webshop, keep them updated with your latest products or articles. If a pet news site linked to your blog post '*Best Dog Foods in 2023*', inform them about your updated 2024 guide to encourage a fresh link.

- **Scheduled Reviews for Backlink Profile Maintenance:** Set regular intervals, like every three months, to check and update the backlink profile of your pet food webshop. This helps in removing outdated links, assessing the current value of existing links, and ensuring alignment with the latest SEO trends.
- **Leveraging Unlinked Mentions:** Monitor the web for mentions of your brand, products, or executives that are not linked. Reach out to the authors of these mentions and politely ask if they can include a link back to your website. You can set up Google Alerts to receive notifications about these mentions within your mailbox.

Link Building Techniques

But what if you notice you have few links and you want to build new links. Let us explore various link building techniques, their advantages, and pitfalls, along with real-world examples.

- **Content Marketing**: This involves creating compelling content like detailed blogs, infographics, or videos, which naturally attract backlinks. For example, a health and wellness website might publish an in-depth article on meditation benefits, garnering attention and backlinks from various health-focused blogs and forums. The advantage here is establishing authority and providing value, leading to organic link growth. However, the challenge lies in the need for significant resources and time to create high-quality content, with no guaranteed return in terms of links. Transforming existing content into different formats can attract a wider range of backlinks. For example, turning a popular blog post into an infographic, video, or even a webinar can make it more appealing for different types of websites to link to your content. But remember the following quote of Rand Fishkin: "*The best links are earned, not built.*"
- **Influencer Outreach:** This strategy entails partnering with influencers to gain backlinks. A classic example is a fashion brand collaborating with a popular Instagram fashion influencer, who then links back to the brand's website in a blog post. This approach can quickly amplify your reach and add credibility. The pitfall, however, is the difficulty in finding the right influencer fit and managing the costs involved. Beyond the usual email outreach, consider strategies like co-authoring content with industry experts or influencers, which can lead to links from high-authority sites.
- **Guest Blogging:** Writing articles for other sites in your niche can attract a new audience. For instance, an expert in digital marketing might write a guest post

for a well-known marketing blog, including a link back to their consultancy website. The benefit is direct traffic and reaching new audiences.

- **PR Campaigns:** Engaging in PR campaigns, like using Haro (Help a Reporter Out), can lead to high-quality backlinks from media outlets. A tech startup might use Haro to provide expert insights to journalists, resulting in mentions and backlinks from major tech publications. The advantage is gaining authoritative backlinks, but effective PR can be complex and may not always yield backlinks.
- **Collaborations:** Partnering with other businesses or entities can result in mutual backlinking. An online cooking school collaborating with a kitchenware retailer for a joint cooking class series online, where both parties link to each other's websites, is a good example. This method opens up new audiences and shared resources, but finding compatible partners with mutual benefits can be challenging.
- **Press Releases**: Distributing press releases about significant company news, product launches, or events can earn backlinks from media outlets and news websites. For example, a software company releasing a revolutionary app might use a press release distributed through a platform like PR Newswire, resulting in multiple backlinks from tech news sites. The advantage of press releases is the potential for widespread coverage and backlinks from numerous sources. The pitfall is that if the news is not compelling enough, it might not attract the desired media attention or backlinks. Also, even if your article gets published, it may not contain a link to any of your pages. A trick may be to put in the press release itself a link to one of the pages on your website and hope the news publisher will just copy paste it.

To provide a clearer overview, here is a table summarizing each technique, its advantages, and pitfalls:

Technique	Advantage	Pitfall
Content Marketing	Establishes authority, organic link growth	Time-intensive, no guaranteed link return
Influencer Outreach	Amplifies reach, adds credibility	Finding right influencers, cost management
Guest Blogging	Direct traffic, new audience reach	Potential for diluted brand voice
PR Campaigns	High-quality, authoritative backlinks	Complexity, not always link-guaranteed
Collaborations	New audiences, shared resources	Finding compatible partners
Press Releases	Widespread coverage, numerous backlinks	Requires compelling news, no guaranteed pickup

***Table 5.4**: Link Building techniques*

In conclusion, while each link building technique offers unique advantages, they also come with specific challenges. The key to a successful link building strategy lies in diversifying your approaches and consistently providing value to your audience and collaborative partners. By doing so, you can significantly enhance your website's backlink profile and overall online presence.

Brand Authority Strategy for Link Building

While previous techniques were more on the tactical level, we can ask ourselves a more strategic question: how to become a brand authority that would naturally gain links.

Indeed, when your brand is viewed as an authority in your field, gaining backlinks becomes a more organic and seamless process. Also, links are for Google actually just a proxy to determine authority. By improving your real-world authority, you are improving on the exact goal which Google wants to convey. Here is how you can leverage social media to enhance your brand's authority and subsequently use this brand authority to build new links.

- **Consistent and Valuable Content:** Regularly post content that is both informative and engaging. This could range from industry insights, how-to guides, thought leadership articles, to the latest news updates. For example, a health food brand might share regular posts about nutrition tips, healthy recipes, and the latest research in the field.
- **Engaging with the Community:** Actively engage with your followers and industry influencers. Respond to comments, participate in relevant discussions, and even host live Q&A sessions. This interaction not only builds trust but also encourages your followers to share your content, increasing its reach.
- **Collaborating with Influencers and Industry Leaders:** Partner with influencers and leaders in your field. Their endorsements can elevate your brand's credibility. For instance, a tech company could collaborate with a well-known tech influencer for a product review or a webinar.
- **Utilizing Multimedia and Live Streaming:** Use various multimedia formats such as videos, live streams, and infographics. These formats tend to have higher engagement rates and shareability, thus increasing your brand's visibility and authority.
- **Promoting User-Generated Content:** Encourage and share user-generated content. It not only engages your audience but also serves as social proof, further establishing your authority.
- **Social Media as a Platform for Outreach:** Leverage your social media connections for outreach. Engage in conversations with other brands and

influencers, who might be more willing to link to your content due to your established relationship and authority.

By strategically leveraging social media to build and showcase your brand authority, you not only enhance your online presence but also create fertile ground for organic link-building opportunities. The key is to maintain a consistent, engaging, and value-driven approach that resonates with your audience and positions your brand as a go-to authority in your field.

Let us examine an approach to becoming a thought leader on LinkedIn and then leverage this position to attract backlinks involving a strategic blend of content creation, active networking, and community engagement. Here is a step-by-step guide on how to achieve this:

1. **Act as a Personal Brand:** As LinkedIn is a person-to-person network, it is easier and more personal to act as a person representing the brand, rather than only use company updates. So, think about making you and your colleagues brand ambassadors rather than having only a company brand presence.
2. **Define Your Niche:** Identify your area of expertise within your industry. This could be anything from digital marketing strategies to sustainability in business. The key is to focus on a domain where you have substantial knowledge and insights to share.
3. **Create and Share Valuable Content:** Regularly post articles, updates, and insights on LinkedIn that add value to your audience. Your content should address current trends, offer solutions to common industry challenges, content related to events within your industry or provide unique perspectives. For example, if you specialize in cybersecurity, you could write about emerging threats or data protection strategies.
4. **Engage with Industry Leaders and Influencers:** Connect and interact with other thought leaders and influencers in your field. Comment thoughtfully on their posts, share their content with your insights, and participate in discussions. This helps in building your network and establishing your presence in the industry.
5. **Join and Contribute to Relevant Groups:** Participate in LinkedIn groups related to your niche. Contribute to conversations, answer questions, and share your content when relevant. This not only showcases your expertise but also helps in reaching a wider audience.
6. **Personal Branding:** Your LinkedIn profile should reflect your expertise and thought leadership. This includes having a professional profile photo, a compelling bio, and showcasing your achievements and endorsements. Be aware that on social media, people act with people, so involve employees to become brand ambassadors.

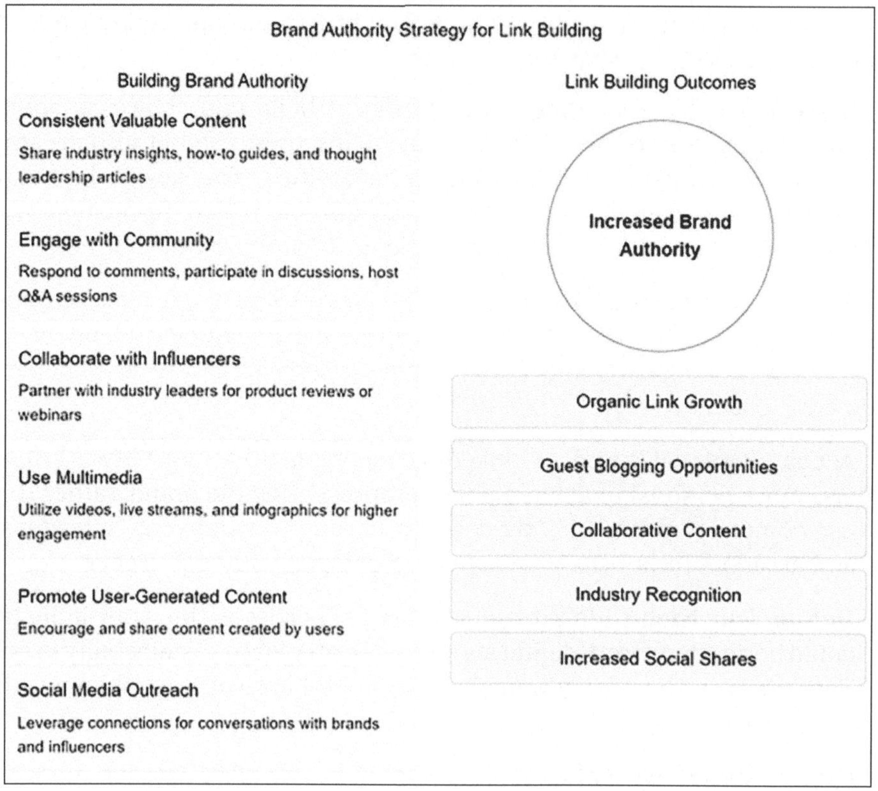

Figure 5.2: *Brand Authority Strategy*

Once you have established yourself as a thought leader, your content is more likely to be shared across platforms. Other websites, blogs, or LinkedIn members might link to your articles or posts as a reference, thereby naturally generating backlinks. You can leverage your LinkedIn connections for guest blogging opportunities or collaborations. Websites often seek out thought leaders for guest posts, interviews, or expert insights, which usually include backlinks to the author's profile or website.

Use LinkedIn messaging and networking events to build relationships with other professionals and website owners. Once a relationship is established, you can explore opportunities for acquiring backlinks, such as through mutual content sharing or collaborations. Share links to your blogs or website content on LinkedIn. If your followers find this content valuable, they might link back to it from their websites or blogs.

When you publish articles on LinkedIn, ensure they are SEO optimized with relevant keywords. This increases the likelihood of your content appearing in search engine results, leading to greater visibility and more backlinks.

By following these steps, you can effectively leverage your position as a thought leader on LinkedIn to not only influence your industry but also to attract valuable backlinks, thus enhancing your digital presence and SEO efforts. As the late Eric Ward once insightfully remarked, the essence of link building lies in fostering relationships. His perspective underscores the significance of connecting authentically with others to establish valuable backlinks. This approach is about more than just technical SEO tactics; it is about creating meaningful connections.

Case Studies on Link Building

In this section, we will have a look at some creative and advanced link building strategies companies have successfully used to attract more links to their content.

- **Backlinko's Skyscraper Technique**, introduced by Brian Dean, is a prime example of enhancing and promoting content to attract high-quality backlinks. This method begins by identifying already popular content in a specific niche, content that has garnered numerous backlinks. The key is then to create a more detailed, more valuable piece of content that provides additional insights or updated information. This superior version is then strategically promoted to the same websites that linked to the original piece, persuading them to link to the new, enhanced content instead. This technique not only focuses on creating high-quality content but also smartly leverages existing content's success, transforming it into a more resourceful and link-worthy piece.
- **Ahrefs utilized a 'Stats' page strategy**, which revolved around creating a page filled with up-to-date, relevant industry statistics. They specifically targeted backlinks that referred to outdated statistics on other websites. By updating these statistics and reaching out to sites that are linked to the outdated ones, Ahrefs could replace those links with ones pointing to their updated statistics. This method not only provided value through updated information but also directly engaged with websites to encourage them to link to the more current, accurate data.
- **Moz's approach with Open Site Explorer** combined tool utility with insightful content creation. By using their backlink analysis tool, they conducted in-depth studies on the effects of link building on SEO. These studies were shared on their blog, offering rich, data-driven content that naturally attracted backlinks from authoritative industry publications. This strategy effectively demonstrated the capabilities of their tool while simultaneously enhancing their online presence and establishing Moz as a thought leader in SEO.
- **Airbnb's User-Generated Content Strategy:** Airbnb encouraged their hosts to create content about their local areas, such as city guides and neighborhood insights. This content was authentic, valuable, and highly relevant to travelers. The genuine and unique nature of this user-generated content caught the attention of travel blogs and websites, leading to high-quality backlinks. Airbnb's approach highlighted the power of authentic, user-centric content in attracting backlinks and improving SEO.

These case studies illustrate the diversity and creativity in SEO link-building strategies. From enhancing existing content to leveraging user-generated contributions and utilizing data-driven analysis, each example provides actionable insights into building successful link-building campaigns.

Link Building Reporting

The effectiveness of link building is not always straightforward to assess. This necessitates a robust system for measuring and reporting on the success of link-building efforts, enabling businesses to understand the return on investment (ROI) and make informed decisions for future strategies.

Effective reporting in link building serves several crucial purposes:

- **Justifies Investment:** Demonstrates the tangible outcomes of link-building efforts, proving the value of the investment to stakeholders.
- **Guides Strategy Adjustments:** By tracking specific metrics, businesses can identify what's working and what's not, allowing for strategic adjustments.
- **Enhances Transparency**: Regular reporting keeps all stakeholders informed about the progress and challenges of link-building campaigns.

When measuring the success of link building, several KPIs are critical:

- **Backlink Quantity and Quality:** Tracking both the number and quality of backlinks is essential. High-quality backlinks from reputable and relevant sites have a greater impact on SEO. Combine Google Search Console data with another tool (for example, Semrush or Ahrefs) to have an idea of the number and quality of backlinks.
- **Referral Traffic:** An increase in traffic from external links is a clear sign of effective link building. Google Analytics is your source.
- **Search Engine Rankings:** Improvement in rankings for targeted keywords often correlates with successful link-building efforts.
- **Domain and Page Authority**: Tools like Ahrefs, Semrush or Moz track these metrics, which are indicative of the strength and reputation of your website's backlink profile.
- **Link Diversity:** A diverse backlink profile, in terms of types and sources, suggests a natural and robust link-building strategy.

Dashboards are invaluable for consolidating data from various sources into a single, visually engaging interface. Platforms like Google Looker Studio or Tableau can be used to create dashboards that provide a real-time view of link-building metrics. These dashboards can display:

- **Backlink Growth Over Time:** A graph showing the increase in the number of backlinks over the campaign period.
- **Referral Traffic**: Charts depicting traffic sources, highlighting the contribution of different backlinks.
- **Ranking Improvements:** A table listing targeted keywords and their changes in rankings over time.
- **Authority Scores:** Visualization of changes in domain and page authority.

While these data and numbers are informative, they become even more insightful when contextualized with real-world implications. So, for a report on link building, include the following topics to make your reporting clearly aligned to the business:

- **Linking Metrics to Business Goals:** Illustrating how increases in referral traffic have led to higher conversion rates or how improved rankings have boosted overall online visibility.
- **Competitive Benchmarking**: Comparing your site's performance with competitors to highlight areas of strength and opportunities for improvement.
- **Incorporating Real-World Examples and Recommendations**

  To make reports more relatable and actionable, showcase specific successful links. Highlight particular backlinks that had a significant impact. For example, a link from a major industry blog that led to a spike in traffic.
- **Provide Actionable Recommendations:** Based on the data, suggest future link-building strategies. If certain types of content have garnered more backlinks, recommend increasing focus on those formats.

  In conclusion, reporting on link-building ROI is not just about presenting data; it is about telling a story. A compelling report combines hard metrics with narrative elements like specific examples and recommendations. This approach not only demonstrates the value generated from link-building efforts but also provides a clear path forward, ensuring that link building remains a dynamic and integral part of the broader digital marketing strategy.

Consider an e-commerce site focusing on sustainable products that launched a six-month link-building campaign through guest posts, influencer partnerships, and high-quality content creation. The campaign led to a 35% increase in quality backlinks, a 25% rise in referral traffic, and improved rankings for several key search terms. The domain authority increased from 25 to 34. This is the information that should be readily available within your dashboard.

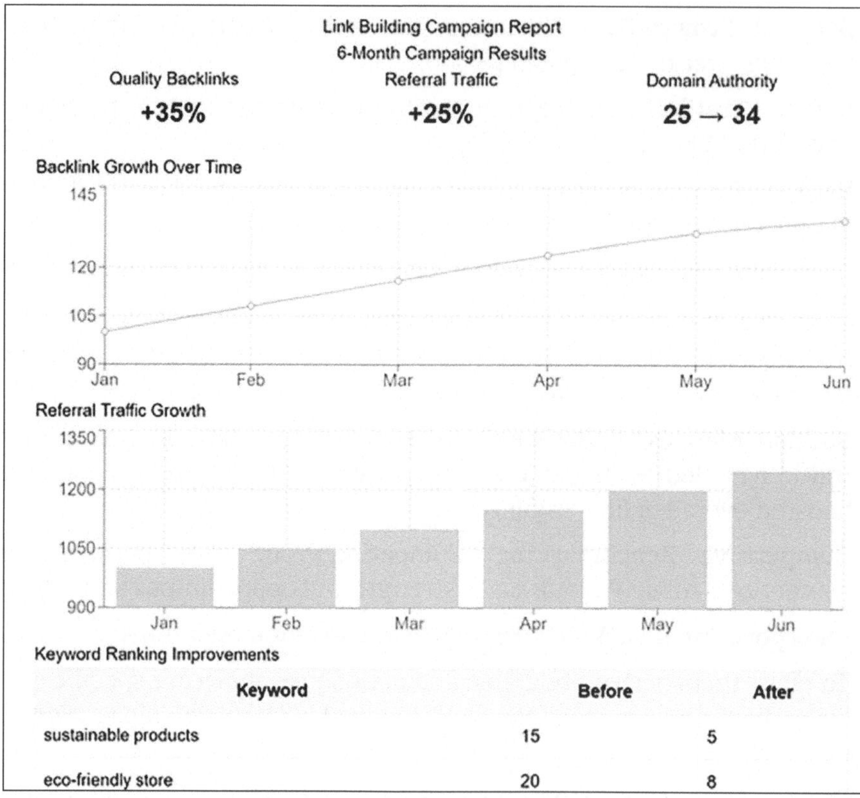

Figure 5.3: *Link Building Report*

A comprehensive report on this campaign would also showcase the most successful content and partnerships, and link these achievements to an increase in online sales and customer engagement. The report would conclude with suggestions for the next steps, such as targeting higher-authority sites or exploring new content formats.

Conclusion

Mastering the art of creating effective backlinks is important for boosting your website's SEO. We have covered a lot, from the types of backlinks and their benefits to ensuring their quality, optimizing internal links, conducting thorough backlink audits, and exploring advanced link-building techniques.

The key takeaway is that successful link building is not just about getting as many links as possible. It is about focusing on the quality and relevance of these links. We discussed how to do this through various methods, such as content marketing, working with influencers, engaging in PR campaigns, and collaborating with others in your industry. All these methods aim to make your site more popular and respected online.

Another important point is the importance of internal links. While the importance of external links in terms has reduced, the importance of internal links is improving and unlike external links, internal links are in your control.

We also looked at how powerful social media, especially LinkedIn, can be in making your brand a recognized authority, which in turn helps in gaining more backlinks naturally.

Now, as we move on from the world of link building, we are going to shift our focus to Local SEO in the next chapter. Here, we will discuss how to make your website stand out in local searches.

Chapter 6
Local SEO

Introduction

Local Search Engine Optimization (Local SEO) is a powerful strategy for businesses aiming to reach customers in their immediate geographic area. In this chapter, you will learn Local SEO for businesses targeting local markets. We will delve into how Local SEO differs from general SEO practices, focusing on its unique aspect. We will explore how Local SEO leverages local search trends, emphasizing the importance of appearing in local search results. Understanding Local SEO is essential for businesses to effectively connect with their local audience, driving foot traffic and boosting local online visibility. This chapter sets the foundation for mastering Local SEO techniques, tailored for businesses seeking to dominate their local market.

Structure

In this chapter, we will cover the following topics:

- Local SEO and the Map Pack
- Importance of Local SEO
- Local SEO Keywords and Rankings
- Local webpage Optimization
- Google Business Profile optimization
- Attracting Reviews on Google Business Profile
- Managing Reviews
- Linkbuilding for Local SEO
- Other Platforms
- Monitoring and Reporting Local SEO

Local SEO and the Map Pack

Local Search Engine Optimization (Local SEO) is a subset of SEO focused on optimizing a business's online presence to attract more customers from relevant local searches. These searches occur on Google and other search engines and are distinguished by their geographical constraints. Unlike standard SEO, which focuses broadly on reaching a national or global audience, local SEO is about increasing visibility for businesses that serve their communities face-to-face, such as local brick-and-mortar stores or service-area businesses.

Key differences between Local SEO and Standard SEO include:

- **Geographical Targeting:** Local SEO targets specific locales, aiming to appear in searches in a specific area, city, or region.
- **Local Keywords:** Emphasizes keywords that are specific to the local area or community.
- **Business Directory and Google Business Profile Optimization:** A major part of local SEO involves setting up and optimizing a Google Business Profile (formerly Google My Business) for increased local search visibility as well as other business directories (example, Bing Places for Business).

The Map Pack, also known as the Local Pack, is a feature in Google's search results that shows a map with pinned locations of businesses along with additional information such as business names, ratings, and hours. It is prominently displayed for local search queries and is separate from Google Maps, although it utilizes Google Maps technology.

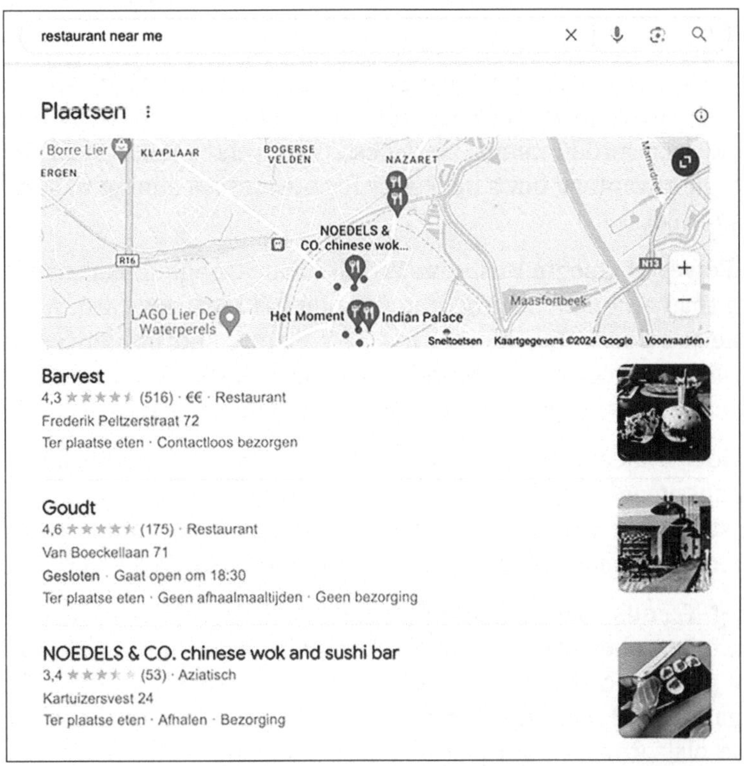

Figure 6.1: *Local Search Result*

The Map Pack appears in Google Search results when a query has local intent, such as "*coffee shops near me*" or "*plumbers in [City]*". It typically displays three business listings and is highly valued due to its prominent placement and the direct information it offers, like business hours, reviews, and quick links to call or get directions.

The Map Pack should not be confused with Google Maps. While Google Maps is a standalone application providing comprehensive geographical information and navigation services, the Map Pack is an integrated feature in Google's search results, specifically designed to showcase local businesses relevant to a user's search query.

Google decides when to display the Map Pack based on the perceived intent of the search query. If Google believes the searcher is looking for a local service or business, it will likely display the Map Pack at the top of the search results, making it a critical target for local SEO efforts.

Importance of Local SEO

Let's see why local SEO is important:

- **Role of Local SEO:** Local SEO focuses on capturing the attention of customers in a specific geographical area. This approach is crucial for businesses ranging from small independent cafes to well-established local branches of larger companies.

  The surge in smartphone usage has led to a paradigm shift in consumer behavior, with an increasing number of people turning to online searches to find local products and services. This trend makes local SEO not just a strategic advantage but a necessity for businesses aiming to stay relevant and competitive.

- **The Power of Google Business Profile:** Your Google Business Profile is much more than an online listing; it is your digital business card. A well-optimized profile provides vital information at a glance and influences how potential customers perceive your brand. It is where first impressions are formed and where the journey from discovery to engagement begins.

  Consider a local restaurant. By optimizing the Google Business Profile with stunning images, updated menus, and prompt responses to reviews, you can almost double your number of reservations. Such stories underscore the transformative power of an effective Google Business Profile.

- **Rising Trends in Local and Google Maps Searches:** With over 46% of all Google searches seeking local information, the importance of local SEO is more pronounced than ever. Additionally, the rise in Google Maps usage for navigation and local discovery has become a game-changer for businesses. These platforms are not just directories but powerful tools for visibility and customer acquisition.

> A staggering 98% of consumers used the internet to find local businesses in 2022, up from 90% in 2019 (On The Map Marketing).
>
> Local searches have a high conversion rate, with 28% of nearby searches resulting in a purchase, according to Google.

Leading SEO experts like Danny Sullivan, co-founder of Search Engine Land, emphasize the critical role of local SEO. Sullivan notes, "*Local SEO is about connecting with your audience at the right place and the right time. In the digital age, that means being visible and relevant in local search results.*" Sarah Bird, CEO of Moz, emphasizes the unique opportunities presented by local SEO. She notes that local intent searches often lead to quicker purchases and highlights the hyper-local nature of modern search results. Bird points out that local search is commercializable and offers much organic opportunity, indicating the critical importance of adapting strategies to the increasingly localized nature of search.

Local SEO is crucial in an AI-driven search landscape where search algorithms increasingly rely on factors like available business information and reviews to rank and present businesses in search results. Efficiently managing these elements can significantly impact a business's local search performance and visibility.

A common challenge in local SEO is the underestimation of its complexity and the time it takes to see results. Many businesses fail at local SEO because 58% do not optimize for local search, and only 30% have an actual plan.

Local SEO Keywords and Rankings

Local SEO Keywords

Local SEO keywords are specific phrases that potential customers use to find local services or businesses. These keywords include geographical locations or local intent, which distinguishes them from broader, non-localized keywords used in standard SEO. For example, "*coffee shops in downtown* Los Angeles" is a local SEO keyword, whereas "*best coffee brewing methods*" is a standard SEO keyword.

Key aspects of Local SEO Keywords:

- **Geo-Targeted Phrases:** Local keywords often contain specific names of cities, neighborhoods, or regions. For instance, "*plumbers in Brooklyn*" targets a specific service in a defined location.
- **Local Intent**: Some keywords may not include a geographical term but still have local intent. Searches like "*dentists near me*" or "*restaurants open now*" signal local intent and are vital in local SEO. On these terms, the map pack will have a prominent place within the search results and thus a broad term as "*restaurant*" may be considered a local SEO keywords, as this term will trigger a map pack and localized results.

Rankings in Local SEO

Local SEO rankings refer to a business's position in search engine results for local queries. These rankings are crucial for driving foot traffic and local business and differ from standard SEO rankings in several ways:

- **Geographical Factors:** Local SEO rankings are heavily influenced by the searcher's location. A business might rank highly for a search conducted nearby but may not appear for the same search in a different location.
- **Google Business Profile Listings:** A well-optimized Google Business Profile can significantly influence local rankings. Elements like NAP consistency (Name, Address, Phone Number), customer reviews, and local content play a pivotal role.
- **Local Map Pack Rankings**: A high ranking in the Local Map Pack can be more beneficial than organic search rankings for local businesses. The Map Pack has its own set of ranking criteria, including proximity, relevance, and prominence.
- **Local Link Building**: Links from locally relevant websites, like local newspapers or community websites, hold more value in local SEO compared to standard link-building practices.
- Still, some on-page factors will also help you to improve your local SEO ranking.

You can find the ranking factors according to research of HOTH at: https://www.thehoth.com/learn/local/seo/ranking-factors/.

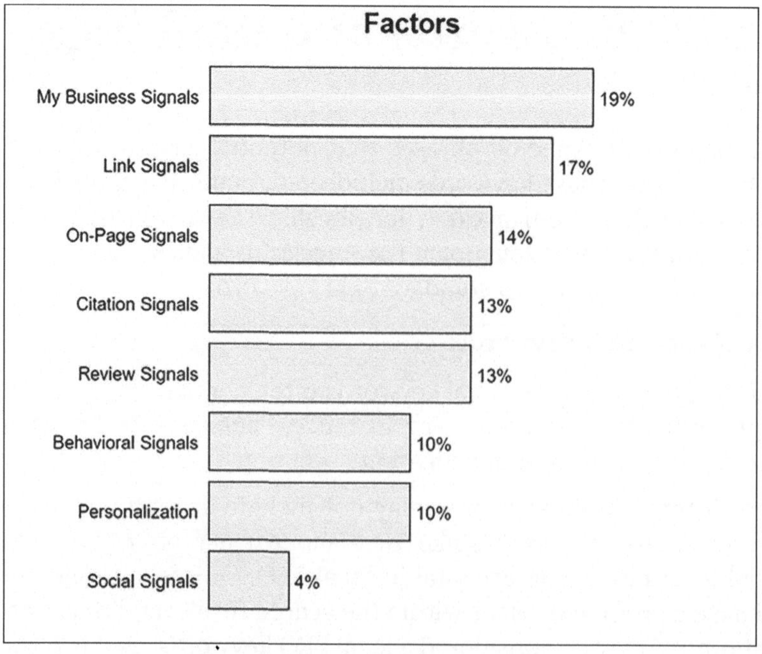

***Figure 6.2**: Local Ranking Factors*

In conclusion, mastering local SEO keywords and understanding the nuances of local search rankings are fundamental for businesses seeking to dominate local search results. This involves optimizing for geo-targeted phrases, ensuring a robust Google Business Profile, generating and managing reviews for your locations and building a local online presence through relevant content and local backlinks.

Local Web Page Optimization

Before diving into Google Business Profile optimizing, start thinking about your local assets on your website. This is often an overlooked step in Local SEO. Just having a place where you list contact details of your different offices or shops won't score you well in SEO. Let us consider the example of '*Happy Paws*', a fictional pet shop chain, to demonstrate how a business can optimize its web pages for local searches effectively.

- **Creating a Dedicated Web Page for Each Location:** For '*Happy Paws*', having a unique web page for each of their locations is essential. Each page acts as a focused platform, providing specific information and services relevant to the local clientele. For example, the page for their Austin store highlights services like pet grooming and locally popular pet food brands, catering to the needs and preferences of the Austin pet owner community. These pages need to have their separate URL and can be optimized with localized metatags.
- **Articulating Services with Local Flavor:** The services offered at each '*Happy Paws*' location are clearly listed, but with a twist. The descriptions are tailored to resonate with the local community. In their Seattle store, for instance, the services include '*Rainy Day Dog Walks*' - a nod to the city's weather patterns, making the service listing not just informative but also relatable.
- **Strategic Use of High-Quality Images:** Visuals play a crucial role. '*Happy Paws*' uses high-quality images of their local stores, featuring staff members with pets, and images of local landmarks with pets, making their web pages visually appealing and locally relevant.
- **Incorporating Local Maps:** Each '*Happy Paws*' location page includes an embedded map. This feature not only assists in guiding pet owners to the store but also reinforces the local nature of the webpage, aiding in local SEO.
- **Optimizing for Local Keywords:** '*Happy Paws*' incorporates specific local keywords into their website content. For their Miami store, they use keywords like "*Miami dog grooming*" or "*tropical fish supplies Miami.*" This strategic placement is not random but carefully woven into the web content, titles, and meta descriptions, aligning with the typical search queries of pet owners in Miami.
- **Local Reviews and Testimonials:** Each store page of '*Happy Paws*' showcases genuine reviews and testimonials from local customers. The San Francisco

store page, for example, features reviews from local pet owners, lending credibility and a personal touch to the site.

Through all these practical steps, '*Happy Paws*' significantly enhances its local online presence. This approach not only improves their visibility in local search results but also fosters a deeper connection with the local community.

Google Business Profile Optimization

Your Google Business Profile is an important asset for optimization. It turns out not every company has this idea yet. My company iO conducted a "2023 *Local SEO Benchmark Report*", a comprehensive analysis of the local SEO performance of retail sectors in the Netherlands and Belgium. A study of nearly 100,000 business locations, focusing on their optimization in local search results. Key findings highlight that over half of these locations are inadequately optimized for local SEO. Only a small fraction effectively utilize tools like Google Posts or engage in review response strategies. The report shows Google Business Profile is often underoptimized. Here you can find some tricks to be sure you optimize your Google Business Profile.

Before you can put your organization on Google Maps and within the map section of the local search result, you obviously need a Google Business Profile. If you are not already registered with Google, you can start by creating a profile:

1. **Creating a Google Account:** Visit Google Business Profile and create a Google Business Profile with your Google account here.
2. **Download the Google Business Profile app to access additional features**: With Google Business Profile, you have access to a number of obvious benefits – the first and most obvious is that users can locate your business more easily. You can get even more out of Google Business Profile. For example, an active Google Business Profile page – which is regularly updated – helps improve your business' ranking in the search results. In other words, if you actively engage with Google Business Profile, you will be rewarded by Google. Here are some tips:
    a. **Your Business Name:** For businesses with physical locations, adding services to your Google Business Profile name can improve local search visibility. For example, if you own a bakery named '*Bockx*', using '*Bakery Bockx*' would be more effective for local searches.
    b. **Complete and Accurate Information:** It is imperative that all foundational details of your business listed on Google Business Profile are meticulously accurate and current. This encompasses not just your business name, address, and contact details, but also extends to subtleties like suite numbers and local phone codes. For example, if "*Bella's Boutique*" moves from 123 Elm St to 456 Oak St, this change must be promptly reflected.

Precision in these details aids in effortlessly guiding customers to your doorstep and ensuring a consistent online presence.

c. **Category and Attributes:** The art of selecting the most fitting category defines how you are perceived. If "*Bella's Boutique*" specializes in handmade jewelry, selecting '*Jewelry Store*' over a generic '*Retail Store*' category can significantly impact visibility in relevant searches. Beyond this, attributes like '*Handmade*,' '*Custom Designs*,' or '*Local Artisans*' can paint a more vivid picture of what Bella's offers, thus magnetically attracting the right clientele. Do not just add one primary category, also think about possible secondary categories: For instance, a restaurant might choose "*Italian Restaurant*" as a primary category and "*Wine Bar*" as a secondary one. Attributes like '*Free Wi-Fi*', '*Wheelchair Accessible*', or '*Outdoor Seating*' provide additional, valuable context to potential customers.

d. **Opening Hours:** It is a good idea to display your opening hours on your Google Business Profile page, so you can communicate clearly when your company is open and temporarily or permanently closed. Make sure to update the opening hours when your company is closed temporarily.

e. **High-Quality Images:** Include a variety of images to give a comprehensive visual overview of your business. This could include:

    i. Your business logo

    ii. Exterior shots of your location

    iii. Interior photos showing the ambiance

    iv. Product images for retail stores or menus for restaurants

    v. Photos of your team or staff in action

    vi. Before/after images for service-based businesses (like beauty salons or auto repair shops)

    vii. Event or promotional images

    viii. Each image type offers a unique perspective of your business and helps to build a more complete and engaging profile.

You can change your Google Business Profile page cover photo, but Google still has the last word on photo choice. Their decision is influenced by the number of views and engagement levels of the photo.

1. **Using Google Posts:** Use Google posts to announce updates, promotions, vacancies, or events that are linked to your company. Standard posts are visible for a week and events expire after the specified end date.

Note: Maintain Your Google Business Profile

Creating your profile is a good first step, but maintaining that profile is another story. Many organizations have a Google Business Profile account but neglect it which puts Google Business Profile benefits at risk. Outdated information can also create a negative impression among users. By regularly writing Google Posts, you make sure your profile looks always up to date.

2. **Google Business Profile Description:** Writing a comprehensive description for your Google Business Profile requires a nuanced approach. Start by identifying the unique aspects of your business that make it stand out from competitors. Incorporate relevant keywords related to your services and location, but ensure they fit naturally within the text. Your description should be clear, succinct, and engaging, providing a snapshot of what your business offers and why it is special. Regular updates are important to keep the description current, reflecting any new services or changes in your business.
3. **Products and Services:** When adding products or services, provide clear, precise titles for each item, followed by detailed descriptions that highlight key features or benefits. Choose the most appropriate categories for each product or service to ensure they are easily discoverable by potential customers. High-quality images of your products or services can significantly enhance their appeal. If applicable, include clear pricing information to provide potential customers with all the details they need to make an informed decision.

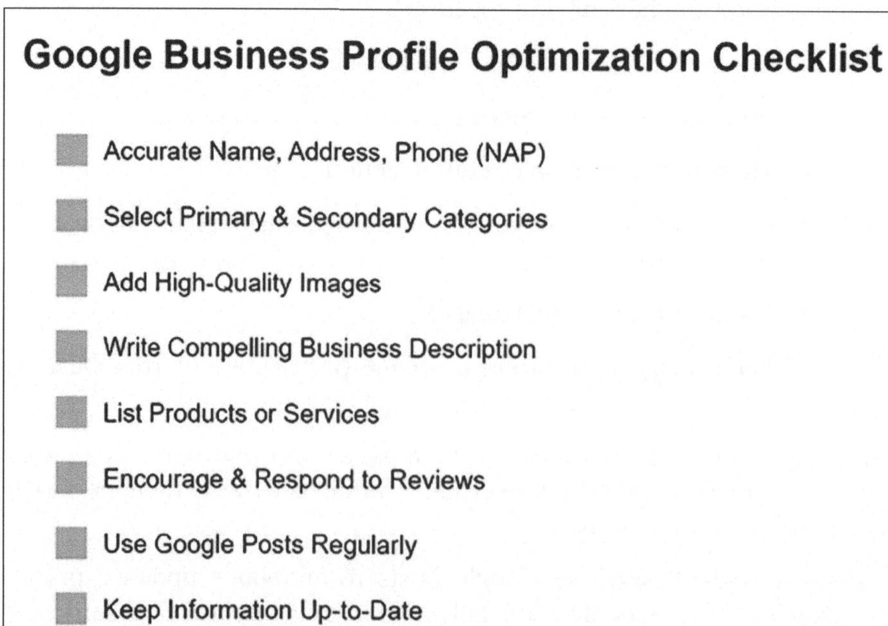

Figure 6.3: *Google Business Profile optimization checklist*

Attracting Reviews on Google Business Profile

Reviews are a key factor in local search algorithms, with positive reviews potentially enhancing a business's visibility and credibility on search platforms. Furthermore, they play a decisive role in influencing customer behavior. Prospective customers often rely on the experiences and opinions of others when making purchasing decisions. Reviews serve as a trust indicator and a reflection of a business's reputation. Therefore, actively receiving reviews is essential for effective local SEO and in attracting and retaining customers. And more, business partners and job seekers will also immediately view your Google Business Profile including your ratings and this may influence how they will perceive you.

Importance of Review Quantity

The quantity of reviews on your Google Business Profile (GBP) is vitally important for several reasons:

- **Enhanced Visibility and SEO:** More reviews can lead to better visibility in Google's local search results. A higher number of reviews, especially positive ones, can positively influence your business's search ranking.
- **Building Trust and Credibility**: A larger volume of reviews often equates to greater trust from potential customers. It shows that a business is well-frequented and has a broad customer base. Many customers prefer companies who have 100 reviews with average score 4 over a company with only two 5-star reviews.
- **Comprehensive Customer Insight**: With a wide range of reviews, businesses can gain a more nuanced understanding of customer needs and preferences. They can identify trends. Patterns in feedback can highlight strengths to capitalize on and weaknesses to address. These insights can be used for improving products and services. By analyzing the diverse and numerous feedback, businesses can make informed decisions to refine their offerings. Understanding different customer segments through their feedback can help in customizing experiences and marketing strategies. In summary, a large and varied collection of reviews not only enhances a business's online presence but also serves as a crucial tool for continuous improvement and customer-driven innovation. In this aspect, even negative reviews may be worth receiving. Like Bill Gates says "*Your most unhappy customers are your greatest source of learning.*"

Getting More GBP Reviews

To effectively increase reviews on your Google Business Profile, you can combine some actionable strategies to encourage customers to leave reviews on your profile.

First, think about your post-transaction follow-up. Send emails with direct review links after purchases or services.

When you have a store, you could set up interactive kiosks for immediate feedback.

Furthermore, highlight customer reviews in your promotional materials.

Actively use your social media platforms to encourage reviews. Share links to your GBP review page, and regularly post about the importance of customer feedback. You can also feature positive reviews on your social media channels. Provide direct links to your GBP review on receipts, or via QR codes in-store or your print publications.

A last trick would be to embed a review widget on your website that directs visitors to your Google Business Profile review page. Highlight positive reviews on your site, showing new visitors the positive experiences of previous customers.

Managing Reviews

Positive Reviews

Thank each reviewer personally. This acknowledgment not only shows appreciation but also reinforces a positive relationship. For example, "*Thank you, [Reviewer's Name], for your kind words!*"

Share glowing reviews on your website, social media, or in promotional materials, always with the reviewer's permission. This showcases real customer satisfaction and can attract new customers.

Example: A restaurant received a review praising their attentive service and unique menu. They added this review on the homepage which leads to increased trust.

Negative Reviews

Addressing concerns in negative reviews involves a strategic approach to maintain professionalism and brand image. It is very common for every business to get a negative review, so do not panic. What makes your brand image is the way you handle those negative reviews. You don't want to argue, deny or ignore negative reviews, as these may make people perceive you as even worse. The best way to deal with negative reviews is by showing understanding and offering solutions when you encounter a negative review.

Here are five types of negative reviews and diverse ways to manage them:

- ***Service Complaints***: Service was unprofessional.

  Example Response: "*We apologize for your experience. We have addressed this with our team to ensure better service in the future. Please contact us directly so we can make this right.*"

- ***Product Issues***: Product broke after 2 months.

  Example Response: "*We are sorry to hear about your issue with [product]. We would like to learn more and find a solution. Please reach out to our customer service for assistance.*"

- ***Delay in Service***: We had to wait for hours.

  Example Response: "*Thank you for bringing this to our attention. We are working on improving our service speed and appreciate your patience. We would love to offer you [a discount/free service] on your next visit.*"

- ***Staff Unfriendly***: "*The cashier was unfriendly*".

  Example Response: "*This is concerning to hear, as we train our staff to be courteous and professional. We will address this internally and hope you will give us another chance to show our true customer service standards.*"

- ***Unmet Expectations***: "*We expected more for the price they were asking*".

  Example Response: "*We regret that we did not meet your expectations. We are continually striving to improve and would value any additional feedback you could provide.*"

In each case, the response is prompt, acknowledges the issue, offers a solution or compensation, and maintains a professional tone. By effectively handling negative reviews, businesses can turn challenging situations caused by negative reviews into opportunities for improvement and customer retention and show off their responsiveness by answering these reviews.

Spam Reviews

In handling spam reviews on your Google Business Profile, first, identify them by their irrelevant or promotional content. For instance, a review might read, "*Great place! Also visit [Unrelated Business] for amazing deals!*" When you encounter such reviews, it's advisable not to engage directly, as this can lend credibility to the fake review. Instead, report the review to Google using their reporting feature. It is crucial to monitor your reviews regularly to quickly identify and report spam, maintaining the integrity and accuracy of your business's online reputation.

Questions

Managing questions on your Google Business Profile enhances customer engagement and SEO. It involves monitoring your profile for new questions, responding promptly and accurately, and ensuring that your answers provide value to both the person asking and potential future customers. Regularly checking for new questions and updating your responses when necessary, helps maintain an active and informative profile. Additionally, create a FAQ section on your website, addressing these questions. This dual approach not only serves customers directly on Google but also drives traffic to your website, providing comprehensive information in both places and improving overall user experience.

Linkbuilding for Local SEO

Local PR and Outreach

In the digital age, local public relations (PR) and outreach remain vital components for enhancing local SEO. There are multiple ways you can use to boost your online visibility.

- **Building Relationships with Local Media**: Engage with local newspapers. Offer your business as a source for local news stories or as an expert in your field. This creates opportunities for mentions and links in local media, which are highly valuable for SEO.
- **Community Involvement and Sponsorships**: Actively participate in local community events, festivals, and charity drives. Sponsorships or partnerships with these events can lead to mentions in local media and on event websites, increasing your visibility. Be sure to request a link when sponsoring a local organization or local event.
- **Leveraging Press Releases**: Use press releases for significant business events or contributions to the community. Distribute these to local news outlets and post them on your website, creating additional content that can be linked back to.
- **Networking with Local Organizations**: Join local business groups, chambers of commerce, or trade associations. These connections can lead to backlinks from their websites and increase your business's exposure in the local community.
- **Creating and Sharing Local Content**: Develop content that resonates with the local audience, such as guides to local attractions or coverage of local issues. Share this content with local media and on social media to increase engagement and backlinks.
- **Engaging with Local Bloggers and Influencers**: Identify and collaborate with local bloggers and influencers in your niche. They can provide valuable backlinks and increase your reach within the community.

In conclusion, local PR and outreach are about creating meaningful connections within your community and with local media. These efforts not only enhance your business's local SEO but also build a strong, positive reputation in your local area.

NAP

In local SEO, NAP stands for Name, Address, and Phone Number. It is critical for Google as it uses this information to create a '*knowledge entity*' – a digital representation of a business. For example, think about a company '*City Florist*'.

For '*City Florist*', variations in their name across different platforms could include listings as "*City Florist and Gifts*," "*City Flower Shop*," or "*City Floral Designs*." These differing names create inconsistencies in how Google and potential customers perceive and find the business online. Such variations can confuse search algorithms and customers, leading to challenges in search engine rankings and local business visibility. By standardizing their name to "*City Florist*" on all platforms, they would ensure a consistent, easily recognizable presence both for search engines and customers. NAP data is essential in forming a reliable knowledge entity for Google, impacting a business's digital presence and customer engagement. Maintaining a precise and consistent NAP profile is a fundamental aspect of an effective local SEO strategy.

Other Platforms

Apart from Google Business Profile, there are some other platforms for local searches, such as Yelp, Foursquare, Waze, and Apple maps. It is key to not forget these platforms when executing a SEO strategy. Here is a table outlining the differences between various local platforms:

Platform	Main Use	Key Features	Primary Audience	SEO Focus
Google Business Profile	Business listings and reviews	Search visibility, Reviews, Posts, Q&A	General internet users	Search engine rankings
Yelp	Customer reviews and ratings	User reviews, Business ratings, Reservations	Consumers seeking reviews	Reputation and review management
Foursquare	Local discovery and reviews	Check-ins, Tips, Reviews	Local explorers and travelers	Local engagement and discovery

Waze	Navigation and traffic information	Real-time traffic, Routing, Business ads	Drivers and commuters	Location visibility for drivers
Apple Maps	Mapping and navigation	Navigation, Business listings, Siri integration	Apple device users	Visibility on Apple devices

Table 6.1: *Other local platforms*

Optimization

For business owners looking to enhance local SEO on platforms like Waze, Yelp, Foursquare, and Apple Maps, consider these strategies:

- **Accurate and Consistent Information**: Ensure your business's name, address, and phone number (NAP) are consistently and accurately listed across all platforms.
- **Engage with Reviews**: Regularly monitor and respond to reviews on platforms like Yelp and Foursquare. Personalized responses to customer feedback demonstrate engagement and can positively influence potential customers.
- **Utilize Platform-Specific Features**: Each platform has unique features. For instance, offer check-in specials on Foursquare, or ensure your business is correctly marked on Waze for easy navigation.
- **Optimize for Keywords**: Include relevant keywords in your business descriptions to improve searchability.
- **Encourage User Interaction**: Motivate customers to check in, leave reviews, or post photos on these platforms.
- **Keep Content Fresh**: Regularly update your profiles with news, offers, and relevant information to keep them engaging and current.

These tactics help in maximizing visibility and engagement across various local search platforms, contributing significantly to a robust local SEO strategy.

Bing Places for Business

Bing is the second biggest traditional search engine. Bing Places for Business is a free service offered by Microsoft's Bing search engine, designed to help business owners manage their online presence across Bing and Yahoo. Similar to Google Business Profile, it allows businesses to add their listings to Bing's search engine, enabling customers to find them more easily. The verification process for Bing Places can be quicker and less cumbersome for some businesses, especially those already verified through Google Business Profile. Bing allows businesses to import their Google Business Profile listings directly, simplifying the initial setup process. So, once you created a top-notch Google Business Profile, you can import this information into Bing Places for Business.

Monitoring and Reporting Local SEO

KPI's

When monitoring and reporting Local SEO, you have to start with defining your KPI's. Some possible KPI's for local SEO are the following:

- **Local Search Visibility**: Track how often your business appears in local search results for relevant keywords. This metric is key for understanding your local online presence.
- **Website Traffic from Local Searches**: Monitor the volume and quality of traffic coming to your website from local searches. This includes assessing which local keywords are driving traffic. Also, you can look at the number of incoming visitors on your local pages.
- **Google Business Profile Insights**: This includes the number of views your listing gets, click-through rates for calls, direction requests, and website visits.
- **Conversion Rate from Local Traffic**: Measure how effectively local search traffic converts into tangible actions like calls, store visits, or purchases.
- **Customer Reviews and Ratings**: Keep track of reviews and ratings on local directories and your Google Business Profile. This includes the number of reviews, average rating, and response rate to reviews.

Figure 6.4: *Local SEO KPI dashboard*

Local SEO Tools

For monitoring the results, some tools are essential. These include:

- **Google Analytics**: Essential for tracking website traffic sources, user behavior, and conversions. It helps in understanding how local SEO efforts are impacting overall web traffic.

- **Google Business Profile Insights**: Provides valuable data about how customers are finding and interacting with your business listing on Google. This includes information on search queries, views, and customer actions like calls and direction requests.
- **Uberall**: Offers features for managing and optimizing online presence across various directories, platforms, and maps. Useful for tracking NAP consistency and online reviews
- **Localfalcon**: Specifically designed for Google Business Profiles, this tool provides detailed insights into local search rankings, helping businesses understand their visibility in different geographical areas.
- **BrightLocal**: It is a powerful tool for enhancing citation signals, which account for 13% of local ranking factors. It streamlines the process of building and managing citations, crucial for local SEO. BrightLocal offers comprehensive citation audits, identifying inconsistencies in business information across the web. It facilitates the creation of new citations on relevant platforms while ensuring NAP (Name, Address, Phone) consistency. This tool also provides ongoing monitoring and cleanup services, helping businesses maintain accurate online presences.

These tools play a crucial role in monitoring various aspects of local SEO, providing actionable insights that can help in refining and enhancing local SEO strategies.

UTM Tags for Local SEO

Traffic from Google Business Profile is automatically added to your organic traffic in Analytics, which doesn't clearly show the impact of your GBP page on your traffic. This can be resolved by using UTM tags in your links, allowing Analytics to keep data from each link separate. For instance, adding the following to your URL:

```
utm_source=google&utm_medium=organic&utm_campaign=gbp&utm_content=lv_riga
```

The first three bold words are mandatory to specify the source (google), medium (organic traffic), and campaign. The last part, useful for tracking traffic from multiple locations, can specify content, like a location in Riga, Latvia.

Conclusion

Local SEO is super important for businesses because it helps them show up in search results when people nearby are looking for what they offer. This can lead to more people visiting the store or website.

First, we discussed making your website friendly for local searches. This means adding information and keywords that let people know where your business is and what it does. Making sure your business's name, address, and phone number (NAP) are the same everywhere online is also another key aspect explored.

Then, we dived into Google Business Profile, which is a free tool that lets your business show up on Google Maps and search results. We learned that filling out your profile with up-to-date info, photos, and responding to customer reviews can make your business more attractive.

Next, we looked beyond Google to other places on the internet where you can list your business, like Bing or directories. This helps make sure even more people can find you, no matter where they search.

Lastly, we talked about reporting your local SEO efforts. This means regularly checking results of your Local SEO efforts and adjusting strategy based on that.

Now that we have covered all the basics of SEO, in the following chapters, we will delve into the more strategic side of SEO. We will start with the important topic of SEO and Business alignment.

CHAPTER 7
Business Strategy and SEO

Introduction

The wisdom of Sun Tzu in "*The Art of War*" finds its place in modern business strategies. His quote "*All men can see these tactics whereby I conquer, but what none can see is the strategy out of which victory is evolved*," reflects the hidden power of strategic SEO. This chapter is all about the fusion of SEO with business strategy, a critical intersection for a next-level SEO professional. We will explore how strategic planning, aligned with the practical application of SEO, transcends conventional SEO tactics to really achieve business outcomes. Through engaging with this chapter, you will understand the importance of stakeholder engagement, the nuances of integrating SEO with broader business objectives, and how to leverage this synergy to dominate the digital landscape. Prepare to uncover the strategic frameworks that will guide in your journey to become a strategic SEO professional and really start generating business impact.

Structure

In this chapter, we will cover the following topics:

- Introduction to Good Strategy
- Goals Setting for SEO
- Strategy Models Applied to SEO
- Market Analysis for SEO
- Stakeholder Management and SEO Strategy

Introduction to Good Strategy

Strategic SEO targets the right audience, enhances brand visibility in relevant search queries, and contributes to achieving specific business objectives like lead generation, sales, and customer engagement. Without alignment to the audience or the business strategy, SEO might bring traffic that does not convert into meaningful business outcomes, wasting resources and missing opportunities for growth and competitiveness. In short, SEO needs to be strategic and aligned with business strategy because it ensures that SEO efforts support business goals, rather than just driving generic traffic. But what is a good strategy?

The book "*Good Strategy Bad Strategy*" by Richard Rumelt outlines a clear distinction between what constitutes a good strategy and what falls under a bad strategy. A good strategy, as defined by Rumelt, consists of a set of coherent actions aimed at getting unique insights and resources to tackle obstacles and achieve significant objectives. It is composed of three elements: a diagnosis that defines the nature of the challenge, a guiding policy for dealing with the challenge, and coherent actions designed to carry out the guiding policy.

Conversely, a bad strategy is characterized by a lack of clarity, disguising the absence of strategic thought with jargon, failing to face the challenge, or setting objectives without a coherent plan to achieve them. Rumelt emphasizes the importance of recognizing and avoiding these pitfalls to formulate strategies that are not only clear and focused but also actionable and aligned with the organization's goals and challenges.

An example of a bad strategy (outside of SEO) could be a company aiming to "*become a market leader*" without specifying the market, the competitors, the timeframe, or the means to achieve this goal. It lacks a clear diagnosis of the current market position, a guiding policy for how to navigate the market, and a set of coherent actions to achieve the objective.

In SEO, a bad strategy might be aiming to "*double website traffic*" without identifying the target audience, relevant keywords, or content strategy. This approach lacks specificity, fails to address how to attract quality traffic, and does not outline the actions needed to achieve the goal, such as optimizing for specific high-intent keywords, improving website UX/UI, or creating content that addresses the target audience's needs and search intent.

Let us explain the three components of a good strategy:

- **Diagnosis**: This defines the nature of the challenge. It simplifies the complexity of reality by identifying the critical aspects of the current situation that need attention.
- **Guiding Policy:** This outlines an approach for dealing with the challenge. It is an overarching principle that steers the efforts and actions towards overcoming the obstacles identified in the diagnosis.
- **Coherent Actions:** These are the steps or measures taken to follow the guiding policy. They are coordinated efforts designed to work together in achieving

the strategic objectives, ensuring that resources and actions are aligned and focused on the path outlined by the guiding policy.

Applying the "*Good Strategy Bad Strategy*" framework to, for example, an online running shoes webshop involves:

- **Diagnosis:** Evaluate the current online market for running shoes, identifying key challenges such as high competition, customer preference for physical shoe fitting, or specific needs of niche markets (for example, trail runners versus urban joggers).
- **Guiding Policy:** Decide on a strategic approach, such as focusing on a niche market with specialized needs (for example, trail running shoes) or offering unparalleled customer service (for example, virtual fitting tools, detailed shoe guides, and personalized recommendations).
- **Coherent Actions:** Implement actions aligned with the guiding policy, like curating a selection of high-quality trail running shoes, developing an interactive online fitting tool, creating content that addresses the concerns and interests of trail runners, and employing SEO tactics targeted at keywords relevant to trail running enthusiasts.

You immediately see this approach is on a strategic level and transcends tactics like "*let's have good rankings by optimizing our content and technique*". By using a good strategic framework, the SEO strategy will be integrated within the overall business strategy.

In the example of the running shoes, following elements tell you the strategy is well researched.

First, there's acknowledgement of the challenge that getting high rankings will be difficult because of the high competition. By focusing on a specific niche, like trail running, offering unique products or services that competitors don't, you acknowledge that you likely won't rank well for very broad and general keywords.

Another element is seeing the pain point for the customers buying shoes online, which is the customer preference for physical fitting. This can be overcome with a virtual fitting tool and a robust return policy to reduce the hesitation of buying shoes online.

Then, a strategy can be further refined by addressing the new niche market's needs. This can be addressed by curating a specialized inventory and creating expert content that resonates with the specific interests and needs of trail runners, such as guides on selecting shoes based on terrain.

These actions directly tackle the challenges identified in the diagnosis, adhering to the guiding policy, and are executed through coherent, strategically aligned actions. As Rumelt says "*A goal is not a strategy*", but clever goal setting is an important part of strategy. Let us learn more about goal setting.

Goals Setting

In this section, we will show you some inspiration to think about your goal setting. A well-known framework, often used in digital marketing is SMART goals. SMART goals stand for Specific, Measurable, Achievable, Relevant, and Time-bound. This framework helps in setting clear and attainable objectives. In the context of SEO, applying SMART goals involves defining precise targets, such as increasing organic search traffic or improving keyword rankings, ensuring these goals are quantifiable, realistic given your resources, aligned with broader business aims, and set with a deadline for completion. For example, aiming to "*Increase organic search traffic by 20% within the next quarter by optimizing for long-tail keywords related to trail running shoes*" follows the SMART criteria, making it a well-defined and actionable goal. In following table, we compare non-SMART Goals with SMART Goals to give you a better feeling about setting good SMART goals.

Criteria	**Non-SMART Goal Example**	**SMART Goal Example**
Specific	Improve SEO	Increase organic search rankings for 5 primary keywords related to trail running shoes in 3 months.
Measurable	Get more website visitors	Achieve a 30% increase in organic traffic to the trail running shoes category within the next quarter.
Achievable	Rank #1 for all keywords	Improve keyword rankings for the trail running shoes category to appear on the first page of Google search results within six months.
Relevant	Do linkbuilding	Enhance the website's backlink profile by acquiring 20 new backlinks from running-focused websites in three months.
Time-bound	Increase sales	Grow online sales of trail running shoes by 25% over the next fiscal year.

Table 7.1: SMART Goals

An extension of SMART goals are OKR's (objectives and key results)

Investor John Doerr, in his book "*Measure What Matters,*" emphasizes the transformative power of Objectives and Key Results (OKRs) in setting and achieving goals. He states that "*Objectives and key results are the yin and yang of goal setting,*" highlighting the balance between ambitious objectives and measurable results. This approach can be especially powerful in an SEO context, where clear, ambitious goals (Objectives) are balanced with specific, quantifiable outcomes (Key Results) such as improved rankings, increased organic traffic, or higher conversion rates from search engine visitors. By applying Doerr's insights, an online running shoes webshop can strategically align its SEO efforts with the company's broader objectives, ensuring every action taken is measurable and directly contributes to the overarching goals.

For a trail running shoes webshop, OKRs could be:

Objective 1: Establish the webshop as the top online destination for trail running enthusiasts.

> **Key Result 1**: Increase organic search traffic to the trail running shoes category by 30% within the next quarter.
>
> **Key Result 2**: Achieve first-page search engine rankings for 10 key trail running shoe-related terms by the end of the year.
>
> **Key Result 3**: Grow customer reviews in the trail running category by 50% within six months.

Objective 2: Enhance customer satisfaction and retention for the trail running segment.

> **Key Result 1**: Achieve a customer satisfaction score of 90% for purchasers of trail running shoes within the next quarter.
>
> **Key Result 2**: Increase repeat customer rate by 30% for the trail running shoes category within the year.
>
> **Key Result 3**: Reduce return rates for trail running shoes by 20% in six months through improved sizing guides and virtual fitting tools.

These OKRs combine ambitious, strategic goals (objectives) with specific, measurable outcomes (key results) that directly contribute to the overarching objectives of the webshop. By starting from the strategic objectives, you can group initiatives around certain goals so your initiative will be aligned with business goals.

A bad OKR approach for the shop might be overly vague, unrealistic, or not directly actionable, such as:

Objective 3: Increase the shop's popularity online.

> **Key Result 1**: Get more website visits.
>
> **Key Result 2**: Sell more shoes.
>
> **Key Result 3**: Be recognized as a top webshop.

These OKRs lack specificity, measurability, and time frames, making it difficult to track progress or determine when objectives have been achieved. Furthermore, they don't inspire direct actions.

Market-Adjusted Goals

Another wisdom, especially for long-term strategy, would be to include other factors within your market. In SEO goal setting within a dynamic market, understanding both controllable and uncontrollable factors is crucial. You can't control branded searches, market interest, or competitor actions directly. For example, a pandemic may lead to a decrease in event-related searches. Therefore, in goal setting you should focus on controllable aspects like on-page optimizations, technical SEO, content strategy, and link-building. These efforts can enhance your site's organic visibility and competitiveness. Recognizing the importance of these insights allows for more strategic, flexible goal setting, enabling quick adaptation to market changes and leveraging areas within your control to optimize performance and achieve SEO goals effectively.

Controllable Factors	**Uncontrollable Factors**
On-page optimizations	Branded searches
Site architecture	Market interest
Technical SEO (site speed)	Competitor actions
Content strategy	Emerging market trends
Link-building efforts	Changes in search algorithms
Mobile-friendliness	Economic factors

Table 7.2: *Factors of SEO performance*

As you can see the overall market in which you operate will also determine whether you reach your SEO goals or not. SEO does not create market demand, it captures market demand!

Business Strategy Models Applied to SEO

One way to align SEO-strategy with business strategy is to start from the business strategy - and then look into the SEO-actions which can follow along with this business strategy. To know which SEO actions can be prioritized to suggest, we will examine well-known strategic business frameworks and apply them to SEO.

The Ansoff Matrix is a strategic planning tool that provides a framework for businesses to plan and evaluate growth strategies. It consists of four quadrants based on market and product dimensions: Market Penetration (existing markets, existing products), Product Development (existing markets, new products), Market Development (new markets, existing products), and Diversification (new markets, new products). This model helps businesses assess risk and strategy alignment with their growth objectives.

New markets	Market developments	Diversification
Existing markets	Market Penetration	Product development
	Existing products	New products

Table 7.3: *Ansoff Matrix*

One can apply this strategy model to SEO.

Strategy	Description	SEO Application
Market Penetration	Increase market share with existing products in existing markets.	Optimize existing content and keywords to increase traffic and conversions.
Product Development	Offer new products to the existing market.	Create new content or optimize for new keywords related to new products or services.
Market Development	Enter new markets with existing products.	Target new geographical locations or demographics with existing content.
Diversification	Introduce new products to new markets.	Develop and optimize content for completely new markets and product lines.

Table 7.4: *Marketing strategy models applied to SEO*

Let us give a concrete example for a health and wellness company offering fitness equipment and online training programs:

- **Market Penetration:** They stick to their existing products/markets. The SEO strategy would be to further optimize existing online training program pages for search engines to increase visibility and capture a larger share of the current market.
- **Product Development**: They make new products for their current market, for example, launch new wellness supplements or fitness equipment. Create SEO-optimized content focused on the benefits and uniqueness of these new products. Don't forget video- SEO with demonstrations of this product.
- **Market Development**: They want to address a new audience. Target new geographical markets by localizing website content and using SEO strategies to rank for region-specific fitness and wellness queries. Or think about a specific demographic they now want to focus on (for example, senior people) and optimize for this demographic with separate landing pages/tips.
- **Diversification**: Enter a completely new market, like corporate wellness programs, developing a new section on the website with targeted SEO content to attract business clients. The SEO expert should in this case help to study the audience of this market, their wants, questions and pain points to come up with SEO ideas.

So, it can be worthwhile to know where the overall business strategy is heading to before making strategic SEO choices.

SWOT Analysis

A SWOT analysis is a strategic tool used in marketing to identify and evaluate the Strengths, Weaknesses, Opportunities, and Threats related to business competition or project planning. This method helps marketers and businesses pinpoint internal factors (strengths and weaknesses) that impact their operations and external factors (opportunities and threats) that affect market position and success. Leverage your strengths, address your weaknesses, seize your opportunities, and neutralize your threats–that's the power of SWOT.

You can also use the SWOT analysis for SEO as a means of story-telling to marketing managers.

For a health and wellness company, an example of a SWOT analysis to SEO might look like:

Strengths: Strong brand reputation in wellness, high-quality content on fitness and health.

Leverage this by optimizing existing content and increasing internal linking to improve site authority. Use the brand's authority to enhance SEO by creating comprehensive guides and resources on trending health topics, and build link partnerships based on this authority.

Weaknesses: Poor mobile website optimization, slow load times.

Address these technical SEO weaknesses to improve user experience and rankings. Implement technical SEO improvements like optimizing for mobile, reducing page load times, and improving site structure to enhance user experience and search engine rankings.

Opportunities: Emerging trends in home workouts and wellness apps.

Capitalize on the rising interest in home workouts by developing targeted content campaigns, utilizing keyword research to identify emerging trends, and creating video content for better engagement. Person skilled in creating videos available within the company, but quantity of video content can still be improved.

Threats: Competitors with strong SEO presence and possible new competitors.

Conduct competitor analysis to identify gaps in their strategies and opportunities for your SEO efforts. Create a SEO dashboard containing keyword rankings and competitor rankings to follow up on competitor strategies.

This approach helps identify internal and external factors that can impact SEO strategy and prioritize actions to enhance online visibility and competitiveness.

Resource-Based and Market Demand Strategy

Basically, there are two ways you could build a competitive advantage: resource-based and market-demand. In a business both should complement each other.

- Building the best internal resources (resource-based)
- Capturing the market demand (market-demand)

A resource-based business strategy focuses on leveraging a company's internal resources and capabilities to gain competitive advantage, whereas a market demand business strategy prioritizes aligning offerings with current market needs and customer demands.

There are three types of resources which can be analyzed before making your SEO strategy, including:

- **Business Resources**: This includes brand awareness. With brand awareness, it may be easier to gain additional links from media and partners, which will be more interested in you because of your brand.
- **Content Resources**: Do you have resources to develop unique, high-quality content that leverages the company's specific expertise or resources, setting it apart from competitors in search engine results. For example, an in-house videographer can be used as a strategic resource for Video SEO
- **Technical Resources**: Leverages in-house technical skills to ensure the website outperforms competitors on speed, mobile optimization, and user experience, directly impacting SEO rankings.

For capturing the market demand, your SEO strategy should be focused on following three topics:

- **Trend Adaptation**: Focuses on identifying and quickly adapting to changing search trends and customer interests, optimizing content to match emerging queries and topics.
- **Customer-Centric Content**: Prioritizes creating content that answers the specific questions and needs of the target market, aiming to attract and retain traffic by meeting user search intent.
- **Competitive Analysis**: Regularly analyzes competitors' strategies to identify gaps in the market and adjust SEO tactics to capture unserved or underserved demand.

Both strategies can complement each other in an SEO context. For instance, making use of unique resources (resource-based) to create content that meets specific market demands (market demand-based) can provide a strong competitive edge in search engine rankings. Example, if you have access to video team, you create videos for a new trend, while if you have a strong development team you can create an interactive tool that may answers questions of their customers. When you use your unique resources to attract market demand, you can build up strategic advantage.

Value Disciplines Model and SEO

By focusing on being the leader in either product innovation, customer experience, or efficiency, businesses can carve out a sustainable competitive advantage. This strategic focus is crucial for companies aiming to establish a strong market presence and achieve long-term success. When doing SEO, it is very good to know what kind of strategy the companies follow to get alignment. We will show you some practical examples of how the value disciplines model can be used to form a SEO strategy.

- **Product Differentiation in SEO**: A boutique tea company with unique products uses SEO to highlight its unique selling proposition of handcrafted, organic teas by creating content around the benefits of organic ingredients and artisanal production methods. This approach helps the company stand out in search results for "*organic artisanal tea*," attracting a niche market.
- **Customer Service Strategy and SEO**: An online electronics retailer focusing on customer service enhances its SEO strategy by incorporating a comprehensive FAQ section that addresses common customer queries. This not only improves their search rankings for specific questions about electronics but also boosts customer satisfaction by providing valuable information upfront.
- **Operational Excellence and SEO Efficiency**: A travel agency known for their pragmatic approach optimizes its website's loading speed and mobile responsiveness, recognizing that these technical SEO aspects significantly impact user experience and search engine rankings. By focusing on operational improvements, the agency sees an increase in organic traffic and a higher conversion rate from mobile users.

Aligning your SEO strategy with your company's focus area ensures coherence between SEO and overall business strategy. In a market with three companies, if one focuses on product innovation and another on customer intimacy, focusing on operational excellence positions you to dominate in searches related to efficiency, reliability, and cost-effectiveness. For all price-related queries, you should be able to outcompete the competition. Similarly, a company prioritizing product innovation would likely excel in searches for the latest or most advanced products, while one emphasizing customer intimacy could dominate in searches for personalized services or customer care excellence or reviews around products, attracting distinct customer segments.

A SEO strategy that aligns with the business should start with focusing on the segment you are able to service the most well. It will be both easier and more profitable to first focus on the most aligned segment.

Market Analysis and SEO

A step further than aligning SEO with business strategy is to let SEO play a pivotal role in shaping and informing business strategy. By providing insights into customer behavior, market trends, and competitive landscapes through data-driven analysis, SEO can help identify new opportunities for product development, market entry, and customer engagement. This relationship ensures that the business strategy is responsive to the digital environment and customer needs, ultimately leading to more effective targeting, enhanced brand visibility, and improved business outcomes.

SEO can inform and influence business strategy through market insights and customer behavior analysis. For example, if SEO data shows a high volume of searches for sustainable products, a company might pivot towards eco-friendly product lines. Another instance is using geo-targeting insights from SEO to expand into new markets or regions showing increased interest in the company's offerings. Additionally, competitive analysis through SEO can uncover gaps in competitors' offerings, suggesting areas for differentiation or innovation. These concrete examples highlight how SEO not only supports but can actively shape business strategy.

SEMrush's keyword gap analysis can identify opportunities for product differentiation by revealing search terms competitors are not ranking for. Using these tools, businesses can make data-driven decisions, such as entering new markets or developing products aligned with search trends, demonstrating the tangible impact of SEO insights on strategic planning.

For example, a fashion company may utilize SEO data to understand fast-changing fashion trends. By analyzing search trends and social media buzz around specific styles or materials, the fashion retailer can quickly adapt its inventory and marketing strategies to match consumer interest, ensuring they remain at the forefront of the fast-fashion industry. This agile approach to product development and marketing, informed by SEO insights, showcases how closely aligning SEO with business strategy can drive success.

SEO can also inform or influence business strategy by identifying under-served customer needs through search query analysis. For example, if an online retailer notices a high volume of searches for eco-friendly packaging that are not well-addressed by current offerings, the company might decide to develop or source products that meet this demand. Additionally, SEO insights into the language and terms used by potential customers can guide the development of improved marketing messages and product descriptions, enhancing brand relevance and customer engagement.

The Lean Startup and SEO

The Lean Startup methodology, developed by Eric Ries and Steve Blank, emphasizes rapid product development cycles, customer feedback, and iterative design to discover a viable business model. The Lean Startup is often used by internet startups and in cases when there are still a lot of unknowns to the business and the customers. The aim for Lean Startup is building a rapid framework for testing and experimentation to build and grow a business. When you follow the lean startup you come up with assumptions about your business and test them as soon as possible. A practical example is Zappos, which validated its business model by selling shoes online without actually holding an inventory of shoes. Zappos could already learn from the customers before investments in a shoe inventory are needed.

SEO professionals should study the Lean Startup methodology because it emphasizes agility, customer feedback, and iterative development, which are crucial for adapting SEO strategies in a constantly changing digital landscape. By applying Lean Startup principles, SEO experts can more effectively test hypotheses, measure results, and refine their tactics to better meet user needs and business goals, ensuring their efforts are always aligned with the most current market demands and search engine algorithms.

This quick testing and hypothesis strategy for SEO involves creating assumptions on how changes can impact your website's SEO performance, then systematically testing these hypotheses through controlled experiments.

An SEO professional could execute the Lean Startup methodology by conducting A/B testing on different SEO tactics for a subset of pages. For instance, they might create two versions of a page with different keyword strategies or meta descriptions, then monitor which version performs better in search rankings and user engagement. This data-driven approach allows for quick learning about what SEO modifications most effectively improve visibility and traffic, embodying the Lean principle of validated learning through rapid experimentation.

For the Lean Startup principle of "*Build-Measure-Learn*," an SEO example could involve creating content clusters around a new, speculative keyword theme that's gaining traction. The SEO team builds a series of articles or pages (Build), uses analytics to track their rankings, traffic, and engagement (Measure), then analyzes this data to decide whether to expand the content cluster, adjust the SEO tactics, or pivot to a new strategy based on what resonated most with the audience (Learn). This cycle promotes continuous improvement and adaptation within your SEO strategy.

Stakeholder Management

A SEO expert is not working on an island. Stakeholder management for SEO involves identifying and engaging with individuals or groups who have an interest in your SEO action and outcomes. This includes internal teams (like content, web development, and marketing) and external stakeholders (such as partners or agencies). Effective management includes clear communication of SEO goals, strategies, and performance metrics. It is crucial to align SEO activities with broader business objectives, ensuring that all stakeholders understand the value of SEO efforts and how they contribute to the organization's success. Engaging stakeholders through regular updates, involving them in strategic discussions, and soliciting feedback can foster collaboration and support for SEO initiatives.

Each of the stakeholders can bring a unique perspective to a SEO project, but also may have some obstacles to overcome. In the following table, we list some common stakeholders within a SEO project.

Stakeholder	Perspective They Bring	Obstacles to Overcome	Way to Work Together
Marketing Manager	Oversight of SEO's alignment with marketing goals.	Balancing SEO with broader marketing objectives.	Establish clear communication channels; align SEO goals with marketing KPIs.
Content Creators	Content relevance and quality.	Balancing SEO with creativity and brand voice.	Host creative workshops to integrate SEO without compromising creativity.
Web Developers	Website technical optimization.	Resource allocation for SEO-driven changes.	Schedule regular technical SEO audits and prioritize updates based on impact.
UX/UI Designers	User experience and design optimization for SEO.	Design constraints versus SEO requirements.	Collaborate on design that enhances both user experience and SEO.
Senior Management	Business impact and ROI from SEO investments.	Justifying SEO budget and timelines.	Provide regular reports on SEO progress and its impact on business goals.

***Table 7.5**: SEO stakeholders*

For managing these stakeholders within an SEO project, you can address each stakeholder in a targeted way.

- **Marketing Manager**: Regular strategy meetings to ensure SEO objectives are aligned with overall marketing goals, using shared dashboards for real-time updates.
- **Content Creators**: Conduct SEO training sessions to integrate keyword research into content creation processes, encouraging feedback on content performance. Create a SEO content dashboard suited towards copywriter so they can follow up results on optimized pages and keyword rankings.
- **Web Developers:** Implement a ticketing system for SEO-related site updates, ensuring priority fixes are understood and scheduled. Always give for each technical point the reasoning behind it, so the developer can think along and sees the priority.

- **UX/UI Designers**: Jointly review user session recordings to identify areas for improvement, blending SEO insights with design enhancements. Create strategic workshops on how to improve UX for people coming from organic sources.
- **Senior Management**: Create nice looking and short SEO performance presentations, highlighting key achievements and impact on business objectives, to secure ongoing support and resources.

To be on the same starting point, you should consider educating these stakeholders: Helen Politt makes a distinction between three categories:

- **Operational Profiles**: Web developers and content creators who need knowledge of SEO skills.
- **Strategic Profiles**: UX designers and marketing managers who needs to understand the context of SEO
- **Senior Management**: They need to understand the importance of SEO

Consider initiatives like setting up SEO dashboards for marketing managers to monitor campaign progress, hosting quarterly SEO trend webinars for content creators to inspire new content strategies, organizing technical SEO workshops for web developers to discuss site optimization practices, and facilitating user experience feedback sessions with UX/UI designers to align on SEO-friendly design principles.

These activities not only educate but also actively engage stakeholders in the SEO process, making the collaborative effort within your organization more effective and aligned with your business goals.

Conclusion

This chapter explores the integration of SEO within business strategy. With strategic frameworks like the Ansoff Matrix and SWOT analysis, businesses can align SEO efforts with broader objectives, ensuring digital marketing initiatives contribute directly to growth and competitiveness. The chapter advocates for a synergistic approach, where SEO not only complements but actively influences business strategy through insights into market trends, customer behavior, and competitive landscapes.

To truly harness the power of SEO in shaping business strategy though, it is essential to move beyond the frameworks and put these into action. A critical way is effective stakeholder management. Engaging stakeholders – ensuring they understand and support SEO's strategic role – transforms theory into actionable insights. This approach not only bridges the gap between strategy and execution but also fosters an environment where SEO becomes a shared priority, integral to achieving business objectives and driving long-term success. In the next strategic chapter, you will learn how to form a content strategy and content plan.

CHAPTER 8
Content Strategy and SEO

Introduction

How do your potential customers find you among all the noise and competition? Writing articles with your primary keyword throughout the text or hopping on today's trending SEO hack is only a small part of the game. For one, you want to create the right kind of content that connects with your audience - which naturally results in said content ranking well on search engines. Content strategy is about creating a plan to structure what you say and how you say it for search engines to easily recognize and reorder it. A content strategy is not only about your words but also about their meaning and your target audience and how, what, where, when, and why they read your words.

The content marketing institutes define content marketing as "*Content marketing is a strategic marketing approach focused on creating and distributing valuable, relevant, and consistent content to attract and retain a clearly defined audience – and, ultimately, to drive profitable customer action.*"

So instead of just tricking Google with keyword optimization, a strategic content-driven approach provides relevant and useful content to your prospects and customers to help them solve issues in their work (B2B content) or personal lives (B2C content).

A content strategy for SEO is about creating a valuable resource for your audience that search engines recognize and reward. As we unpack the layers of a successful content strategy in this chapter, remember, the aim is to craft content that serves dual purposes - to delight your audience and to signal search engines that your site is a credible, authoritative source on the topics you cover. This journey is about aligning your brand's expertise and your audience's needs in a way that naturally enhances your SEO. Arjun Basu wisely said: "*Without strategy, content is just stuff, and the world has enough stuff*". So, let us learn to make a content strategy that will help you rank in search engines.

Structure

In this chapter, we will cover the following topics:

- Steps to Form a Content Strategy
- Types of Content
- Content Audit
- Competitor Analysis
- Content Plan and Stakeholder

Steps to Form a Content Strategy

Creating a content strategy consists of multiple steps. It involves, defining goals, getting to know the audience, auditing your current content, developing a content plan, defining a tone-of-voice, making a distribution plan and analyzing your content. We will explain these steps by using an example for a SAAS accounting software targeted towards small companies.

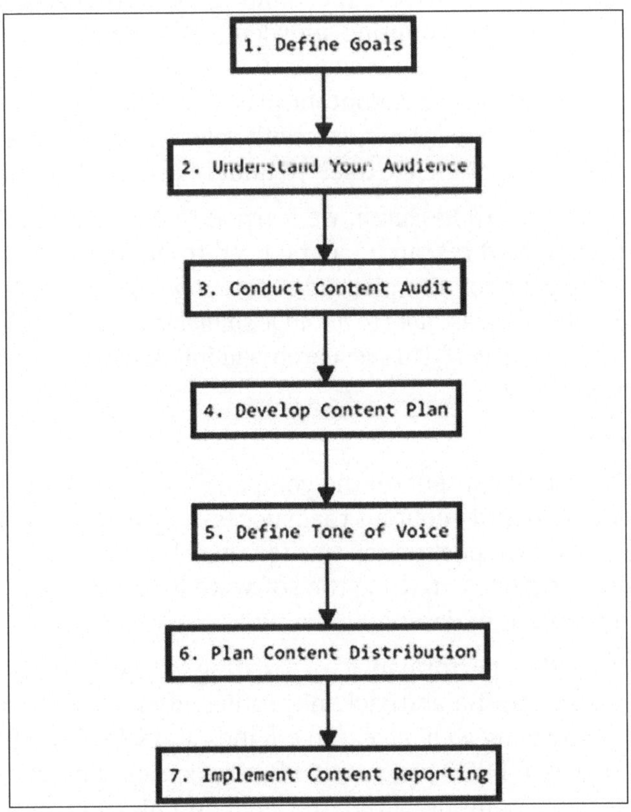

Figure 8.1: *Content strategy steps*

1. **Defining Goals**

   The first step is to define goals. For a SaaS accounting software, goals might include:

   - **Increase Traffic**: Attract small business owners seeking accounting solutions.
   - **Boost engagement**: Encourage interaction with product demos and free trials.
   - **Enhance Brand Awareness**: Establish the brand as a trusted, easy-to-use accounting solution for small businesses.

   Do not forget to incorporate specific SEO goals such as improving keyword rankings for accounting-related queries, increasing organic search traffic for non-branded keywords, traffic on new and updated blog and product pages, and enhancing domain authority through backlinks. Use SEO tools to set baseline metrics and track improvements.

2. **Understand Your Audience**

   The target audience of our SAAS accounting software is small business owners, perhaps with limited accounting knowledge or resources to hire accountants. Pain points might include managing finances efficiently, understanding tax obligations, and invoicing. A content plan that will address the pain points of your audience will help. Also speak with sales of customer support persons - or even better - the audience itself to understand your customer even better.

   In *Chapter 3, Keyword Research*, we learned to conduct keyword research. Of course, this keyword research can be used to understand your audience and form a base of your content plan. Look for long-tail keywords that match their specific queries, such as "*how to manage small business taxes*" or "*easy invoicing software for freelancers*." This research will inform your content creation with SEO-focused topics.

3. **Content Audit**

   Assess the existing content on the company's website, blog, help articles, and tutorial videos. Identify content that successfully drives traffic or engagement – like a popular blog post on tax tips for small businesses – and areas that are lacking, such as guides on using the software for invoicing. This audit helps in prioritizing content updates and identifying new topics.

   Evaluate the SEO performance of existing content by checking keyword rankings, organic traffic, and backlink profiles. Identify which pages and content types are performing well in search engines and why. Use this information to replicate successful SEO practices in future content and update or repurpose underperforming content with better SEO optimization. In this step, you may also consider having a look at top performing content of competitors.

4. **Content Plan**

   Plan content that addresses the identified needs and gaps. With insights from your audience and keyword research, plan to create content that fills SEO gaps. For instance, if you find high-volume searches around "*small business accounting software features*," plan blog posts, videos, or infographics that address this topic, ensuring to optimize for related keywords.

   Think about different content types you can use within your content plan. Your content plan likely will contain different content types, for example:

   - **Educational Blog Posts**: Topics on financial management, tax tips, and industry insights.
   - **Tutorial Videos**: Step-by-step guides on using the software for various accounting tasks.
   - **Case Studies**: Success stories of small firms that have streamlined their accounting processes using the software.

   More possible content types will be discussed later in this chapter.

5. **Define Your Tone of Voice**

   First, articulate the brand's tone-of-voice. For a SaaS accounting software aimed at small businesses, the tone might be professional yet approachable, knowledgeable yet understandable, and trustworthy with a hint of friendliness. This tone should reflect in all content to resonate with small business owners who may not have deep accounting knowledge but are eager to learn and apply best practices to their operations.

   Create detailed tone-of-voice guidelines that describe how your brand's personality translates into written content. Include examples of phrases or stylistic choices that embody this tone. For instance, use active voice to make content more engaging, opt for layman's terms over jargon to ensure accessibility for business owners with limited financial knowledge, and inject a bit of humor where appropriate to make the content more relatable.

6. **Content Distribution**

   Choose channels like the company blog, YouTube, email newsletters, and LinkedIn for distribution, ensuring these channels align with where the target audience spends their time. Define on which types of content an additional push or advertisement budget may be needed, you don't want to spend thousands of dollars shooting a video with only 100 views.

   For our accountancy software, your content will likely be reused in multiple channels like email marketing, social media platforms where business owners are active (like LinkedIn), and SEO optimization to ensure high visibility in search engine results.

As you produce content, optimize it for search engines by incorporating targeted keywords naturally into titles, headings, meta descriptions, and throughout the content body. Also, optimize images and videos with descriptive alt texts and file names. For distribution, select channels that can boost your SEO efforts, such as your website for blog posts or YouTube for video content.

7. **Content Reporting**

   Use analytics tools to measure the SEO impact of your content. Look at metrics such as keyword ranking changes and organic traffic growth. We will discuss reporting in *Chapter 11, SEO Reporting.*

Types of Content

In the following table, we make a list of possible content types that can be used within a content plan. We apply this to the accountancy software example.

Content Type	Description	SEO Impact
Calculation Tools	Interactive tools that allow users to calculate important financial metrics, like tax deductions, loan interest, or profit margins, based on their inputs.	• Increases time on site and user engagement. • Attracts backlinks as a useful resource. • Targets specific, often searched financial calculation queries.
Category Pages	Pages that aggregate content or products into specific categories, such as tax advice, payroll management, or accounting software tutorials.	• Improves site structure and navigation, enhancing user experience. • Targets broad category keywords. • Increases internal linking opportunities, spreading SEO value site-wide.
Programmatic SEO Content	Automatically generated content for a wide range of keywords, especially in areas with numerous variables like geographic locations or industry-specific financial advice.	• Targets long-tail keywords at scale. • Can capture a vast array of niche searches. • Enhances content offering without manual content creation for each scenario.

Blog Posts	In-depth articles on topics like tax tips, accounting best practices, and financial planning for small businesses.	• Drives organic traffic through targeted keywords. • Increases dwell time and engagement. • Potential for backlinks from reputable sites in the finance sector.
How-To Guides	Step-by-step tutorials on using the software for specific accounting tasks, such as invoicing, tax filing, and financial reporting.	• Targets long-tail, how-to search queries. • Enhances user experience by providing value. • Increases time on site and page views.
FAQ Sections	Answers to common questions about accounting software, troubleshooting, and general accounting advice.	• Captures traffic from voice and conversational search queries. • Reduces bounce rate by directly addressing user queries.
Videos	Tutorial videos, feature overviews, and customer testimonials.	• Increases engagement and time on site. • Videos can rank in both Google's video search and YouTube. • Enhances content shareability and link acquisition.
Infographics	Visual content that simplifies complex accounting concepts or data, like tax deadlines, expense categorization, or financial planning timelines.	• Attracts backlinks and social shares. • Enhances user engagement and understanding of complex topics. • Can rank in Google's image search.
Case Studies	Success stories of small businesses that have benefitted from using the software.	• Builds trust and credibility • Targets specific industry-related keywords. • Potential to attract backlinks from featured businesses and industry blogs.
Newsletters	Regular email content that updates subscribers on new blog posts, software updates, and accounting tips.	• Drives repeat traffic to the site. • Enhances user engagement and brand loyalty. • Can indirectly affect SEO through increased site interactions.

E-books	Comprehensive guides on accounting principles, software usage, or industry insights, available for download.	• Attracts targeted traffic and generates leads. • Potential for backlinks and citations. • Enhances brand authority and expertise.
Webinars	Live or recorded sessions covering accounting topics, software training, or financial planning advice.	• Increases brand engagement and authority. • Generates high-quality leads. • Webinar pages can rank for specific queries and attract backlinks.

***Table 8.1**: Content types*

- **Calculation Tools**: Develop a simple tax savings calculator for small businesses to use, providing instant value and encouraging users to explore the software further.
- **Category Pages**: Create a category page for "*Small Business Accounting*" that curates blog posts, videos, and tutorials relevant to small business owners, making it easier for them to find useful information. Optimize each category page with SEO-friendly descriptions and meta tags that target high-volume keywords related to the category.
- **Programmatic SEO Content**: Use programmatic techniques to generate pages for "*Accounting advice for [Industry]*" for various industries like retail, hospitality, and freelancing, targeting specific needs and keywords. Ensure programmatic pages are quality-checked to align with Google's guidelines on auto-generated content, focusing on providing genuine value to users.
- **Blog Posts**: Develop a content calendar focusing on regular publication of blog posts that address common accounting challenges, industry news, and tips for small businesses. Utilize keyword research to inform topics and ensure SEO optimization of titles, headers, and content.
- **How-To Guides**: Create comprehensive how-to guides for complex accounting tasks simplified for the non-accountant, integrating step-by-step instructions, screenshots, and video tutorials where applicable.
- **FAQ Sections**: Compile a robust FAQ section based on common customer inquiries, focusing on accounting software usage, financial compliance, and troubleshooting. Regularly update the FAQ section based on new customer questions and changes in accounting regulations.
- **Videos**: Produce high-quality videos covering software tutorials, feature updates, and expert interviews on financial management topics. Ensure videos are optimized for SEO with keyword-rich titles, descriptions, and tags. Host

videos on both the company website and a dedicated YouTube channel to capture traffic from the world's second-largest search engine. Embed videos in relevant blog posts and guides to increase on-page time.

- **Infographics**: Design visually appealing infographics that break down complex accounting principles, software features, or industry statistics into easily digestible content. Share infographics on social media and with industry influencers to encourage shares and backlinks. Include embed codes to facilitate easy posting by third-party sites, enhancing link-building efforts.
- **Case Studies**: Publish detailed case studies highlighting how different small businesses successfully utilized the software to solve specific accounting challenges. Target industry-specific keywords within each case study to attract niche markets.
- **Newsletters**: Curate monthly newsletters that aggregate new blog posts, videos, feature updates, and exclusive tips for subscribers.
- **E-books**: Develop in-depth e-books covering topics like small business financial management, tax planning, and getting the most out of accounting software. Offer e-books as free downloads in exchange for email sign-ups, directly supporting lead generation efforts. Optimize landing pages for e-book downloads with targeted keywords and repurpose pages within the e-book as landing page.
- **Webinars**: Host live webinars on topics of significant interest to small business owners, such as end-of-year tax planning, integrating accounting software with other business tools, and financial forecasting.

Of course, strategy is also about "*what not to do*", so focus on the content types with the largest impact first.

Content Inventory and Audit

Before defining your future content strategy, it can be worthwhile to have a look back in time and make an inventory of your already existing content.

A critical step in this process is the content audit, a review of your site's content to evaluate the impact and effectiveness of your content. This not only helps in identifying what works but also in uncovering hidden opportunities for improvement. Let us dive into how conducting a thorough content audit can pave the way for a more refined and successful content strategy.

Your website content inventory acts as your map, outlining the terrain you will navigate as you assess each piece's value and performance. A tool many SEO-experts use to build a content inventory is Screaming Frog. With Screaming Frog, you can crawl your whole website to make a content inventory. Screaming Frog will automatically collect data on every page of your website. This data includes URLs, page titles, meta descriptions, headings, wordcount, and more. This data forms the basis of your content inventory, allowing you to assess and organize your website's content effectively.

But don't stop at Screaming Frog. Use your Google Search Console account to find all of the pages with impressions in goals. By combining both lists, you have an overview of your website content with SEO value. For even more metrics, you can integrate additional Google Analytics data within your table.

A content audit is usually presented in a spreadsheet where every row has multiple columns with possible metrics and actions.

- **URL:** The specific address of the content on the website. This allows readers to locate and review the individual pieces of content directly.
- **Clicks/Impressions:** A combined metric showing the total number of clicks a piece of content received alongside the number of times it was shown (impressions) in search results. This provides insight into traffic volume and visibility.
- **CTR (Click-Through Rate):** The percentage of impressions that resulted in a click. A high CTR indicates that the title and description are compelling to users.
- **Keyword:** The primary keyword or phrase the content targets. This reflects the content's focus and its intended search query relevance.
- **Content Type:** The format of the content (example, blog post, video, and product page), indicating the method of information delivery.
- **Last Updated:** The date when the content was last revised. Regular updates are crucial for maintaining relevance and accuracy.
- **Action Required:** Recommendations for improving the content, such as updating information, optimizing for additional keywords, or enhancing user engagement.
- **Keyword Rankings:** The search engine ranking positions for the content's targeted keywords. Higher rankings increase visibility and traffic potential.
- **Comments/Feedback:** A summary of user feedback or notable comments on the content. This qualitative data can provide insights into reader perceptions and areas for improvement.

Here is a table with an example row:

URL	Clicks/ Impressions	CTR	Keyword	Content Type	Last Updated	Action Required	Rankings	Feedback

/example-url	100 / 1,000	10%	Example	Blog Post	Jan 1, 2021	Update stats for 2024	#5 for "*example*"	Positive feedback, after small update this webpage should continue to exist.

Table 8.2: *Content Performance Overview*

Once you have compiled this comprehensive overview, you are positioned to take actionable steps toward improving your site's performance, both in terms of SEO and user engagement.

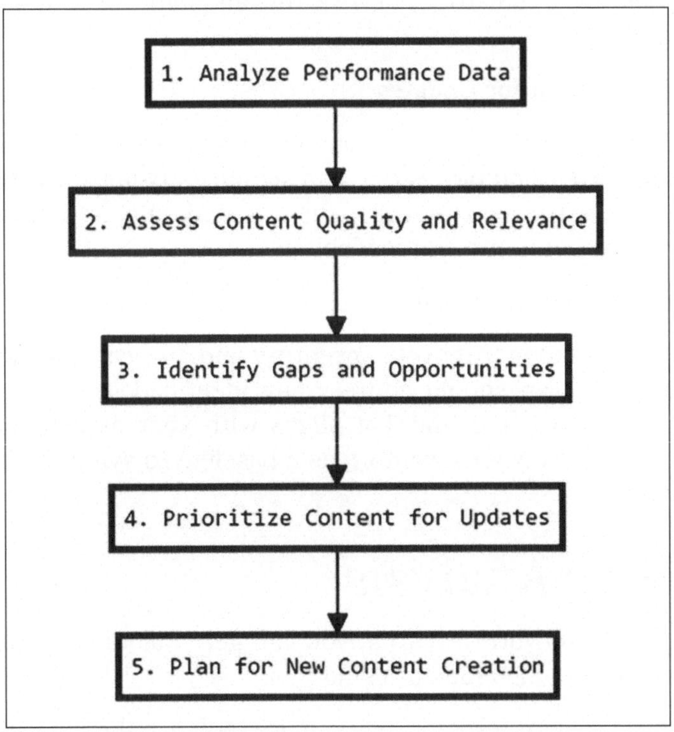

Figure 8.2: *Content inventory - next steps*

Here's what to do next:

1. **Analyze Performance Data**

   Start by analyzing the performance data you've gathered (clicks, impressions, CTR, conversion rate, and more) to identify patterns. Look for content that performs exceptionally well or falls short of expectations. This analysis can reveal insights into topics that resonate with your audience, types of content that drive engagement, and areas where your content strategy may need adjustment.

2. **Assess Content Quality and Relevance**

   Review each piece of content for its quality, accuracy, and relevance to your target audience. Content that is outdated, off-brand, or no longer relevant may require updating or removal. This step ensures that your site remains a valuable resource for visitors and maintains a consistent tone and message.

3. **Identify Gaps and Opportunities**

   Use your inventory to identify gaps in your content coverage. Are there important topics within your niche that you haven't addressed? Are there questions frequently asked by your audience that you haven't answered? Filling these gaps can attract new visitors and improve your site's authority in your niche.

4. **Prioritize Content for Updates**

   Based on your performance analysis and content assessment, prioritize content for updates. Focus on pieces that can significantly impact your SEO and user engagement with minor tweaks, such as updating statistics, incorporating new keywords, or improving readability.

5. **Plan for New Content Creation**

   Armed with insights from your inventory and analysis, plan for new content creation. This plan should address any identified gaps and opportunities, aiming to produce content that aligns with your audience's interests and search intent. Use your inventory as a baseline to avoid duplicating existing content.

Competitor Analysis

Once you have done keyword research, you can get your rankings and rankings of your competitors using a SEO rank tracking tool.

Even without prior keyword research, you can use tools like the SEMrush keyword gap and organic domain reports to get top keywords of your competitors.

Through a comprehensive competitor analysis, where you compare your rankings against those of your competitors will provide you further insights that can inform and refine your content strategy.

Creating a quadrant for SEO competitor analysis is a strategic way to visualize where you stand in relation to your competitors regarding keyword rankings, content gaps, and the competitiveness of certain keywords. This visualization helps identify opportunities for improvement and areas where you're already performing well.

	Competitor top rankings	Competitor bad rankings
Your top rankings	Top keywords	Unique strengths
Your bad rankings	Content gaps	Difficult or unaddressed keywords

***Table 8.3**: Ranking quadrant*

The quadrant can be divided into four sections:

Top Left Quadrant: Top Keywords

This quadrant represents keywords where both you and your competitors are performing strongly. It signifies areas of strength in your SEO strategy where you should continue to invest to maintain your lead.

Bottom Left Quadrant: Content Gap

This section highlights areas where your competitors are strong, but your site has not fully capitalized on these opportunities. These represent content gaps or topics that your competitors are ranking for, but you're not, indicating potential areas for content development.

Bottom Right Quadrant: Difficult Keywords

Here, both you and your competitors struggle to rank well. These might be highly competitive keywords that are challenging to break into due to high authority sites dominating the rankings. This quadrant helps in deciding whether to focus efforts on these difficult keywords or to find alternative long-tail keywords.

Top Right Quadrant: Unique Strengths

This quadrant shows keywords where your site performs well, but your competitors do not. These are your unique strengths and represent niche areas that you have successfully captured. Maintaining or even increasing focus here can solidify your authority and ranking. It is also worth trying to increase conversion ratio on these keywords.

Now, we provide an example for the SAAS small business accountancy software with four different keywords in the quadrants.

Quadrant	Keywords	Your Rank	Competitor's Rank	Possible action
Your Top Keywords	*"best accounting software"*	1	2-5	Monitor for rank changes; update with fresh stats and user testimonials.
Content Gap	*"tax saving for small businesses"*	50	1-3	Create comprehensive guide and checklist for tax saving tips, as probably your competitors now provide better content than you do.
Difficult Keywords	*"free accounting tools"*	20	15-20	Research long-tail keywords like "free accounting tools for freelancers" for targeted content.
Unique Strengths	*"accounting software for freelancers"*	1	50+	You already have the top keyword. Make sure your top landing page leads to conversion.

***Table 8.4**: Keyword quadrants*

Content Planning and Stakeholders

A content calendar for SEO is pivotal, acting as a roadmap aligning your content strategy with your SEO goals. It ensures the planned and strategic distribution of keywords throughout your content over time, covering a variety of targeted keywords to enhance visibility across different search queries. Search engines favor websites that consistently publish fresh content, and a content calendar helps maintain a regular publishing schedule. This consistency signals to search engines that your website is active, providing up-to-date information, which can positively impact your rankings.

Additionally, a content calendar allows you to capitalize on seasonal trends and events relevant to your audience and industry. Planning content around these times can improve visibility and engagement by appearing in search results for timely and trending queries. It also ensures that your SEO efforts are synchronized across all platforms, including your website, blog, and social media, amplifying your reach and effectiveness.

By planning your content in advance, resources can be allocated more efficiently, ensuring that writers, designers, and SEO specialists have clear directives and timelines. This efficiency leads to higher quality content, crucial for SEO success. Moreover, with a content calendar, you can track the performance of different types of content and topics over time, allowing for data-driven adjustments.

An example for the content planning calendar for the SAAS software could be:

Date	Content Topic	Format	Keywords	Publication Channel
Sept 1	*"5 Common Accounting Mistakes by Small Businesses"*	Blog Post	Small business accounting	Company Blog
Sept 15	*"Streamlining Your Invoicing Process"*	Video	Invoicing software	YouTube, Social Media, Website
Oct 1	*"Tax Preparation Tips for Small Businesses"*	Blog Post	Business tax software	Company Blog
Oct 15	*"Live Demo: Maximizing [Software Name] for Your Business Finances"*	Webinar	Accountancy software demo	Company Website

Table 8.5: *Example for the content planning calendar*

This calendar ensures content is prepared and distributed consistently across channels.

When developing a content calendar, involving key stakeholders in the planning process is crucial for ensuring the content strategy aligns with broader business objectives and meets the needs of all parts of the organization. Following is an example of a stakeholder table for content planning and calendar development, followed by an explanation of each role's contribution and expectations.

Stakeholder	Interest in Content Planning	Role
Content Team	Producing engaging, valuable content	Develop and maintain the content calendar; create and curate content
SEO Team	Ensuring content is optimized for search engines	Provide keyword research; optimize content for SEO
Marketing Team	Aligning content with marketing campaigns and goals	Integrate content with marketing strategies; promote content
Sales Team	Using content to generate leads and close sales	Offer insights on customer pain points; use content in sales processes
Customer Service	Addressing common customer questions and concerns	Suggest topics based on frequent customer inquiries
Product Team	Highlighting product features and updates	Contribute product knowledge for accurate, up-to-date content
Executive Leadership	Ensuring content aligns with overall business strategy	Approve high-level content strategy and direction

External Partners	Co-creating content or sharing content to wider audiences	Collaborate on content projects; distribute content through their networks

Table 8.6*: Content stakeholders*

Involving a diverse group of stakeholders in the project significantly enriches the content calendar. Their varied perspectives and expertise ensure the content strategy is well-rounded, aligns with broader organizational goals, and addresses the needs of different segments of your target audience. After defining the content calendar and identifying key stakeholders, the content creation and publication process can start.

This critical step involves transforming the strategic insights gathered during the planning phase into compelling content pieces and ensuring their timely publication across the selected channels. To execute this effectively, consider the following enhanced approach:

- **Content Creation Workflow:** Establish a clear workflow for content creation, involving ideation, research, drafting, editing, and final approval. Assign specific roles and responsibilities to team members, leveraging the unique strengths of your content creators, SEO specialists, and designers to produce high-quality, optimized content.
- **Editorial guidelines:** Develop comprehensive editorial guidelines that ensure consistency in tone, style, and quality across all content pieces. These guidelines should also include SEO best practices, such as keyword usage, meta data optimization, and linking strategies, to ensure content is search engine friendly.
- **Collaborative Tools and Platforms:** Utilize collaborative tools and content management systems (CMS) to streamline the content creation and review process. These tools facilitate seamless collaboration among team members, allowing for real-time feedback, revisions, and approvals.
- **Content SEO Optimization:** Work closely with SEO specialists to optimize each piece of content for search engines. This includes incorporating targeted keywords, optimizing titles and meta descriptions, and ensuring content is structured in a way that enhances readability and user engagement.
- **Publication Scheduling:** Utilize the content calendar to schedule publication dates and times that align with your audience's content consumption habits and your marketing objectives. Consider seasonality, industry events, and product launches when scheduling content for publication.
- **Multi-Channel Distribution:** Plan for the distribution of content across multiple channels, including your website, social media platforms, email newsletters, and partner sites. Tailor content formats and messaging for each channel to maximize reach and engagement.

- **Performance Tracking and Analysis:** After publication, closely monitor the performance of each content piece using analytics tools. Track key metrics such as traffic, engagement, conversion rates, and SEO rankings to gauge the effectiveness of your content.
- **Feedback and Iteration:** Encourage feedback from stakeholders and the target audience to continually refine and improve the content creation and publication process. Use insights from performance data and feedback to iterate on content strategies, optimizing for both user engagement and SEO performance.

By following these enhanced steps, you can ensure that your content not only resonates with your target audience but also contributes to achieving your SEO and business objectives.

Conclusion

In this chapter, you learned about the steps needed to create a strategy that connects with your audience and boosts your online visibility through SEO. We discussed how to define your strategy and assess your existing content. Then, we explained how to plan out your content, involve the right people in the process, and the importance of making and sharing content that both people and search engines will love.

A big part of our discussion was on creating a content calendar. This tool helps you keep track of what to publish, when to publish it, and where it should go. It is all about getting the right information out at the right time to catch the attention of your audience and the search engines. We also talked about choosing topics that matter to your audience, the impact of certain content types, and making sure it gets seen by distributing it on different platforms.

Next up, we will dive into Technical SEO Strategy. This is all about making sure your website itself is technical optimized. However, as always, alignment and stakeholder management are crucial for successful execution within this field of SEO.

CHAPTER 9
Technical SEO Strategy

Introduction

In this chapter, we will explore the essential but often overlooked aspects of technical SEO. This includes making your website fast, organizing your website data clearly, migrating to a new website platform, and stakeholder management.

We will explain the key steps to make your website better and easier to find by search engines and people. This chapter will show you how to use technical details to your advantage and attract more visitors.

As we navigate through the complexities of auditing, prioritization, and stakeholder engagement, prepare to uncover the strategies from which technical SEO victory has evolved.

Structure

In this chapter, we will cover the following topics:

- Structured Data
- PageSpeed and Core Web Vitals
- Website Migration
- SEO Auditing

Structured Data

Structured data is a standardized format for providing information about a page and classifying its content. Technically, structured data is code added to your website, which organizes your content into labeled boxes so search engines can easily understand each part of your site.

With structured data, your search result can transform from a simple blue link into a rich snippet, featuring stars for reviews, prices for products, or images for recipes, making your listing more eye-catching.

While it is not a direct ranking signal, structured data can lead to higher search visibility and click-through rates, indirectly improving your SEO.

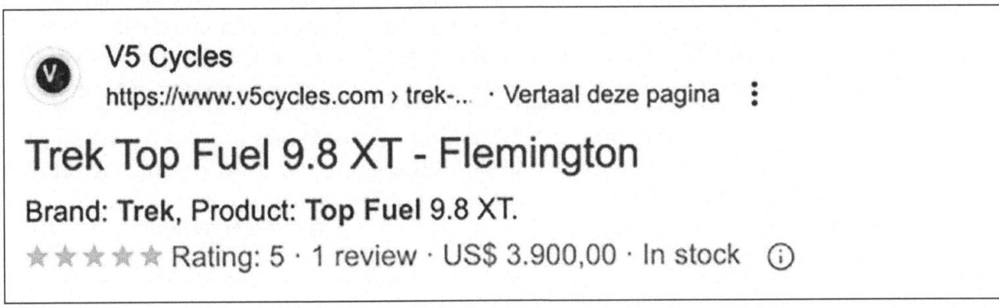

Figure 9.1: *Search result with structured data*

For example, by adding stock status and ratings, this result stands out in the search results. The website achieved this with the use of structured data.

The following table lists the commonly used structured data types in SEO.

Structured Data Type	**Purpose**	**Example Use Cases**	**Benefits of Implementing**
Organization	Provides information about an organization, including name, URL, logo, and contact info.	Company profiles, local businesses	Enhances brand visibility in search results with detailed information, potentially leading to a knowledge graph entry.
Local Business	Details about local business operations, such as address, phone number, and opening hours.	Restaurants, shops, service providers	Improves local search presence and visibility on Google Maps, making it easier for customers to find and visit the business.
Breadcrumb	Indicates page hierarchy and helps users understand their location within a site.	E-commerce sites, blogs, informational websites	Improves user navigation and can enhance search result listings, making them more informative and clickable.
Product	Information about a product, including price, availability, and reviews.	Online retailers, e-commerce platforms	Enhances product visibility in search with rich snippets, including price and stock status, which can improve click-through rates.

Article	Describes articles on a site, including the headline, author, and publish date.	News sites, blogs, informational content	Increases chances of appearing in top stories and rich results, driving more traffic to content.
Event	Details about an event, such as location, date, and ticketing information.	Concerts, conferences, community events	Makes event information stand out in search results, helping to increase attendance and interest.
Recipe	Provides details about recipes, including ingredients, cook time, and nutritional information.	Food blogs, recipe sites, culinary guides	Allows recipes to appear in rich snippets and the recipes carousel, increasing visibility and engagement.
Review	Displays information about reviews for a product or service.	Consumer products, services, entertainment	Showcases product or service ratings directly in search results, enhancing trust and credibility.
FAQ	Frequently asked questions and their answers.	Health and government websites	Can lead to direct answers in search results, and expanding improving click-through rate and user experience.
Job posting	Details about job openings, including description, location, and salary.	Companies, job boards	Increases visibility of job listings in Google for Jobs, making it easier for potential applicants to find relevant job information.
Person	Information about individuals, including their job title and affiliation.	Professional portfolios, author pages	Enhances personal brand presence in search results, potentially leading to a knowledge panel with detailed professional information.
Video	Provides details about videos, including description, thumbnail URL, and upload date.	Media sites, instructional content	Improves the likelihood of video content appearing directly in search results and video search features, driving more views and engagement.

***Table 9.1**: List of structured data types*

For an up-to-date list of featured snippets supported by Google, you can refer to the following link: https://developers.google.com/search/docs/appearance/structured-data/search-gallery

To effectively monitor and analyze the structured data types on your site and compare them with what your competitors are using, follow a streamlined approach that integrates several tools and techniques:

- **Check Your own Structured Data**: Start with your own website by utilizing Google's Search Console. This platform provides a comprehensive view of the types of structured data recognized on your site, highlights any implementation errors, and offers improvement suggestions. For example, if you run an e-commerce site, you should see structured data types such as Product, Review, and Price in your reports, which are crucial for product-rich snippets in search results.
- **Testing and Validation:** Tools such as Google's Rich Results Test can help you verify the correct implementation of your structured data. This step is vital to ensure that your structured data is not only correctly implemented but also capable of producing rich results in Google's search. For instance, if you manage a recipe blog, testing your pages to see how recipe structured data (like ingredients and cooking time) appears in search results can give you an edge by enhancing visibility.
- **Analyze Competitor Structured Data:** You can also add the competitor webpages to Google's Rich Results Test to uncover the structured data schemes your competitors are employing. For example, observing a competitor's hotel booking site might reveal extensive use of structured data types such as Reviews, Ratings, and Availability.
- **SERP Analysis for Practical Insights:** Engage in a routine analysis of search engine results pages (SERPs) for key business-relevant queries. Notice which types of rich snippets appear and which structured data types are driving those enhancements. For example, a local business owner might notice that search results frequently appear with rich snippets featuring operating hours and star ratings, indicating the effective use of organization and review of structured data.

By integrating these methods, you will not only ensure that your structured data is optimally deployed but also maintain a competitive edge by aligning your SEO strategy with visible trends and effective practices in your industry. This comprehensive approach helps you stay proactive in adapting to search engine trends and user preferences, ultimately enhancing your site's visibility and engagement.

PageSpeed and Core Web Vitals

Another crucial aspect of technical SEO is page speed and core web vitals. These are essential for several key reasons:

- **Core Web Vitals as Ranking Signals:** Google explicitly incorporates these metrics, which measure real-world user experience elements like loading performance (Largest Contentful Paint), interactivity (Interaction to Next Paint), and visual stability (Cumulative Layout Shift)–into its ranking criteria. A site that scores well on these metrics is considered more likely to offer a good user experience, which Google aims to prioritize in its search results.

- **Mobile Experience**: With the dominance of mobile browsing, a fast and responsive site is vital. Page speed is especially critical on mobile devices, where network conditions can vary significantly. For example, a restaurant's website that loads quickly on mobile will more effectively attract customers searching on the go, potentially increasing reservations.
- **Enhanced Conversion Rates:** Speed and stability directly impact conversion rates. Fast-loading websites that offer a smooth user experience reduce frustration and encourage users to complete purchases or sign-up processes. For example, a travel booking site with quick page loads and minimal layout shifts during the booking process will likely experience higher completion rates.
- **SEO and User Engagement Metrics:** Google uses various user engagement metrics as part of its ranking algorithms. Sites that load quickly and have good Core Web Vitals scores often have better engagement metrics, such as longer time on site and lower bounce rates. A blog that loads quickly and has stable content as users scroll is more likely to keep users engaged, increasing the chances they will read more articles or subscribe to a newsletter.
- **Crawling:** How faster the web page load, the lesser time it takes for Googlebot to crawl and render a page. So as it takes the Google bots less time, Googlebot can crawl more pages within your website's crawl budget.

In short, improving page speed and optimizing for core web vitals should be a priority for any business looking to enhance its online presence, improve user satisfaction, and achieve better SEO results. These factors not only help meet search engine standards but also align with providing the best possible experience to users, which is the ultimate goal of SEO strategies.

Auditing your website's page speed is essential to identify opportunities for improvement and ensure optimal performance. Here are several tools and techniques to effectively audit page speed. The first four tools are commonly used for SEO and are free Google tools.

- **Google PageSpeed Insights:** This is one of the most popular tools for checking the speed of your web pages, especially for SEO. It provides scores for both mobile and desktop versions of your site and offers detailed suggestions on improving performance. The tool measures aspects of web performance such as server response times, rendering and scripting times, and the efficiency of your code and images.

- **Chrome DevTools Lighthouse**: Integrated into Chrome DevTools, Lighthouse is an open-source, automated tool for improving the quality of web pages. It includes audits for performance, accessibility, progressive web apps, SEO, and more. You can run it against any web page, whether public or requiring authentication. It provides insights into load times, interactivity, and content stability as the page loads.
- **Chrome DevTools Network Panel:** The network panel in Chrome DevTools can be used to manually inspect the loading behavior of each page element. You can see how long resources take to load, which can help pinpoint files that might require optimization, such as images, JavaScript, or CSS that could be minified or compressed.
- **Chrome UX Report:** The Chrome User Experience Report (CrUX) consists of real user measurement (RUM) data for how actual users experience popular destinations on the web. This dataset is collected from users who have opted-in to sync their browsing history and have usage statistic reporting enabled. The data includes various user experience metrics across millions of websites and is aggregated from users of Chrome browsers on different devices and network conditions around the world. This is in contrast to previous tools that use lab data generated in a controlled environment with predefined device and network settings.

Other tools (not from Google) are:

- **WebPageTest:** This tool allows for more detailed testing across different browsers, connection types, and locations. WebPageTest breaks down page load into stages, giving you a detailed view of each element's impact on overall speed. It is particularly useful for simulating user interaction in different environments and provides visual performance charts, such as waterfall views of asset loading.
- **GTmetrix:** Combining the power of Google PageSpeed Insights and YSlow, GTmetrix analyzes your page's speed performance and provides actionable recommendations. It offers a comprehensive look at load times, page sizes, and request counts, providing a clear picture of what might be slowing your site down.
- **Pingdom Tools**: Pingdom offers a suite of reliable tools for website performance monitoring, including speed testing from multiple locations around the world. It provides similar insights to GTmetrix, with detailed reports on the causes of slow performance and historical performance data, which can be useful for tracking speed improvements over time.
- **Real User Monitoring (RUM) Tools:** Solutions like New Relic, Akamai, and Cloudflare provide real-user monitoring, which collects and analyzes the performance data from actual site visitors. This data can offer insights into

how performance varies in real-world scenarios, which can differ from what synthetic tests project.

Lastly, dashboarding can assist with analyzing page speed. One programmatic way of checking PageSpeed is through the Google PageSpeed Insights API. This API can be used to check your web pages on PageSpeed and core web vitals in bulk (up to a usage limit of 1000 web pages per day). The SEO tool Screaming Frog has an option where you simply need to enter your PageSpeed API key to connect PageSpeed data with your webpages. This will help you detect the slowest-loading pages of your website. You can develop custom dashboards that pull data from the API to visualize performance metrics across different pages of your site. This makes it easier for non-technical stakeholders to understand and prioritize performance improvements.

Improving PageSpeed

Improving website speed is essential for enhancing user experience and boosting search engine rankings. Here are common PageSpeed issues and effective solutions:

- **Large Images and Media Files**: High-resolution images and videos can slow down page loads. Optimize and compress media files using formats like WebP for images. Implement lazy loading for below-the-fold images so they load only when they enter the browser's viewport. Use appropriately sized images for mobile to increase mobile page speed. Avoid loading large images (example, 1000x1000px) on small screens (example, 100x100px).
- **Unoptimized Code**: Heavy JavaScript and CSS can delay interactivity. Minify these assets to remove unnecessary data, strip unused code, and ensure scripts are loaded asynchronously to avoid blocking page rendering.
- **Excessive HTTP Requests**: Multiple files require multiple HTTP requests, each adding to load time. Consolidate CSS and JavaScript files to reduce the number of requests.
- **Lack of Caching**: Without caching, browsers may repeatedly download resources. Use browser caching for static assets like images.
- **Poor Server Response Times**: Slow server responses delay everything. Optimize server performance by using server caching, HTTP/2, and connection keep-alive. Implement a Content Delivery Network (CDN) for international websites to reduce load times by serving files from locations closer to users. Consider upgrading to a more powerful server to improve response times.
- **Render-Blocking Resources**: Resources that block rendering until fully loaded can cause delays. Identify and eliminate these resources by inlining critical CSS and deferring the loading of non-critical CSS and JavaScript.
- **Too Many Ads or Widgets**: Third-party scripts for ads or widgets can significantly slow down your site. Evaluate the necessity of each script, delay

third-party content until after primary content loads, and load third-party scripts asynchronously.

- **Not Using Compression**: Uncompressed content increases data transfer. Enable server-side compression like GZIP for HTML, CSS, and JavaScript.

By systematically addressing these issues, you can significantly improve your site's page speed performance.

Improving Core Web Vitals

Let us look at some actionable tips to improve LCP, CLS, and INP as these are core web vitals which are reported in Google Search Console and used within the Google algorithm.

LCP measures the load performance by timing how long it takes for the largest content element visible in the viewport to become fully visible. Often this is the largest image above the fold. To improve LCP, you may execute the following actions:

- **Optimize Images**: Compress and resize images appropriately. Use modern image formats like WebP, which provide high quality with smaller file sizes.
- **Prioritize Loading of Important Resources**: Utilize the preload attribute to prioritize loading key assets that contribute to LCP, such as large images or background videos.
- **Improve Server Response Time**: Use a CDN to distribute content closer to users and optimize your server configuration. Consider upgrading your web hosting if response times are consistently slow.
- **Minimize Render-Blocking Resources**: Inline critical CSS and defer non-critical JavaScript and CSS to prevent them from blocking the time to first paint.

CLS measures the visual stability of a page as it loads. To minimize layout shifts, the following steps are recommended:

- **Set Size Attributes for Media**: Define explicit width and height attributes for images and videos to allocate space while loading, preventing shifts when media loads.
- **Reserve Space for Ad Elements**: Use placeholders or skeleton screens for ads and embeds to ensure space is allocated before content loads.
- **Avoid Injecting Content Above Existing Content**: Especially after site load, dynamically injected content can cause shifts, so modify content flow as little as possible. For example, a live chat or a cookie banner that pops up may influence CLS negatively.

For INP, we recommend the following actions:

- Minimizing CPU load, which involves running more of your code asynchronously. This approach helps keep the interface responsive, as the main tasks are handled in the background without disrupting the user's interaction. Additionally, using tools like Chrome's DevTools can help you pinpoint where your page might be slowing down, allowing you to make targeted optimizations.
- Reducing input delay. To tackle this, consider breaking up large tasks into smaller chunks. This prevents long tasks from monopolizing the CPU and keeps the interface interactive. Monitoring metrics such as Total Blocking Time can also provide insights into what might be causing delays, helping you fine-tune the performance. Furthermore, optimizing the loading and execution of third-party scripts can prevent them from becoming a bottleneck.
- Updating the user interface promptly before initiating heavy processing tasks can significantly improve perceived performance. Providing visual feedback, such as spinners or progress indicators, informs users that the system is working even if it is performing a long process. Implementing web workers is another effective method to offload heavy tasks from the main thread, keeping the user interface smooth and responsive.
- Non-blocking user interface elements are essential for maintaining interaction flow. Replacing traditional, blocking alerts with non-blocking UI components ensures that user interactions are not disrupted, enhancing the user experience.
- It is also crucial to streamline content display. By prioritizing the loading of important content first, you can significantly reduce the time it takes for users to see useful information. Managing how tasks and interactions are queued is vital to prevent them from piling up and causing delays, keeping the site responsive at all times.

With these actions, you can improve core web vitals. Of course, for some websites (for example, ad-heavy and media-heavy news websites) a perfect score is not achievable.

Website Migration

Once upon a time, an e-commerce company decided to migrate their website to a more advanced platform. They were focused on improving the look and feel of the site, excited by the new features that promised a better user experience. However, they overlooked something crucial: the SEO fundamentals that had helped their site thrive.

The migration day came and went, and at first, everything seemed fine, until problems started creeping in. The new website had changed URL structures but did not redirect the old ones, causing dead links and lost traffic. Essential metadata like page titles and descriptions had not been transferred over, stripping the pages of their ability to communicate effectively with search engines.

As a result, their once highly visited site began to lose visitors. Search rankings plummeted as search engines could no longer find or understand the content as well as before. Without the crucial backlinks and properly indexed pages, the website dropped off the radar for many potential customers.

Realizing the disaster, the company scrambled to fix these issues. They had to manually set up 301 redirects for every changed URL, rewrite all the metadata, and restore lost content. This was a huge effort that took considerable time and resources, and it was a painful lesson in the importance of SEO.

The recovery process was slow and expensive, and it taught the company a vital lesson: never ignore SEO during a website migration. It is not just about making a site look good; it is about maintaining its foundation in search engines to ensure it remains visible and viable. This story serves as a cautionary tale for all businesses planning to update or migrate their websites.

Indeed, when it comes to website migrations, the technical SEO aspects are often overlooked due to several reasons that stem from both organizational and technical challenges. Firstly, there is a common lack of awareness about the connection between SEO health and the technical undertakings during a migration. Many stakeholders involved in the process might focus predominantly on visual updates and user experience enhancements, underestimating how foundational SEO is to the site's visibility and traffic.

Additionally, website migrations are typically seen as a complex task. With numerous moving parts, including design, content, and infrastructure changes, the technical SEO tasks can seem less urgent or secondary, especially when immediate visual and functional results are prioritized. This perspective leads to a scenario where SEO fundamentals such as URL mapping, redirect implementation, and link updates are sidelined or rushed through without adequate attention.

Resource constraints also play a significant role. Migrations require substantial time and effort, and in many cases, budgets are tight and timelines are strict. Under these pressures, teams may choose to allocate resources to areas that promise the most immediate and noticeable improvements, leaving the less tangible SEO tasks for later consideration – which often means they get insufficient focus or are completely forgotten. Take the scenario where a launch date and launch party have been set months beforehand, and developers barely managed to get the website working, with no time left to focus on potential SEO issues.

Furthermore, the repercussions of neglecting SEO during migration may not be immediately apparent, which can lead teams to mistakenly believe that the migration was successful without these considerations. It is only later when site rankings drop and traffic decreases that the impact of inadequate SEO attention becomes evident. This delayed impact contributes to the underestimation of technical SEO's importance during the planning and execution phases.

Given these factors, it is crucial for project leaders and teams to recognize the vital role of SEO from the outset. Educating all stakeholders about the implications of SEO on a site's long-term health and success is essential to ensure these tasks are given the attention they deserve during the migration process. This approach not only prevents potential setbacks but also paves the way for a smoother transition and a stronger post-migration presence in search engine results.

Website Migration Steps

Website migration, whether it involves moving to a new domain, changing content management systems, or even transitioning to HTTPS, requires careful planning and execution to ensure minimal impact on search engine visibility and user experience.

Here, we explore key technical SEO aspects that are crucial during the migration process to maintain and potentially improve your search rankings.

- **Pre-Migration Audit**: Before making any changes, conduct a thorough audit of your current website. This includes documenting your site structure, metadata, URLs, and any existing SEO issues. An audit helps in setting a benchmark against which you can measure the migrated site's performance.

  Use a tool like Screaming Frog to crawl your entire website, cataloging every URL along with their title tags, meta descriptions, and headers. Add URLs from your sitemap and your Google Search Console and Analytics account so you won't forget any links. This data will serve as your reference to ensure no critical content is lost or altered unfavorably during the migration.

- **URL Mapping**: Developing a comprehensive URL mapping strategy is essential. Each URL from the old site should have a corresponding new URL in case of changes. This map will guide the redirection process, ensuring that all old URLs properly redirect to the appropriate new URLs, preserving link equity and user access.

  Create a spreadsheet that lists every old URL and its corresponding new URL. For instance, if you're consolidating several product pages into a single new category page, this document will guide you in setting up the necessary redirects.

- **301 Redirects**: Implementing 301 redirects is critical for maintaining your site's authority by permanently passing the existing rank and link equity from the old URLs to the new ones. Ensure that redirects are set up correctly and tested extensively to prevent any broken links.

After migration, search for old web pages within Google to find out if they got redirected correctly to the new platform. Do a manual check by clicking on Google links or use Screaming Frog to instantly check the status code for the top 1000 visited pages.

- **Handling Duplicate Content**: Migrations can often result in duplicate content issues, especially if not all old URLs are correctly redirected. Utilize canonical tags to point search engines toward the primary versions of your content, preventing them from indexing duplicate pages.

If both `example.com/page` and `example.com/page/exist` after migration, choose one as the canonical version and implement a `<link rel="canonical" href="https://example.com/page/">` tag on both versions to signal the search engines which version should be prioritized. Ideally, there should also be a redirect to avoid any confusion with Google.

- **Updating Internal Links**: Ensure that all internal links point to the new URLs. This step is vital for maintaining the link authority throughout your site and providing a seamless user experience. Automated tools can help update these links more efficiently than manual updates. For external links, consider contacting the most important link partners to ensure the links will continue working and give you additional domain authority.

- **XML Sitemap and `robots.txt` Update**: Update your XML sitemap to reflect the new URLs and submit it to major search engines. This helps them discover and index the new site structure more quickly. Also, review and update the `robots.txt` file to ensure it accurately reflects the directives for crawling the new site.

  Generate a new XML sitemap that includes all the new URLs and does not contain any of the old URLs. Update the `robots.txt` file to exclude directories or pages that should not be crawled by search engines in the new structure.

- **Monitoring and Testing**: Post-migration, it is crucial to monitor the website for errors actively. Use tools like Google Search Console to track indexing status and crawl errors. Regularly check for issues with redirects, broken links, or any fluctuations in search rankings.

  After migration, set up daily crawls with Screaming Frog or a similar tool for the first few weeks to check for 404 errors or redirect chains. Also, keep an eye on Google Search Console for any increase in crawl errors or manual actions.

- **Re-engage with Google Search Console**: Set up and verify the new domain (if changed) in Google Search Console. This step is crucial for submitting sitemaps, monitoring performance, and being alerted to potential issues directly from Google.

If the domain has changed, add and verify the new domain in Google Search Console and submit the XML sitemap.

- **Communication with Stakeholders**: Keep all relevant stakeholders informed throughout the migration process. This includes internal teams and external partners like hosting providers and domain registrars. Clear communication ensures that everyone is aligned on timelines and expectations.
- **SEO Performance Benchmarking**: After the migration, closely monitor the SEO performance of the new site against the pre-migration benchmarks. This monitoring helps in quickly identifying and rectifying any downturns in traffic or rankings due to the migration.

By paying close attention to these technical SEO aspects during a website migration, you can ensure a smoother transition with minimal disruption to your site's search engine performance. This proactive approach not only protects your SEO efforts but can also pave the way for future growth and enhancements post-migration.

The following table highlights the interconnectedness of various website migration tasks and underscores the importance of a comprehensive approach to avoid common pitfalls that could undermine the site's performance and search visibility.

Task	Why Needed	Potential Pitfall
1. Pre-migration SEO Audit	To assess and document the current state of the website's SEO, including its structure and performance. This ensures that any positive aspects of the old site are retained.	Neglecting this task can lead to a loss of SEO equity, as valuable elements like optimized content and meta tags may be overlooked or improperly configured in the new site.
2. URL Mapping	To ensure all old website URLs are accounted for and redirected to appropriate new URLs. This helps maintain link equity and user access continuity.	Without proper URL mapping, the new site can have broken links, leading to a poor user experience and loss of search engine rankings.
3. Implement 301 Redirects	To permanently move SEO value from old URLs to new ones, maintaining the integrity of inbound links and rankings.	Failing to set up 301 redirects correctly can lead to 404 errors, severing existing backlinks and causing a drop in traffic.

4. Update Internal Links	Ensures all links within the website point to the correct new URLs, which helps maintain the site's internal structure and user navigation.	Overlooking internal links can lead to many broken links within the site, harming the user experience and SEO performance.
5. Handling Duplicate Content	To manage and mitigate any duplicate content issues that can arise during migration, ensuring search engines index the preferred versions of content.	Duplicate content can dilute SEO efforts and confuse search engines, potentially leading to penalization or decreased rankings.
6. Update XML Sitemap and Robots.txt	Sitemaps help search engines quickly find and index new pages, while the robots.txt file directs their crawling efforts.	An outdated sitemap or robots.txt can misguide search engines, delaying the indexing of the new site or crawling unwanted pages.
7. Monitor and Test Post-Migration	To identify and fix any issues that arise after migration, such as broken redirects, missing content, or SEO performance issues.	Failure to monitor the new site can result in unresolved errors persisting, which may negatively impact site performance and rankings.
8. Re-engage with Google Search Console	To ensure the new site is properly connected with Google for monitoring and issue detection. It is important for submitting sitemaps and tracking indexing status.	Not updating the Google Search Console can lead to a lack of data on how well the new site is performing and delay the discovery of critical issues.
9. Communication with Stakeholders	Keeps everyone informed about the migration process and expectations, which is critical for a coordinated effort.	Poor communication can lead to misunderstandings, incomplete tasks, and a migration that does not meet business or technical requirements.
10. SEO Performance Benchmarking	To compare pre- and post-migration SEO metrics, ensuring that the migration has not negatively impacted the site's performance.	Without benchmarking, it is difficult to measure the impact of the migration and identify areas that need improvement.

Table 9.2: *Migration checklist*

Technical SEO Auditing

Technical SEO auditing is a critical process that dives deep into the infrastructure of a website to ensure it's optimized for search engine indexing and performance. This type of audit focuses on examining the technical aspects of a site – everything from site structure and indexing to mobile optimization and security. The goal is to identify and rectify any elements that could hinder the website's ability to be fully understood and prioritized by search engines.

An effective technical SEO audit not only highlights issues that may affect a site's visibility and ranking but also offers actionable insights to enhance overall digital health and user experience. By thoroughly assessing factors such as crawlability, site speed, content quality, and security, businesses can ensure their site adheres to SEO best practices and performs optimally in search engine results. This proactive approach helps maintain a robust online presence, attracts more organic traffic, and ultimately drives better engagement and conversions. Whether you are preparing for a site migration, recovering from a traffic drop, or simply aiming to improve your website's search engine rankings, a comprehensive technical SEO audit is an essential step.

Parts of an SEO Audit

Here are the parts of SEO audit:

- **Site Architecture Analysis**

  Purpose: Evaluate the website's structure for effective search engine crawling and user navigation.

  How to: Analyze the hierarchy of your site, URL structure, and internal linking strategy. Ensure that navigation is logical and that content is grouped in a way that enhances discoverability.

- **Indexing**

  Purpose: Confirm that key pages are indexed by search engines.

  How to: Look in Google Search Console how many pages are indexed, and check which pages within the sitemap are not indexed.

- **Site Speed**

  Purpose: Guarantee fast loading times for better user experience and SEO.

  How to: Measure page load times using tools like Google PageSpeed Insights. Optimize images, leverage browser caching, and minify CSS and JavaScript files to improve speed.

- **Security**

  Purpose: Secure the website and protect user data. Avoid websites being hacked, as this has a negative SEO effect.

  How to: Implement HTTPS across your site. Check for valid security certificates and resolve any security warnings that browsers might show. Use tools like SSL-labs and securityheaders.com to check how secure the website is.

- **Content Analysis**

  Purpose: Evaluate content quality and SEO effectiveness.

  How to: Identify and resolve duplicate content issues. Make sure headings are used correctly and content includes targeted keywords without stuffing.

- **On-Page SEO Elements**

  Purpose: Optimize on-page elements to improve rankings.

  How to: Ensure that every page has a unique and descriptive title tag and meta description. Check that header tags are used hierarchically and that images have descriptive alt attributes. With Screaming Frog, you can make an overview of these problems in bulk.

- **URL Structure**

  Purpose: Assess URL clarity and SEO effectiveness.

  How to: Review URLs to ensure they are concise, free of unnecessary parameters, and include relevant keywords. Avoid using underscores and instead use hyphens to separate words.

- **Internal and External Links**

  Purpose: Analyze the link profile within the site and from external sources.

  How to: Use tools like Ahrefs or Screaming Frog to find and fix broken links. Review all redirects to avoid unnecessary redirect chains. Assess the quality of backlinks and remove or disavow harmful ones.

- **Sitemaps**

  Purpose: Ensure sitemaps are accurate.

  How to: Check status codes of sitemaps, see if recently published pages are present within the XML sitemap.

- **Structured Data**

  Purpose: Ensure structured data is applied correctly on the website.

  How to: Check the current use of structured data, possible errors and structured data types to add.

- **Analytics and Tools**

  Purpose: Make sure tracking and analysis tools are correctly configured.

  How to: Verify that Google Analytics and Google Search Console are properly set up and tracking data. Ensure that all conversion points are being tracked and that data appears to be accurate.

By methodically addressing each of these areas, you can effectively conduct a technical SEO audit that will identify potential issues and opportunities for enhancing your site's search engine performance.

Now, by executing the parts written before, you will get a standard technical SEO audit. If you want to really make a great technical SEO audit, there are two different approaches you can take. The first one is to align your technical SEO audit with the business goals of your customers. The second one is by being more technically savvy within your technical SEO audit.

Next Step: Business-Proof SEO Audit

We now give for each section within your technical audit the difference between a good approach and a great approach for SEO auditing. A great SEO audit will think along with the business goals.

- **Site Architecture Analysis**

  Good: Examining site structure for SEO effectiveness.

  Great: Aligning the site architecture with the customer journey to facilitate easier navigation and improve conversion paths. For instance, simplifying the structure to reduce the number of clicks from the homepage to product pages can directly increase sales, aligning with business goals like enhancing user experience and boosting conversions.

- **Crawlability and Indexing**

  Good: Ensuring all important pages are accessible to search engine crawlers.

  Great: Prioritizing crawlability for high-value pages that directly contribute to business goals, such as lead generation forms or key product categories. This includes strategic use of the **`robots.txt`** file to direct crawlers towards these high-impact pages, improving their visibility and effectiveness.

- **Site Speed**

  Good: Running a page speed test and giving recommendations.

  Great: Linking speed enhancements directly to customer satisfaction and conversion rates. For example, improving load times on mobile for a quicker checkout process can reduce cart abandonment rates, directly impacting sales and customer retention.

- **Content Analysis**

  Good: Checking for SEO-friendly content practices.

Great: Not only checking standard SEO practices on content, but analyzing whether content serves strategic business functions, such as educating users, reducing support calls, or nurturing leads. For instance, creating detailed how-to guides for products can drive SEO traffic while also reducing post-purchase customer support queries.

- **On-Page SEO Elements**

  Good: Analyzing use and length of metatags.

  Great: Check if metatags are using language and calls-to-action that align with business goals as well as search intent.

- **Link Profile Analysis**

  Good: Identifying broken links.

  Great: Strategically building and maintaining a link profile that supports business goals, such as partnering with industry leaders for backlinks that enhance both SEO and brand authority, directly contributing to the goal of market leadership.

- **Analytics and Conversion Tracking**

  Good: Ensuring accurate tracking of traffic and basic conversions.

  Great: Setting up detailed tracking that ties specific SEO improvements to changes in business metrics, such as lead quality or customer lifetime value. This helps demonstrate the ROI of SEO initiatives in terms directly relevant to business stakeholders.

Next Step: Technical Savvy SEO Audit

Another approach to elevate a technical SEO audit from good to great is by leveraging advanced tools and strategies to uncover hidden opportunities for optimization. Here are examples that illustrate the difference between a good and a great technical SEO audit, and how to make the difference by being more technical savvy.

- **Crawlability and Indexing**

  Good: Checking for crawl errors using Google Search Console, ensuring the **`robots.txt`** file is not blocking important pages, and that the XML sitemap is up-to-date and submitted.

  Great: Going further by simulating different search engine crawlers (mobile and desktop) to understand how they navigate and index the site across various platforms. Implementing a crawl analysis to see how search engine bots are actually interacting with the site, identifying wasted crawl budget, and optimizing it by adjusting the **`robots.txt`** directives. Creating a list of pages with their indexation status.

- **Site Speed**

  Good: Using tools like Google PageSpeed Insights to identify page speed issues and following its generic recommendations to improve load times.

  Great: Conducting a segmented speed analysis for different types of content and webpages across various devices and network conditions. Advising advanced performance optimizations such as critical CSS, image optimization based on content visibility (lazy loading), and fine-tuning server performance through technologies like HTTP/2. Use the Google PageSpeed API to get insights in bulk and present the results in a PageSpeed dashboard.

- **Content Analysis**

  Good: Check for duplicate content issues and missing metatags using SEO tools like Screaming Frog or SEMrush.

  Great: Implement NLP (Natural Language Processing) tools to analyze content quality, readability, and metatags quality more deeply. Utilize AI-driven content analysis tools to benchmark content against top competitors and uncover deeper insights into content gaps and opportunities.

- **Comprehensive Link and Architecture Review**

  Good: Checking for broken links and ensuring proper internal linking using standard SEO tools.

  Great: Conducting a thorough audit of site architecture using graph databases to visualize site structure and identify inefficiencies. Applying complex algorithms to optimize internal linking and enhance PageRank flow across the site, thereby improving the overall authority distribution.

These technical tools of course are not easy to use for every marketeer, but learning and utilizing them helps you to stand out as a professional SEO expert.

Implementation of Technical SEO Proposals

It is one thing to list technical SEO action points, but it is often more difficult to get these points executed. In this section, we further focus on ways to make sure technical SEO action points are picked up.

The Business Value of Technical SEO

Integrating business outcomes into a technical SEO audit is crucial to getting recommendations implemented. Furthermore, business-driven audits ensure that the technical adjustments not only boost SEO performance but also contribute directly to business growth, customer satisfaction, and revenue generation. Not every point you get from an automated SEO audit from an SEO tool needs to be addressed, only the real issues that can impact business outcomes need to be implemented.

Here are effective ways to include business outcomes within a technical SEO audit:

- **Define Business-Specific Goals:** Start by understanding and defining the specific business goals. These could range from increasing direct sales, generating more leads, enhancing customer engagement, or expanding into new markets. Having clear objectives allows you to tailor the SEO audit to directly support these goals, such as prioritizing pages that drive conversions or focusing on markets indicated by regional SEO efforts.
- **Segment Data by Business Priority:** Segment and analyze SEO data based on business priorities. For example, if certain product lines are more crucial for revenue than others, focus your crawl analysis, speed optimization, and content audits on those sections of the site. This helps prioritize SEO efforts where they can have the most significant impact on the business's bottom line.
- **Align Technical Issues with Business Impact:** Identify and highlight how specific technical issues can affect business outcomes. For instance, slow page load times on a best-selling product page can lead to higher bounce rates and lost sales. Present technical findings in a way that relates them to business metrics like conversion rates, average order value, or customer retention rates.
- **Use Business KPIs to Measure SEO Success:** Instead of only using traditional SEO metrics like rankings and organic traffic, incorporate business Key Performance Indicators (KPIs) such as lead conversion rates, customer acquisition costs, and return on investment (ROI). This helps to demonstrate the real-world impact of SEO improvements on business outcomes.
- **Incorporate Competitor Insights:** Include a competitive analysis that looks at how competitors are achieving their business goals through SEO. Identify gaps in their strategies that your business can exploit and areas where they are strong that your business may need to improve on. This not only enhances SEO but also provides strategic business insights.
- **Collaborate with Other Departments:** Work closely with other departments such as sales, marketing, and customer service to get a broader understanding of business challenges and objectives. For instance, integrating input from the sales team can help you understand which product features are most important to highlight in your SEO content strategy.
- **Customize Reporting for Stakeholders:** Develop SEO audit reports that speak directly to different stakeholders within the company by focusing on the aspects of SEO that impact their specific interests and responsibilities. For instance, a report for the finance department might focus on the cost-

effectiveness and ROI of SEO initiatives, while a report for the marketing department might focus on traffic growth and engagement metrics.

- **Forecast and Set SEO Goals:** Based on the audit findings, set realistic SEO goals that align with business objectives for the upcoming period. Include forecasts of how reaching these SEO goals could impact business metrics like market share, revenue growth, and customer engagement.
- **Ongoing Optimization and Learning:** Treat the technical SEO audit as an ongoing process rather than a one-time event. Continuously test and learn from the SEO initiatives, using business outcomes to guide future optimizations. This ensures that the SEO strategy remains aligned with dynamic business goals and adapts to changes in the market and consumer behavior.

By incorporating these strategies, a technical SEO audit becomes a vital tool not just for improving search engine visibility but for driving measurable business success. This approach helps to secure buy-in from across the organization, as the value of SEO is clearly linked to strategic business outcomes.

The Technical SEO Action Plan

Creating a technical SEO action plan that effectively prioritizes tasks and organizes team responsibilities is essential for enhancing website performance and aligning with business objectives. Here is a streamlined approach to crafting this plan, emphasizing clarity and accountability without relying heavily on bullet points:

Step 1: Set Clear Priorities

Start by identifying the most critical issues found during the SEO audit. Prioritize these tasks based on their potential impact on your key business metrics such as revenue, user engagement, and traffic. For example, high-priority tasks might include fixing crawl errors on high-traffic pages and implementing 301 redirects for outdated URLs. Medium and lower-priority tasks can include optimizing load times on less critical pages and updating meta descriptions to improve click-through rates.

Step 2: Summarize Action Items

List each SEO task along with a brief description that includes the tools or resources needed for completion. For instance, to implement 301 redirects, you would need access to the website's CMS and a comprehensive URL mapping file. Clearly defining each task helps in assigning and executing them without confusion.

Step 3: Develop a RACI Chart

A RACI chart is crucial for defining roles clearly within your team. Assign roles such as:

- **Responsible**: The person or team doing the actual work (example, Web Developer).

- **Accountable**: The individual who delegates the work and is ultimately accountable for its completion (example, SEO Manager).
- **Consulted**: Those whose opinions are sought; typically, these are subject-matter experts (example, Content Creators).
- **Informed**: Those who are kept up-to-date on progress (example, Marketing Manager).
- This structure helps streamline communication and ensures everyone understands their roles and responsibilities.

Step 4: Set Deadlines and Metrics for Success

Define a deadline for each task to keep the project on track. Also, establish clear metrics for success to quantify the impact of your SEO efforts. These metrics might include improved site speed metrics, a decrease in bounce rates, or an increase in page rankings.

Step 5: Monitor and Adjust

Continuously monitor the outcomes of the implemented changes using tools like Google Analytics and Google Search Console. Regular check-ins allow you to adjust your strategies as needed and address any new issues that arise. Keeping a flexible approach ensures your SEO efforts remain aligned with evolving business goals and search engine algorithms.

By following this structured yet flexible approach, your technical SEO action plan will not only improve your site's search engine visibility but also contribute to your overall business success. This methodical process ensures that all team members are clear on their tasks and deadlines, fostering a collaborative and productive environment.

Presentation of Technical SEO Findings: The REBUS Framework

The REBUS framework is a structured approach for analyzing and solving problems, particularly useful in contexts where clear understanding and methodical action are required. REBUS stands for Reason, Example, Business Understanding, Business Value, and Solution. Each component of the framework plays a crucial role in ensuring comprehensive problem-solving. Here is how each part functions:

- **Reason**: This is the starting point of the framework. It involves identifying and articulating the underlying cause or reason behind a specific issue or challenge. By clearly defining the reason, you can set a focused context for addressing the problem, ensuring that any subsequent actions are directly aimed at the root cause rather than just the symptoms.

- **Example**: Providing a specific, real-world example of the problem in action helps to illustrate the issue more vividly. This makes it easier for stakeholders to grasp the practical implications of the issue, see how it manifests in a real context, and understand the urgency or impact of addressing it. Examples serve as a tangible reference point that can make abstract or complex issues more relatable.
- **Business Understanding**: This component involves translating the technical or specific aspects of the problem into understandable terms for all stakeholders. It is about breaking down the issue into simpler, non-technical language that can be easily understood by people not familiar with the specific jargon or technical details of the field. This ensures that everyone involved has a clear understanding of what the problem is and why it needs to be addressed.
- **Business Value**: Here, the focus shifts to the impact of the problem on the business. This part of the framework outlines the potential or actual consequences of the issue on business operations, profitability, customer satisfaction, or other relevant business metrics. It helps stakeholders appreciate the importance of the problem in terms of its potential to affect the bottom line or other critical business outcomes.
- **Solution**: The final component of the REBUS framework is about proposing actionable solutions to address the identified problem. Solutions should be practical, feasible, and tailored to effectively tackle the root cause identified under the Reason section. This part also often includes a plan for implementation, including who will be responsible for each action, timelines, and any resources required.

The REBUS framework is particularly useful for ensuring that all discussions around an SEO problem are comprehensive and grounded in both the technical realities and the business implications. By systematically addressing each aspect – Reason, Example, Business Understanding, Business Value, and Solution – the framework ensures that proposed actions are both effective and aligned with business goals.

Using the REBUS (Reason, Example, Business, Understanding, Solution) framework provides a structured way to diagnose and address technical SEO issues found during an audit. To illustrate this, we apply this method to a common issue: improper use of 301 redirects, specifically for a product page.

Now, we will use the REBUS framework to explain this issue with the wrong 301 redirects within an SEO audit, which will make your SEO audit more actionable.

- **Reason**: Improper implementation of 301 redirects for product pages can arise when websites undergo updates, such as changing URL structures for better SEO or site hierarchy. Incorrect or missing redirects can lead to broken links, loss of specific product page traffic, and decreased search engine visibility.

- **Example**: The URL was www.example.com/products/widget1, but it was updated to www.example.com/gadgets/widget1 to reflect a new product categorization. Unfortunately, the redirect from the old URL to the new one was misconfigured to lead to the general category page (www.example.com/gadgets) instead of the specific product.
- **Business Value**
    - **Loss of Targeted Traffic**: The specific product page loses traffic that was originally intended for it, impacting the visibility and sales of that product.
    - **Decreased Conversion Rates**: Visitors landing on a broader category page rather than the specific product page are less likely to make a purchase, reducing overall conversion rates.
    - **SEO Impact**: The loss of direct links to the specific product page weakens its SEO authority, potentially lowering its rankings in search results. This diminishes the product's online presence and can lead to decreased organic search traffic.
- **Understanding**: In simple terms, because the redirect was set up incorrectly, customers and search engines trying to access the specific widget through the old URL didn't reach the intended product page. Instead, they landed on a more general page, which likely did not meet their specific needs or expectations. This misdirection can confuse customers and search engines, making it harder to find the specific product.
- **Solutions**
    - **Review and Correct Redirects**: Conduct a thorough review of all redirects, especially for high-value product pages. Correct any misconfigured redirects by ensuring that old URLs map directly to the new product-specific URLs, not just general categories.
    - **Verify Redirect Implementation**: Use tools like Screaming Frog SEO Spider to test that the correct 301 redirects are in place and functioning as intended.
    - **Monitor Performance**: Keep an eye on the performance of the corrected URLs using Google Analytics to track traffic and conversion rates, and Google Search Console to ensure proper indexing.
    - **Ongoing Education and Protocol Development**: Provide training for the development team on the importance of accurate redirect mapping and establish clear protocols for URL changes to prevent future issues.

By applying the REBUS framework with these adjustments, the technical SEO audit not only identifies critical issues but also aligns the solutions with broader business goals, enhancing both the customer experience and the product's market performance.

Using the REBUS framework on every issue in your technical SEO audit will increase the chance that the SEO issue will be resolved.

Conclusion

This chapter has guided us through different technical strategies, from leveraging structured data to enhance visibility in search engine results to refining website performance through meticulous attention to PageSpeed and Core Web Vitals. We also navigated through the complexities involved in website migration, ensuring SEO considerations are front and center to prevent the loss of search equity.

One of the chapter's key focuses has been on making SEO audits more actionable and closely aligned with business objectives. By emphasizing not just the identification of technical issues but also their resolution in ways that directly support business goals, the chapter has laid out a path for transforming technical insights into strategic actions.

The chapter has highlighted yet again the importance of aligning SEO strategies with broader business objectives. In technical SEO, it is important not just to bring up problems but to ensure that the technical enhancements are understood, valued, and supported across the organization. This collaborative approach not only fosters a better understanding of SEO's role in achieving business success but also helps in the smooth implementation of technical recommendations. As we look ahead, in the next chapter, we will dive into emerging SEO trends.

CHAPTER 10
SEO Trends

Introduction

In the changing landscape of SEO, adapting is crucial. This ensures you maintain and improve your online presence. Consider recent advancements in artificial intelligence, changes in user behavior, and new platforms. Integrate these into your SEO strategy and action plan.

In this chapter, you will learn about the latest SEO trends. These trends include:

- **AI Transformation:** AI is reshaping every industry, as well as the SEO industry.
- **0-Click Searches:** Users often get their answers directly from search results without clicking links. Optimize for featured snippets to stay visible.
- **Impact of Large Language Models:** Tools like ChatGPT influence SEO jobs. They automate tasks such as content generation and keyword analysis.
- **Social Media and Video SEO:** Platforms like TikTok and YouTube are becoming crucial for SEO. Optimize content for these channels to reach a wider audience.

By understanding these trends, you will future-proof your SEO efforts, stay ahead, and keep your strategies relevant.

Structure

In this chapter, we will cover the following topics:

- Zero-Click Searches
- Large Language Models
- Social Media SEO
- Video SEO
- Advanced AI

Zero-Click Searches

Zero-click searches occur when users get the information, they need directly from the search results page without clicking any links. For example, if you Google the weather, Google displays the forecast automatically. This reduces the likelihood of users clicking on the website.

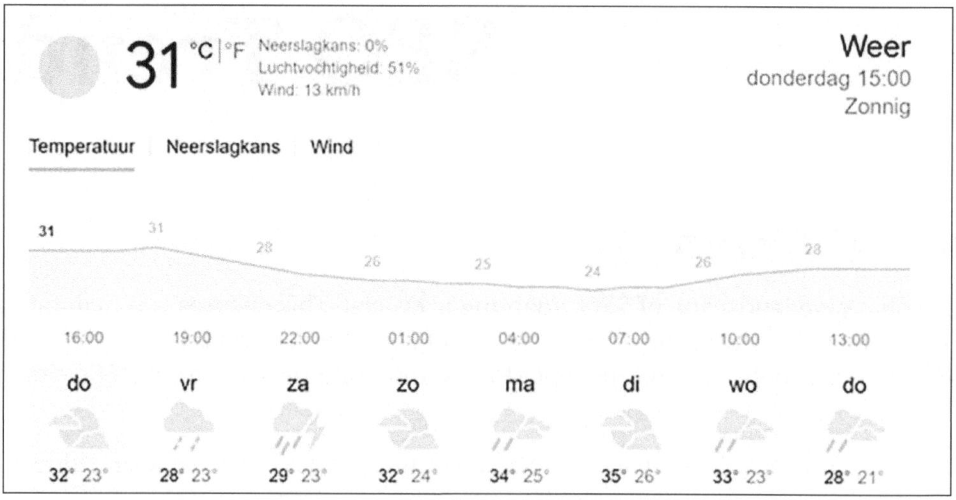

***Figure 10.1**: 0-Click search result*

This trend is driven by smarter search engines providing quick answers, snippets, and rich results on the SERP (Search Engine Results Page). These features include knowledge panels, featured snippets, local packs, and other direct answers that satisfy user queries immediately. With SGE (Search Generative Experience), AI formulates answers within Google Search Results. This trend is likely to continue.

How do 0-click searches change keyword optimization and content creation? Traditional strategies focused on driving clicks to websites are less effective when users get their answers directly from search results. You need to optimize for visibility within these rich results to stay relevant. This trend influences how we approach keyword optimization and content creation.

To adapt to the rise of 0-click searches, optimizing for featured snippets is crucial. Structure your content to provide clear and concise answers to common questions. Use formats like lists and tables, which are often favored for snippets. Including FAQ sections in your content can also improve your chances of being featured.

Utilize structured data for better results. Implement schema markup to help search engines understand and display your content accurately. Aim for rich results like review stars, event dates, and product information to enhance your visibility in search results.

Create multimedia to stand out. Publish and optimize video content, as videos are increasingly featured in search results. Use infographics and other visuals to provide information engagingly, making your content more appealing and accessible to users.

Regularly Google your main keywords to see which snippets appear in the results. This helps identify keywords worth optimizing for and those that are no longer valuable.

Large Language Models

Large Language Models (LLMs) like ChatGPT are set to revolutionize various industries by transforming our interaction with technology. These models, built on advancements in AI, especially deep learning and natural language processing, open new ways for enhancing SEO strategies.

The Evolution of AI and Language Models

AI's journey began in the 1960s with ELIZA, a basic chatbot for medical diagnosis. In 1996, a significant milestone was reached when Deep Blue, a chess computer, defeated grandmaster Garry Kasparov. The real breakthrough came with deep learning algorithms and cloud computing, allowing AI to process vast data sets.

In 2013, Google's Word2Vec was a game-changer. It converted words into vectors, enabling contextual understanding. Then, in 2017, the introduction of the Transformer architecture, followed by models like BERT and GPT, propelled AI capabilities further.

For example, BERT improved understanding of search queries by grasping context, while GPT-3 (and now GPT-4) can generate human-like text, making content creation and keyword optimization more effective.

ChatGPT: AI's iPhone Moment

ChatGPT represents a significant milestone in AI, much like the iPhone revolutionized the mobile industry. Three key factors contribute to its impact. First, generative capabilities: AI can now create content, moving beyond predictive tasks. This enhances creativity and efficiency. Second, broad applications: unlike narrow AI, ChatGPT's versatility spans various functions, from personal assistance to content creation. And third, the accessibility: user-friendly interface democratizes AI making it accessible to non-specialists.

These factors have led to rapid adoption, with ChatGPT reaching one million users within five days, showcasing its potential to transform business processes.

Now as SEO professionals, we should ask how to make the most out of these new technologies.

1. **Automating Repetitive Tasks**

   LLMs can automate repetitive SEO tasks such as keyword research and clustering. For example, at my agency, we developed a keyword clustering tool. AI converts a list of keywords into '*embeddings*' and groups them using the

K-means clustering algorithm. This approach efficiently organizes keywords into topics and subtopics, providing strategic insights into search trends. It saves significant time in executing keyword research.

2. **Enhancing Content Creation**

   LLMs assist in generating content at scale. Businesses can use LLMs to automatically generate product descriptions based on specifications. This saves time and ensures consistency, but on the downside, it creates generic content that won't make you stand out in the search results or even may lead to Google penalties.

3. **Optimizing Meta Descriptions and Titles**

   Using LLMs, businesses can analyze and optimize meta descriptions and titles to better match search queries. This improves relevance and boosts search engine rankings. Our content dashboard project uses language models to ensure visitors' keywords align with meta titles, enhancing site relevance and Google scores.

4. **Sentiment Analysis and Customer Feedback**

   LLMs enable sentiment analysis of customer feedback, helping businesses understand user perceptions. For example, a major car brand used LLMs to process textual feedback from their website and configurator. The language model segmented feedback by theme and sentiment, providing actionable insights to optimize the configurator and improve user experience.

5. **Customer Service Chatbots**

   LLMs can create customer service chatbots tailored to specific industries. The Dutch tourist association ANWB used a customized language model to generate qualitative answers to visitor questions, enhancing customer service. The chatbot provided answers and linked to relevant information sources, making interactions more informative and user-friendly.

Challenges and Ethical Considerations

While LLMs offer immense potential, ethical concerns must be addressed. LLMs can produce factually incorrect or biased outputs. Therefore, human oversight is crucial to verify and correct these inaccuracies. Ensuring ethical use of AI is necessary to maintain trust with your customers. Implementing a human-in-the-loop system is a recommended best practice to maintain accuracy and fairness.

Future Trends and Conclusion

The integration of LLMs into SEO is just the beginning. Future advancements will likely bring more sophisticated models and tools, further automating and enhancing SEO practices. Businesses should stay updated with these developments and continuously experiment with AI to maximize its potential.

LLMs like ChatGPT are transforming SEO by automating tasks, enhancing content quality, and providing deeper insights into customer behavior. By combining the strengths of AI and human creativity, businesses can achieve more efficient and impactful SEO strategies. Staying informed about AI advancements and integrating these tools into your workflow will keep your SEO efforts future-proof.

TikTok SEO

With the rise of searches on social media platforms like TikTok, it is the perfect time to enhance your TikTok visibility using SEO.

TikTok has become one of the most popular social media platforms globally. Millions of users generate and consume content daily. For brands and creators, leveraging SEO on TikTok can significantly enhance visibility and engagement. Here is how to apply SEO strategies on TikTok, offering practical tips to boost your content's ranking.

- **Understanding TikTok SEO:** SEO on TikTok involves optimizing your content to be more discoverable within the platform's search function and recommendation algorithm. TikTok SEO requires understanding how the app's algorithm curates and promotes content. The algorithm is a mix between user interaction, video information, device and account settings as well as content quality and relevance. So in essence, create highly likeable videos on relevant topics and optimize your video information to attract the right audience.
- **Optimizing User Profiles:** A well-optimized profile is the first step. Ensure your username and handle are simple, memorable, and relevant to your brand or niche. Craft a compelling bio that includes relevant keywords and hashtags. This makes your profile more searchable, allowing users to find you easily.
- **Creating SEO-Friendly Content:** Content optimization is key. Use relevant keywords in your video captions, descriptions, and within the video itself. This helps TikTok's algorithm understand and categorize your content. Incorporate trending and niche-specific hashtags, focusing on relevance and popularity without overloading your posts. Engage actively with your audience through likes, comments, and shares. High engagement rates signal the algorithm to promote your content more widely.
- **Participating in TikTok Trends:** Participating in trending challenges and using popular sounds increases your content's chances of being featured on the "*For You*" page. Consistency in posting keeps your profile active and signals to the algorithm that you are a reliable content creator. Additionally, cross-promote your TikTok videos on other social media platforms to drive traffic and increase visibility.

- **Engagement Metrics:** Engagement is crucial. Create engaging content that encourages viewers to watch until the end, as TikTok prioritizes videos with higher watch times. Monitor your engagement metrics closely and adjust your strategy based on insights. Regular posting and active participation in trends help maintain a strong presence on the platform.
- **Cross-Promotion:** Promote your TikTok videos on other social media platforms to drive traffic and increase visibility. Collaborate with other TikTok users or influencers to reach a broader audience. These collaborations introduce your content to new viewers and enhance your overall engagement.
- **Analyzing Performance:** Use TikTok's analytics tools to track the performance of your content. Pay attention to metrics such as views, engagement rates, and follower growth. Adjust your strategy based on insights gained to continually improve your SEO efforts. Regular analysis and strategy adjustments are essential for sustained success on the platform.

Summary

SEO on TikTok requires a blend of creativity and strategic optimization. By focusing on relevant keywords, engaging content, and active participation in trends, you can enhance your visibility and grow your audience on the platform. Implement these strategies to make the most of TikTok's unique algorithm and drive success in your digital marketing efforts.

Incorporating these SEO strategies into your TikTok approach will not only improve your visibility but also ensure your content reaches the right audience, driving engagement and growth.

Bing SEO

Google is the search engine market leader (and probably will be for a while). However, when it comes to search queries, there is a challenger to that monopoly: Bing by Microsoft.

It may seem out of the blue that Bing is taking up space in the search engine market. And yet, Microsoft has been bringing the heat to Google's virtual doorstep for some time now.

Early 2000s, Microsoft attempted to beat Google with products such as MSN Search and Live Search but failed. In 2008, Microsoft took over the search engine Yahoo to increase its search capabilities. Bing, Microsoft's own search engine has turned into a stable player in the search engine arena since its launch on 28 May 2009. Thanks to improved search algorithms and integrations with Windows devices, but also strategic partnerships, integration and innovation, the search engine reached a stable (but insignificant) market share.

The AI-first vision of CEO Satya Nadella is mainly responsible for the transformation within Microsoft with a strong focus on the integration of artificial intelligence in every product and service. Just think of the launch of Copilot, a ChatGPT-like chatbot that handles recent information well and, in that sense, combines the best of Google and ChatGPT. That focus on AI is what turned Bing into a more powerful, personal and integrated search engine. More importantly, the search engine focuses heavily on local relevance and user privacy. Bing's growth is therefore not entirely surprising.

Now that Bing competes with Google, you can use it to your advantage (and maybe even to get ahead). While Bing is still largely ignored or even mocked in the SEO world, there are definitely new opportunities to take advantage of on this platform. By integrating Bing into your SEO and advertising strategies, your company can increase its visibility in a search engine that is increasingly at the top of the list for a considerable portion of the internet population.

But is not Bing optimization the same thing as Google optimization? Doesn't Bing just want to serve its visitors the best and most relevant information, taking content, technical aspects and authority in mind – just like Google does? There are plenty of ways in which both search engines are different to warrant a change in strategy.

Local SEO

One example is local SEO. By adjusting your strategy with Bing Maps in mind, you can increase your visibility in specific markets. Just like Google, Bing shows you a map when you enter a local search query. But Bing's company index is more limited than Google's. More importantly, Bing business profiles often lack essential data, such as opening hours, photos or contact details. A local SEO strategy should, therefore, take Bing Maps results in mind to complement the Google Maps strategy. Luckily, it is very easy to import your already verified Google Business Profile into Bing Places so you don't need to go through a verification process again.

A Smaller Index

Although Bing has indexed a decent number of web pages, the index is smaller than Google's. GoogleBot is the most active crawler – partially because of Google's dominant position in the search engine market. The tech giant has invested considerably in developing advanced crawlers that can search the web efficiently and thoroughly. The frequency of GoogleBot's visits can vary depending on the popularity of the website, content changes, the technical setup of the website, and the PageRank.

The BingBot generally works the same way as the GoogleBot but it doesn't always get the same frequency or coverage. So, don't assume that Bing has indexed your entire website. Indexation may present a few challenges for Bing. Luckily, Bing Webmaster Center offers the option to send in thousands of URLs for high-priority crawling by BingBot in bulk.

Additionally, developers can use the "*IndexNow*"-API to pass on new and updated pages to have them (re-)indexed with high priority. In a perfect scenario, every website would tell Bing when there are new or updated pages available, so the crawler does not waste time randomly crawling numerous web pages.

Keywords and Visitors

Keyword positions and traffic can also differ between Google and Bing. Use the Bing Webmaster Center to analyze which keywords push traffic towards your site. These results may differ from your Google Search Console data. Figure out how Bing brings unique traffic to your site. That can indicate less competitive but valuable niches. Or maybe you will find keywords that already bring your site traffic through Bing, which you can now use for Google as well.

The visitors are also different, by the way. Bing users are often a touch older than Google users. Many Bing users may use the search engine simply because it comes with their Windows control system.

Advertising Strategy

Bing Ads grants you access to a specific demographic segment at (often) lower costs because the competition is less fierce. Bing Advertising and Google Advertising are both powerful online marketing platforms but serve different audiences and offer unique benefits.

Bing is often overlooked, but it offers you cost-efficient access to a new demographic segment that is characterized by higher incomes and a desktop preference. Google Advertising, on the other hand, offers advanced targeting options and it helps you reach a huge group of users. Advertisers should consider using both platforms for a balanced and extensive digital marketing strategy.

Taking Advantage of The Increase in Search Traffic on Bing

Search engines evolve constantly, which is why our SEO approach cannot stagnate. Google will undoubtedly remain one of the leaders in search engine marketing, but the rise of Bing does show that deploying our SEO and SEA strategies across different channels is more important than ever. If you take advantage of the unique opportunities Bing offers, you can increase your range and strengthen your brand in a competitive digital landscape.

Summary

Optimize your strategy with Bing's unique ranking factors in mind. Focus on high-quality content, social cues, and local SEO with Bing Places for Business. And use the Bing Webmaster Center to gain insights and optimize your approach.

Find out how many of your pages are available in the Bing index and have your pages added to the Bing Webmaster Center or use the IndexNow API.

Experiment with Bing Ads to address a different audience than the one you reach through Google Ads (often with lower costs per click).

Monitor your performance on Bing regularly and adjust your strategies based on what works best.

Automation, Generative AI, and Your Team

Generative AI boosts productivity by automating a large portion of work activities. Current estimates suggest it could automate tasks that account for 60% to 70% of employees' time, up from 50% a year ago. This increase is due to generative AI's advanced natural language processing capabilities, which are essential for automating knowledge work and other complex activities. Beyond automating tasks, AI unlocks new capabilities. For instance, AI can generate code, aiding SEOs without programming knowledge.

In this context, SEO responsibilities are shifting from content creation to validation.

As generative AI tools like ChatGPT become more common, roles within SEO teams are changing. Traditionally, content creators and SEO specialists generated and optimized content manually. Now, with AI automating many content-related tasks, the focus is moving from creation to validation.

Content creators are increasingly becoming editors and fact-checkers. With AI generating initial drafts, they ensure the accuracy, tone, and relevance of the content. For example, in an SEO firm, content creators might use AI tools to draft articles but spend more time verifying facts, refining the tone, and ensuring the content aligns with brand guidelines.

SEO specialists are becoming prompt engineers, developing and refining prompts to generate high-quality content. An SEO consultant might create a library of prompts tailored to different types of content, such as blog posts, product descriptions, and FAQs, ensuring consistency and quality in AI-generated text.

Importance of Prompt Engineering Skills

Prompt engineering is critical for maximizing the potential of AI tools. It involves creating precise and context-rich prompts to guide AI in producing relevant and accurate content. Organizations are investing in training sessions to enhance prompt engineering skills among their teams. For example, a marketing agency might conduct workshops on prompt engineering, teaching SEO specialists how to craft effective prompts and troubleshoot common issues in AI-generated content.

Creating a structured approach to prompt engineering requires collaboration and knowledge sharing among team members. Teams use internal communication channels and regular meetings to share successful prompts and strategies, fostering a collaborative environment that enhances AI utilization.

To illustrate, here is an example of an effective prompt for generating a blog post:

"*Write a 500-word blog post on the importance of local SEO for small businesses. Include key strategies such as optimizing Google My Business listings, using local keywords, and encouraging customer reviews. Provide concrete examples and actionable tips. Ensure the tone is professional yet approachable. Each sentence in the generated text should have value, no fluff.*"

This prompt is specific, context-rich, and includes clear instructions, ensuring the AI generates content that meets the desired criteria.

Organizational Success Factors and Barriers

Developing structured workflows for AI integration is crucial. This includes creating prompt libraries, establishing clear guidelines for AI use, and implementing regular training sessions. For example, an e-commerce company might create a centralized repository of prompts and guidelines, ensuring all team members have access to the tools and knowledge needed to use AI effectively.

Having enthusiastic individuals can drive AI adoption and innovation within the organization. A digital marketing firm might identify AI champions within the organization who lead the charge in exploring new AI tools, conducting training sessions, and mentoring colleagues.

Despite the potential benefits, integrating AI into SEO processes faces several barriers. Limited time for testing and implementing AI tools can hinder effective integration. Teams need sufficient time to experiment with prompts and workflows. A content agency might struggle to find time for prompt engineering due to tight project deadlines, resulting in inconsistent AI-generated content quality.

Concerns about the accuracy of AI-generated content and data privacy can create resistance to AI adoption. A financial services firm might be cautious about using AI due to concerns about data security and the potential for factual errors in AI-generated financial advice.

Ensuring the accuracy and quality of AI-generated content requires significant manual effort, which can be a bottleneck in the content creation process. A health information website might use AI to draft articles but must allocate substantial resources to verify the medical information provided by the AI.

Evolving Towards Human-AI Collaboration

The SEO industry is moving towards a model of human-AI collaboration rather than full automation. AI tools are seen as aids that enhance human capabilities rather than replacements for human expertise. AI can handle repetitive tasks and generate ideas, allowing human experts to focus on more strategic and creative aspects of SEO. For example, an SEO agency might use AI to generate keyword ideas and content outlines, freeing up human experts to develop comprehensive SEO strategies and creative campaigns.

Now, let us explore some practical ways to make your AI content human-friendly, thanks to some effective prompting techniques.

It is recommend following these 5 steps for AI content:

1. **Include Facts and Creative Insights**

   Facts provide a solid foundation of trustworthiness, while creative insights add uniqueness that can distinguish your content from competitors.

   Using solid facts like, "*According to our recent survey, 70% of small businesses report increased financial accuracy with our software*," makes your content both informative and compelling.

2. **Imitate Your Tone of Voice**

   Consistent tone builds a recognizable brand identity and trust, making your content feel more personal and engaging.

   So, use a prompt like "*Develop a blog on how our B2B SaaS accountancy software supports small businesses, maintaining a professional yet approachable tone similar to our existing content. First, analyze the tone and writing style of the uploaded PDF. Then, write the new content in this style.*"

   This prompt helps you to mirror the friendly yet knowledgeable tone your audience expects, it feels more relatable and trustworthy.

3. **Include Personal Experiences**

   Personal experiences create authenticity and relatability, helping to forge a deeper connection with your audience.

   "*Write a case study about how using our B2B SaaS accounting software helped hairdresser Sarah, living in Palo Alto, streamline her accounting processes. Earlier, she had to pay her account a monthly fee of 300 dollars which has now been reduced to 20 dollars a month.*"

Sharing a story about how the hairdresser was now able to cut accountant expenses using your software not only highlights the software's effectiveness but also makes your content more engaging and relatable.

4. **Target the Audience and Persona Within Your Prompt**

   Tailored content resonates better with your audience, addressing their specific needs and challenges, which increases engagement and conversion rates.

   "*Create a guide for freelancers on how our B2B SaaS accounting software can simplify their invoicing and tax filing processes. Think about the pain points for freelancers and discuss how the software helps them.*"

   Even human copywriters are often failing to start writing from pain points, by asking AI to generate a text targeting pain point, the result will improve.

5. **Avoid AI fluff Within Your Generated Content**

   Clear, concise content is more engaging and effective. Avoiding unnecessary filler ensures that your message is direct and valuable. By stripping away the fluff, your content delivers clear, actionable insights. AI content has a tendency to add additional fluff to your content, so within your prompts take care of removing this fluff.

   A prompt like "*delete the fluff and yammer of the generated output. Sentence length may vary. Every sentence used within the text needs to provide value*" will make sure you avoid the AI fluff.

   Therefore, by including data, tone of voice, personal stories, the audience and avoiding the AI fluff, you can make your AI-generated content more human-like.

Impact on SEO Strategies and Practices

The SEO industry is moving towards a model of human-AI collaboration rather than full automation. AI tools are seen as aids that enhance human capabilities rather than replacements for human expertise. AI can handle repetitive tasks and generate ideas, allowing human experts to focus on more strategic and creative aspects of SEO. For example, an SEO agency might use AI to generate content outlines, freeing up human experts to develop comprehensive SEO strategies.

New Coding and Data Analysis Skills for Your SEO Team

Coding and data analysis are important skills for SEO professionals working on big projects with a lot of available data. For example, you can use Python to analyze large datasets of keyword performance, traffic patterns, and user behavior. This helps in identifying trends and making data-driven adjustments to SEO strategies. Additionally, learning to code enables you to automate repetitive SEO tasks. You can write scripts to scrape websites for data, automate reporting, or even perform bulk updates to metadata. For instance, a Python script can automatically update meta descriptions across hundreds of web pages, saving hours of manual work.

These types of data analysis and automation work typically are beyond the skillset of the beginning SEO professional. But we have good news. Even if you are not a coder, you can use tools like ChatGPT and AI notebooks (like Colab and Deepnote) to write Python code for automation and advanced data analysis. Start with simple prompts, use AI-generated code, and gradually build your skills through hands-on practice. This approach makes advanced data analysis and automation accessible to everyone.

Summary

Integrating generative AI into SEO is changing team roles, organizational processes, and industry practices. By focusing on human-AI collaboration, businesses can maximize their SEO efforts. Investing in prompt engineering skills and addressing organizational barriers are crucial. Additionally, AI coding skills provide significant benefits.

For example, teams can automate repetitive tasks and analyze data more efficiently. As the industry evolves, adaptability and embracing AI's potential are essential. Staying competitive requires leveraging these advanced tools and techniques effectively.

Real-Life Ranking Signals

Google is incorporating real-life ranking signals into its algorithm. Understanding these signals is crucial for optimizing your SEO strategy. These signals, derived from actual user behavior and website performance, significantly influence search engine rankings. Let us focus on two specific signals: website usage and real-life visits and how they impact rankings.

Website Usage

Website usage metrics like time spent on site, pages per session, and return visits provide insights into user engagement and content quality. These metrics help search engines gauge how valuable and relevant your website is to users.

For example, imagine a user exploring your pet shop's website. They spend time reading multiple pages about different pet care products and return later for more information. This behavior signals to search engines that your website is engaging and valuable, which can lead to higher rankings. To boost these metrics, ensure your content is informative and user-friendly, encouraging users to spend more time on your site and return frequently.

Consider a user who visits your site to learn about your range of pet foods. They read a detailed guide on choosing the best food for their dog, then navigate to the FAQ section to clear up some doubts and come back a few days later to check out customer reviews. This positive engagement indicates to search engines that your site provides valuable content, potentially boosting your rankings.

Real-Life Visits

For businesses with a physical location, driving directions and other local signals can significantly impact local SEO. These signals help search engines determine the relevance of your business to local search queries, improving your visibility to nearby users.

Imagine a pet owner searching for a local pet shop. If your business details, including driving directions and local reviews, are optimized, search engines are more likely to show your pet shop to users in your area. To enhance local SEO, ensure your Google Business Profile is up-to-date and encourage satisfied customers to leave reviews.

If a local dog owner searches for "*pet shop near me*" and your business appears with positive reviews and clear driving directions, they are more likely to visit your shop and consider purchasing from you. Additionally, if people are willing to travel from far away to visit your pet shop in real life, this indicates a high level of trust and satisfaction. These types of real-life signals will also influence your Google Business Profile ranking.

By understanding and optimizing these real-life ranking signals, you can improve your SEO strategy, ensuring better visibility and higher rankings for your pet shop.

YouTube SEO

As video content continues to dominate online consumption, optimizing for YouTube has become a crucial component of comprehensive SEO strategies. YouTube, being the second largest search engine after Google, offers unique opportunities for reaching and engaging audiences through video content.

YouTube's algorithm considers several factors when ranking videos, including watch time, audience retention, click-through rate (CTR), engagement metrics (likes, comments, shares), upload frequency, and keyword relevance in titles, descriptions, and tags. Focusing on these elements can significantly improve a video's visibility on both YouTube and Google search results.

Video titles play a crucial role in both SEO and user engagement. Effective titles are keyword-rich yet natural-sounding, compelling, and under 70 characters to avoid truncation in search results. For instance, rather than using a generic title like "*Dog Training Tips*", a more specific and engaging title such as "*5 Essential Dog Training Tips for New Puppy Owners | Expert Advice*" can be more effective.

YouTube descriptions offer considerable SEO potential. Best practices include front-loading important information and keywords in the first 2-3 sentences, providing a detailed description of the video content, adding timestamps for longer videos, and including relevant links to websites or social media. An example of a well-optimized description might begin: "*Discover 5 essential dog training tips for new puppy owners in this comprehensive guide. Professional dog trainer Sarah Jones shares expert advice on housebreaking, basic commands, and socialization techniques...*"

Tags help YouTube understand video content and context. A mix of broad keywords, specific long-tail keywords, and branded terms is recommended. Choosing the most relevant category for a video aids YouTube in recommending it to the appropriate audience.

While not directly an SEO factor, compelling thumbnails can significantly boost click-through rates, indirectly improving SEO. Effective thumbnails are visually appealing, accurately represent the video content, and often include text overlays to provide context. You can use graphic design software like Canva to generate eye-grabbing thumbnails.

Engagement signals are crucial for YouTube SEO. Encouraging viewers to like, comment, and share videos through clear call-to-actions (CTAs) both in the video and in the description can boost these signals. Creating themed playlists can increase watch time and session duration, both important ranking factors.

With the rise of voice-activated devices, optimizing for voice search has become increasingly important. Including natural language phrases in titles and descriptions can improve performance in voice searches. For example, "*How do I train my new puppy?" is more voice-search friendly than simply "puppy training tips".*

Regular analysis of YouTube Analytics provides insights into video performance, audience retention rates, and traffic sources. These insights can be used to refine content strategy and SEO tactics over time.

Implementing these YouTube SEO strategies can significantly improve video visibility, enhance target audience engagement, and drive traffic not only on YouTube but also through Google's video search results. Consistency in uploading valuable content that addresses audience needs, combined with ongoing optimization efforts, typically leads to improved YouTube SEO performance over time.

Conclusion

In this chapter, you learned how advancements in AI, changes in user behavior, and new platforms are shaping SEO strategies. Zero-click searches have become a significant factor. Search engines now provide instant answers and rich results. This shift necessitates optimizing for featured snippets and using structured data to capture traffic without clicks.

The rise of Large Language Models (LLMs) like ChatGPT has revolutionized content creation and optimization. These models automate repetitive tasks, generate content, and enhance meta descriptions, providing a significant boost to SEO efforts.

Social media SEO, particularly on platforms like TikTok, is gaining importance. By optimizing profiles, leveraging trends, and engaging actively, brands can enhance visibility and engagement on these platforms. With Bing SEO, there is a clear opportunity to tap into a different audience. Focusing on Bing's unique ranking factors and using its advertising platform can help businesses reach a demographic that might be overlooked on Google.

The integration of generative AI in SEO is transforming roles within teams and the industry at large. By fostering human-AI collaboration, investing in prompt engineering skills, and addressing organizational barriers, businesses can effectively utilize AI for more efficient and impactful SEO strategies.

As we look forward to the next chapter on SEO reporting, it is clear that understanding and adapting to these trends is crucial. SEO reporting will equip you with the tools and techniques to track progress, measure strategy effectiveness, and make data-driven decisions for continuous improvement.

CHAPTER 11
SEO Reporting

Introduction

This chapter on SEO *Reporting* is designed to equip you with the tools and knowledge to not just report on your SEO efforts, but to turn those reports into actionable insights that drive real business outcomes.

We will break down why SEO reporting is more than just a checkbox in your marketing strategy – it is the key to understanding how your efforts translate into traffic and conversions. You will discover what metrics matter most, the tools that can simplify your reporting process, and how to craft reports that are not only clear and concise but also impactful.

Whether you are proving your value to stakeholders, fine-tuning your strategy, or keeping an eye on the competition, this chapter will help you master the art of SEO reporting. So, let us dive in and transform your data into stories that not only inform but inspire action.

Structure

In this chapter, we are going to dive into the world of SEO reporting. We will cover:

- Importance of SEO Reporting
- Key Metrics for SEO Reporting
- SEO Reporting Tools
- Tailoring SEO Reports to Your Audience
- Making Effective SEO Data Visualizations
- Communicating SEO Reports

Importance of SEO Reporting

Alright, let us get down to business – literally! You might be wondering, "*Why should I care about SEO reporting?*" Well SEO, is your Digital Report Card.

Remember those report cards from school? SEO reports are kind of like that, but for your website. They show you how well your site is performing in the vast playground of the internet. And just like those school reports, they can help you identify where you are acing it and where you might need a bit of extra study.

- **Proving Your Worth to the Boss:** If you are managing a website or running digital marketing for a company, you will probably need to show the higher-ups that all your hard work is paying off. SEO reports are your secret weapon here. They provide concrete evidence of your efforts and their results. It is like being able to say, "*Look, boss! Our website visits are up 50% since last quarter!*" That is the kind of thing that makes executives sit up and take notice.
- **Guiding Your Marketing Strategy:** SEO reports aren't just about looking back – they are also about looking forward. By understanding what is working (and what is not), you can make smarter decisions about where to focus your efforts. Maybe your blog posts about coffee brewing techniques are bringing in tons of traffic. Great! That might mean it is time to create more content on that topic.
- **Keeping an Eye on the Competition:** In business, it is always good to know what your competitors are up to. SEO reports can give you insights into how you are performing compared to others in your industry. Are they outranking you for important keywords? Are they getting more traffic? This information can help you stay one step ahead.
- **Connecting SEO to Real Business Goals:** Here is where things get really exciting for stakeholders. SEO is not just about rankings and traffic – it is about how those things translate into real business results. A good SEO report can show how organic search is contributing to leads, sales, and revenue. That is the kind of information that gets everyone from the CEO to the sales team excited.
- **Identifying Opportunities and Threats:** SEO reports can reveal new opportunities you might have missed. Maybe there is a keyword you're ranking well for that you didn't even know about. On the flip side, they can also alert you to potential threats, like a sudden drop in rankings for a key term. This allows you to react quickly and protect your digital turf.
- **Justifying Your SEO Budget:** Let us face it – SEO can be a significant investment. Whether you are doing it in-house or working with an agency, it costs time and money. SEO reports help justify this spending by showing the return on investment. When stakeholders can see that every dollar spent on SEO is bringing in $5 in revenue, it becomes much easier to secure budget for future initiatives.
- **Making Data-Driven Decisions:** In today's business world, data is king. SEO reports provide a wealth of data that can inform decisions across your organization. From content creation to product development, insights from SEO can help guide your company in the right direction.

- **Tracking Progress Over Time:** Rome wasn't built in a day, and neither is a successful SEO strategy. Regular reporting allows you to track your progress over time, showing stakeholders the upward trajectory of your efforts. It is incredibly satisfying to see those graphs trending upwards month after month!
- **Aligning Teams and Departments:** SEO doesn't exist in a vacuum – it impacts and is impacted by various parts of your business. Good SEO reporting can help align different teams towards common goals. When the content team sees how their work affects SEO performance, and the product team understands how site structure impacts rankings, magic happens!

So, there you have it – the business case for SEO reporting. Whether you're a small business owner wearing all the hats, or part of a large corporate team, understanding and using SEO reports can be a game-changer.

Remember, knowledge is power, and in the world of digital marketing, SEO reports are your power source. They turn the often-mysterious world of search engine optimization into concrete data that can inform decisions, guide strategy, and ultimately, boost your bottom line.

Let us dive deeper into the world of SEO reporting. In the next section, we will look at the key metrics you should be tracking to get the full picture of your SEO performance.

Key Metrics for SEO Reporting

Now that we know why SEO reporting is so important, let us talk about what exactly we should be measuring. Think of these metrics as the vital signs of your website's health. Just like a doctor checks your heart rate and blood pressure, you will be checking these key indicators to see how your site is doing.

Organic Traffic: Your Website's Visits Count

- **What it is**: This is the number of people who find your website through search engines (not through ads or direct visits).
- **Why it matters**: More organic traffic usually means your SEO efforts are working. It is like having a busy store – the more people coming in, the more chances you have to make sales or achieve your goals.
- **How to use it**: Look for trends over time. Is your traffic growing month over month? Are there any sudden drops or spikes you need to investigate?
- **Advanced**: Measure organic traffic on sections of your website, pages you optimized, divide between branded SEO traffic and non-branded SEO traffic.

Keyword Rankings: Your Position in the Search Race

- **What it is:** This shows where your website appears in search results for specific keywords.
- **Why it matters**: The higher you rank, the more likely people are to click on your site. Being on the first page of Google is like having a shop on the main street instead of a back alley.
- **How to use it**: Track rankings for your most important keywords. Look for opportunities to improve lower rankings and celebrate (but don't get complacent about) high rankings.
- **Advanced**: Compare keyword rankings with your competition, track average position on certain keyword groups.

Click-Through Rate (CTR): Are People Choosing You?

- **What it is**: Out of all the people who see your site in search results, how many actually click on it?
- **Why it matters**: A high CTR means your title tags and meta descriptions are doing their job – they are enticing people to visit your site.
- **How to use it**: If you have a low CTR for a high-ranking keyword, it might be time to optimize your meta title and description. Make them more compelling!
- **Advanced**: Look at pages with high impression and low CTR% and create a plan to optimize these pages for CTR%.

Bounce Rate: Are Visitors Sticking Around?

- **What it is**: The percentage of people who leave your site after viewing only one page.
- **Why it matters**: A high bounce rate could mean that visitors are not finding what they are looking for on your site. It is like people walking into your store and immediately walking out.
- **How to use it**: Look at bounce rates for different pages. If some have particularly high bounce rates, they might need some improvement in content or user experience.
- **Advanced**: Look at the search queries for pages with high bounce rate. Is the webpage relevant for the user typing in the search query?
- **Nice to know**: GA4 doesn't bounce rate, but instead looks at engagement rate.

Average Time on Page: Are People Actually Reading?

- **What it is**: How long, on average, visitors spend on a particular page.
- **Why it matters**: Generally, the longer someone spends on your page, the more engaged they are with your content.

- **How to use it**: Compare time on page across different types of content. Which topics keep people reading longer? This can guide your content strategy.
- **Advanced**: Include scroll tracking in your analytics setup to find if user are scrolling on your webpages.

Page Load Speed: How Fast is Your Site?

- **What it is**: How quickly your web pages load for visitors.
- **Why it matters**: Slow sites frustrate users and can hurt your search rankings. Google likes speedy sites!
- **How to use it**: If your pages are loading slowly, it might be time for some technical optimization. Every second counts!
- **Advanced**: Have a look at the evolution of core web vitals.

Conversion Rate: Are Visitors Taking Action?

- **What it is**: The percentage of visitors who complete a desired action on your site (like making a purchase or filling out a contact form).
- **Why it matters**: This is where SEO turns into actual business results. A good conversion rate means your SEO is bringing in the right kind of traffic.
- **How to use it**: Track conversion rates for different types of traffic and landing pages. This can help you focus your SEO efforts on what's actually driving business results.
- **Advanced**: Map keywords to conversions or use your Search Engine Advertising campaigns to find high converting keywords.

SEO Reporting Tools: Your Digital Swiss Army Knife

Now that we know what to measure, let us talk about the cool gadgets that help us do the measuring. Think of these tools as your SEO Swiss Army knife – each one has different features to help you tackle various aspects of SEO reporting.

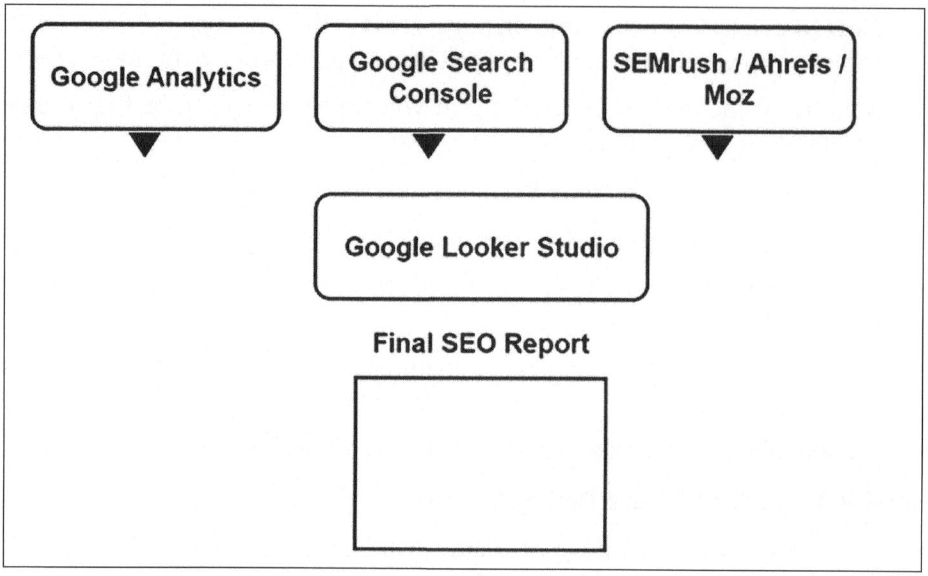

***Figure 11.1**: SEO reporting tools*

- **Google Analytics: The Free Powerhouse**

  Google Analytics is like having a super-smart robot counting and analyzing every visitor to your site. And the best part? It is totally free! This tool tracks your organic traffic, bounce rates, and time on page, showing you which parts of your site are the most popular. It is also great for understanding your audience – where they are from, what devices they use, and how they navigate your site.

  Pro tip: Set up goals in Google Analytics to track conversions. It is like giving your robot assistant a checklist of what success looks like for your site.

  Some alternatives to Google Analytics are Piwik or Adobe analytics.

- **Google Search Console: Your Direct Line to Google**

  Imagine having a backstage pass to how Google sees your site – that's Google Search Console for you. Another free tool from Google, it shows you which queries are bringing people to your site and alerts you to any technical issues Google finds. You can even use it to submit sitemaps and individual URLs for crawling, giving you more control over how Google interacts with your site.

  Pro tip: Check the "`Performance`" report regularly to spot trends in your click-through rates and average positions. It's like getting a regular health check-up for your site's search performance.

- **The Power Trio: SEMrush, Ahrefs, and Moz**

  Now, if you are ready to level up your SEO game, you might want to consider one of the big players in the SEO tools world: SEMrush, Ahrefs, or Moz. These are comprehensive SEO toolkits that cover everything from keyword research to competitor analysis.

These cloud-based software products all offer similar core features: tracking your rankings for hundreds of keywords, providing detailed site audits to find technical SEO issues, and offering competitor analysis tools.

Ahrefs is particularly strong in backlink analysis - it is like having X-ray vision for backlinks. SEMrush shines in its keyword research capabilities and competitive intelligence tools. Moz, one of the pioneers in the SEO software world, offers a user-friendly interface and is known for its Page Optimization Score feature, which gives you quick wins for on-page SEO.

While the tools are similar to each other, each of these tools also has its own unique strengths. The choice often comes down to personal preference and specific needs. They all offer free trials, so don't be afraid to take them for a spin and see which one feels right for you.

Pro tip: Whichever tool you choose, make sure to look into their learning resources. These companies offer a wealth of tutorials, guides, and even certification programs that can help you become an SEO reporting pro.

- **Google Looker Studio: The Report Builder**

  Last but not least, let us talk about Google Looker Studio. This free tool is like being able to paint with data. You can turn all those numbers from Google Analytics and Search Console into beautiful, interactive reports that are easy to read and share.

  The best part? Once you set up a report, it updates automatically. No more spending hours every month copying and pasting data into spreadsheets. You can connect Data Studio with various data sources, create custom dashboards, and easily share reports with team members or clients.

  Pro tip: Start with one of their templates to get a feel for how it works, then customize to your heart's content. Before you know it, you will be creating reports that would make any data scientist proud!

  Remember, you don't need to use all of these tools at once. Start with the free Google tools (Analytics and Search Console) and then explore others as you get more comfortable with SEO reporting. Each tool has its strengths, so choose the ones that best fit your needs and budget.

Know Your Audience: Tailoring SEO Reports for Maximum Impact

Before you dive into creating your SEO report, take a moment to consider who will be reading it. Understanding your audience is crucial for creating a report that not only informs but also resonates and drives action. Let us explore how you can tailor your reports for different audiences to ensure your insights hit home.

The C-Suite: Executive Realness

When your report is destined for the big bosses – we are talking CEO, CMO, or other C-level executives - you need to think big picture and bottom line. These high-flyers care about how SEO is impacting overall business goals, the ROI of SEO efforts, and how you are positioning against competitors in the market.

For this audience, keep it brief. Executives are busy people, so aim for a one-page summary of key metrics and insights. Focus on business impact by translating SEO metrics into business terms. Don't just report a 20% increase in organic traffic; show how that translated to increased revenue or leads. And remember, a picture is worth a thousand words. Use well-designed charts to convey trends much faster than paragraphs of text ever could.

Here is an example of how you might present information to the C-suite: "*Our SEO initiatives have driven a 30% increase in organic traffic, resulting in 250 additional qualified leads this quarter. This puts us ahead of our main competitor in organic search visibility for our top 5 product categories.*"

The Marketing Team: Strategy Central

Your marketing colleagues need more detailed information to inform their strategies and day-to-day decisions. They are interested in the performance of different content types and campaigns, keyword trends and opportunities, and insights into user behavior.

When reporting to the marketing team, don't be afraid to provide more detail. Break down performance by different marketing channels and initiatives. Offer actionable insights by giving specific recommendations for content creation or optimization. Show trends over time to help them understand what's working and what's not.

For instance, you might tell your marketing team: "*Our 'Ultimate Guide to Home Brewing' blog post has generated 45% of our organic blog traffic this month. We recommend creating similar in-depth guides for our top 5 product categories to capitalize on this success.*"

The Development Team: Tech Talk

When reporting to the dev team, it's all about the technical nitty-gritty. These code wizards are concerned with site speed and performance issues, crawlability and indexation problems, and mobile optimization opportunities.

Be specific when talking to developers. Provide exact URLs, error codes, and technical specifications. Help them understand which problems are most critical from an SEO perspective by prioritizing issues. And make sure you are speaking their language - use technical terms accurately and provide context for SEO-specific concepts.

You might report to the dev team like this: "*The average load time for product pages on mobile devices is 5.2 seconds, well above the recommended 3 seconds. Implementing lazy loading for images could potentially reduce this by 40%, significantly improving our mobile user experience and search rankings.*"

The Client: Value Demonstration

If you are agency-side, your reports need to clearly demonstrate the value you're providing. Clients care about progress towards agreed-upon KPIs, how SEO efforts are impacting their business goals, and clear justification for ongoing investment in SEO.

When reporting to clients, always align with their goals by tying your reporting back to their specific objectives. Educate gently – do not assume they understand all SEO concepts, but explain things clearly without being condescending. Show your work by highlighting the specific actions you have taken and their results. Also ask the client what he would like to see in the report.

For a client, you might report: "*By optimizing your product descriptions and implementing schema markup, we have increased your click-through rate from search results by 25%. This has led to a 15% increase in product page visits and a 10% boost in online sales.*"

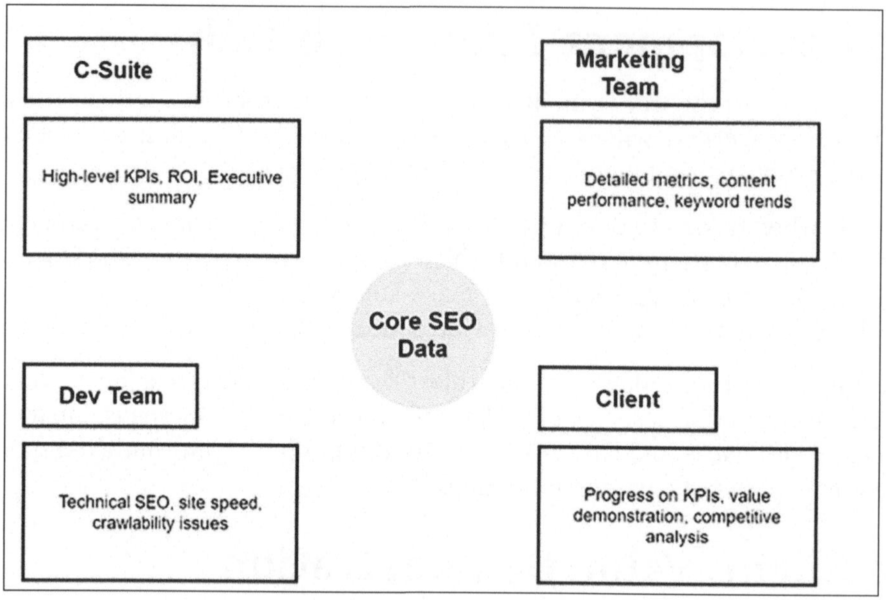

Figure 11.2: *Reporting to stakeholders*

Remember, effective SEO reporting is not just about what you say, but how you say it. By tailoring your reports to your specific audience, you ensure that your insights don't just get read, but drive real action and results. So, before you start your next SEO report, take a moment to consider your audience. What do they care about most? What level of detail do they need? How can you present your insights in a way that will resonate with them? Answer these questions (or even ask them to the client), and you will be well on your way to creating SEO reports that truly make an impact.

Data Visualization: Making Stories Out of Data

Let us face it: SEO reports can be a sea of numbers. But with the right data visualization techniques, you can turn those numbers into compelling stories that captivate your audience and drive action. Let us dive into some best practices for creating visuals that pack a punch in your SEO reports.

Choose the Right Chart for Your Data

Not all data is created equal, and neither are charts. Picking the right type of visualization can make or break your message. Here are some go-to charts for common SEO metrics:

- **Line Charts**: Perfect for showing trends over time. Use these for metrics like organic traffic, rankings, or conversions over weeks or months.

Example: A line chart showing organic traffic growth over the past 12 months, with annotations for major SEO initiatives.

- **Bar Charts**: Great for comparing values across categories. Use these for comparing performance across different pages, keywords, or channels.

  Example: A horizontal bar chart showing the top 10 landing pages by organic traffic.

- **Pie Charts**: Use sparingly! They're good for showing composition when you have just a few categories that sum to 100%.

  Example: A pie chart showing the distribution of organic traffic by device type (desktop, mobile, and tablet).

Remember, the goal is to make your data easy to understand at a glance. If you are spending more time explaining your chart than discussing insights, it might be time to rethink your visualization choice.

Declutter Your Charts

When it comes to data visualization, less is often more. Here is how to keep your charts clean and focused:

- **Remove Chart Junk**: Get rid of unnecessary gridlines, borders, and backgrounds. Let your data take center stage.
- **Use Color Strategically**: Stick to a simple color palette. Use bold colors to highlight key data points and muted colors for context.
- **Simplify Labels**: Don't crowd your chart with labels. Use clear, concise labeling and consider moving detailed information to a legend or footnote.

For instance, instead of labeling every point on a 12-month organic traffic line chart, consider labeling just the first and last months, and any significant peaks or troughs.

Storytelling

Great data visualization is not just about making pretty charts–it is about telling a compelling story. Here is how to narrativize your SEO data:

- **Provide Context:** Don't just show what happened; show why it matters. If organic traffic spiked in March, was it because of a successful content campaign or an algorithm update?
- **Highlight Key Insights**: Use callouts, annotations, or color to draw attention to the most important parts of your visualization.
- **Order Matters**: Arrange your data in a way that makes sense. For bar charts, consider ordering bars by value rather than alphabetically to make comparisons

easier. For example, if you are showing keyword ranking improvements, order keywords from highest to lowest improvement, and use color to highlight the top 3 gainers.

Make it Interactive (When Appropriate)

If you are creating digital reports, consider making your visualizations interactive. This can allow your audience to explore the data themselves. Tools like Google Looker Studio or Tableau can create interactive dashboards where users can filter data, hover for more details, or click to drill down into specifics.

For instance, you could create a dashboard where clicking on a specific keyword in a ranking chart brings up detailed performance metrics for that keyword.

Design for Your Audience

Remember our earlier discussion about knowing your audience? This applies to data visualization too. Here is how to tailor your visuals:

- **For Executives**: Focus on high-level trends and bottom-line impact. A simple line chart showing the correlation between organic traffic and revenue could be perfect.
- **For Marketing Teams**: Provide more detailed breakdowns. A stacked bar chart showing traffic by channel and content type could offer valuable insights.
- **For Dev Teams**: Get technical. A scatter plot showing the relationship between page load time and bounce rate could drive home the importance of site speed.

Test Your Visualizations

Before finalizing your report, put your visualizations to the test. Can someone understand the main point within 5 seconds of looking at your chart? If not, it might need simplifying.

Try the squint test: If you squint at your chart, does the main message still come through? This can help you identify if you're effectively using size, color, and placement to highlight key information.

Remember, the goal of data visualization in SEO reporting isn't to show how much data you have – it is to clearly communicate insights that drive action. By following these best practices, you will create SEO reports that not only inform but also engage and inspire your audience.

Mastering SEO Report Communication: Action Titles and Pyramid Structure

When it comes to SEO reporting, how you present your information is just as important as the information itself. Two powerful techniques can help you create reports that are both engaging and easy to understand: action titles and pyramid communication. Let us break these down and see how they can supercharge your SEO reports.

Action Titles: Your Report's Secret Weapon

Think of action titles as the movie trailers of your SEO report. They give a sneak peek of what's to come and get your audience excited about the content. But what exactly are they?

Action titles are descriptive headings that not only introduce a section but also convey its key message or the action it's promoting. They are dynamic, engaging, and give your reader a clear idea of what to expect.

Here is how to create effective action titles:

- **Start with a verb**: This immediately conveys action and tells the reader what to do.
- **Be specific**: Avoid vague phrases and instead focus on the particular insight or action.
- **Keep it concise**: Aim for about 5-7 words. You want it punchy, not wordy.
- **Make it benefit-oriented**: Show the value or outcome of the section.

Let us look at some examples:

- Instead of: "*Traffic Analysis*" Use: "**`SEO delivers 30% of traffic - Keep optimizing`**"
- Instead of: "*Keyword Performance*" Use: "**`Improved Rankings for High-Potential Keywords`**"
- Instead of: "*Technical* SEO *Issues*" Use: "**`Accelerate Site Speed: Fix Critical Technical Roadblocks`**"

By using action titles, you are not just organizing your report – you are guiding your reader through it and highlighting the most important takeaways.

Pyramid Communication: Building Your SEO Story

Now, let us talk about the structure of your report. Ever heard of the inverted pyramid style in journalism? It is a technique where the most important information comes first, followed by supporting details. In SEO reporting, we're going to flip that pyramid right-side up.

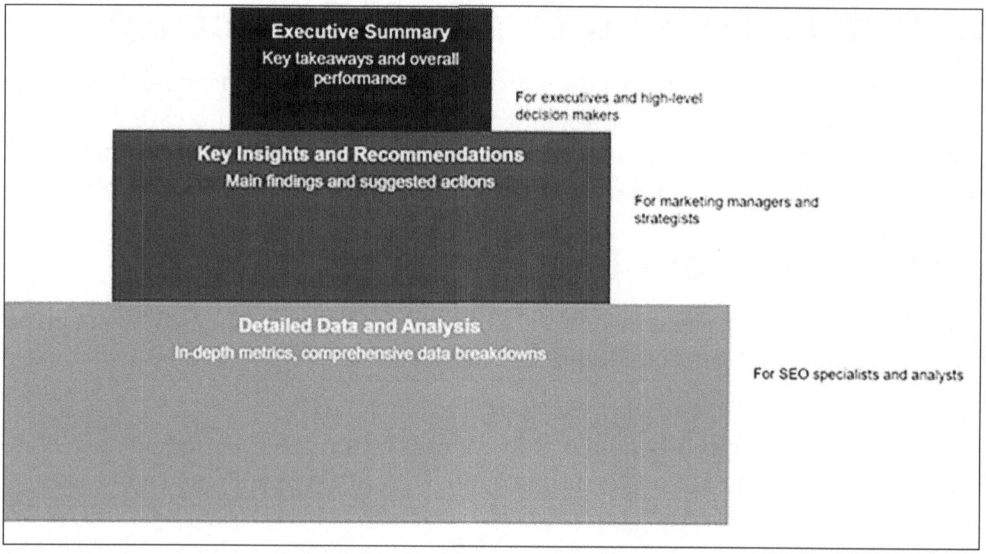

Figure 11.3: *Pyramid communication*

Pyramid communication in SEO reporting means starting with a broad overview and then drilling down into more specific details. Here is how it works:

- **The Peak (Executive Summary)**: Start with the big picture. What are the key takeaways? What is the overall trend in your SEO performance? Example: "*Our SEO efforts have driven a 30% increase in organic traffic this quarter, resulting in 15% more conversions.*"
- **The Middle (Key Insights and Recommendations)**: Next, provide your main insights and top-level recommendations. What are the most important things you've discovered, and what actions should be taken? Example: "*Mobile traffic has surged 50%, but our mobile conversion rate lags behind desktop. We recommend prioritizing mobile optimization for our top-selling product pages.*"
- **The Base (Detailed Data and Analysis)**: Finally, dive into the nitty-gritty. Provide detailed metrics, in-depth analysis, and specific action items. Example: "*Include a breakdown of mobile versus desktop traffic for each product category, page load times for mobile devices, and a prioritized list of mobile optimization tasks*".

This structure works because it caters to different reading styles and time constraints. Executives can get what they need from the peak, managers can dig into the middle, and SEO specialists can explore the base.

Putting it All Together

Now, let us see how action titles and pyramid communication work together in a real SEO report section:

Action Title: Increase mobile engagement for growing smartphone audience

1. **Peak** (Executive Summary): "*Mobile traffic has grown 50% this quarter, now accounting for 65% of all site visits. However, mobile conversion rates are 30% lower than desktop, representing a significant growth opportunity.*"
2. **Middle** (Key Insights and Recommendations):
   - "*Top 5 product pages show 70% higher bounce rates on mobile compared to desktop.*"
   - "*Mobile users spend 40% less time on site than desktop users.*"
   - "*Recommend mobile-first redesign of product pages to boost engagement and conversions.*"
3. **Base** (Detailed Data and Analysis):
   - Detailed breakdown of mobile versus desktop metrics for each product category.
   - Analysis of mobile user behavior flow.
   - Specific UX issues identified through mobile usability testing.
   - Prioritized list of mobile optimization tasks with estimated impact and effort required.

By structuring your report this way and using compelling action titles, you are not just sharing data – you are telling a story about your SEO performance and providing a clear roadmap for improvement.

Remember, the goal of your SEO report is not just to inform, but to inspire action. With action titles and pyramid communication, you are well on your way to creating reports that do just that.

Conclusion

We have explored the importance of SEO reporting, learned how to craft impactful reports, and gained insights into key metrics and visualizations. With this knowledge, you're well-equipped to become an SEO reporting superstar. Let us take a moment to recap the key takeaways:

- SEO reporting is not just about numbers – it is about telling the story of your website's performance and guiding future strategies.

- Knowing your audience is crucial. Whether you are reporting to C-suite executives, marketing teams, dev teams, or clients, tailoring your report to their needs and interests is key.
- The right tools can make your life a whole lot easier. From Google Analytics and Search Console to comprehensive platforms like SEMrush or Ahrefs, choose the tools that best fit your needs and budget.
- Data visualization is your secret weapon. A well-crafted chart or graph can convey complex information at a glance and make your insights more impactful.
- Structure matters. Using action titles and pyramid communication can transform your report from a data dump into a compelling narrative.

Remember, the goal of SEO reporting is not just to show what happened – it is to provide insights that drive action. Your reports should answer the "*So what?*" *and* "*What now?*" questions, guiding your team or clients towards smarter SEO decisions.

As you put these techniques into practice, don't be afraid to experiment and find what works best for you and your audience. SEO reporting is as much an art as it is a science, and your style will evolve as you gain more experience.

Most importantly, keep in mind that behind all the metrics and charts are real people – the users visiting your site, the stakeholders reading your reports, and you, the SEO professional making it all happen. Your reports have the power to influence decisions, shape strategies, and ultimately, improve user experiences.

So go forth and report with confidence! Whether you are celebrating wins, identifying opportunities, or navigating challenges, your SEO reports are your chance to showcase the value of your work and drive your digital presence forward.

Who knows? With your newfound reporting skills, you might just find yourself looking forward to your next SEO report. After all, there is nothing quite like the satisfaction of seeing those trend lines moving in the right direction and knowing you played a part in making it happen.

Index

Symbols

<head> 31
<loc> 23
<url> 23

A

Ansoff Matrix 119

B

B2B Keyword Research 51
B2B Keyword Research, aspects
  Decision-Maker Habits 51
  Decision Stages, considering 51
  Niche Targeting 51
  quality over quantity 52
B2B Keyword Research, strategies
  buyer, mapping 52
  competitors, analyzing 52
  industry jargon 52
  Linkedin, leveraging 52
  Long-Tail, utilizing 52
  problem-solving 52
Backlink 78
Backlink, advantages 87
Backlink Audits, maintenance 83, 84
Backlink, benefits
  authority, establishing 80
  discoverability, aiding 80
  relationship, building 81
  search engine, boosting 80
  traffic, driving 80
Backlink, characteristics 79
Backlink, importance 84, 85
Backlink, insights 85, 86
Backlink Quality, importance 81
Backlink Quality, key factors
  authority 82
  link placement 82
  Relevance 82
Backlink, techniques
  collaborations 87
  content, marketing 86
  guest, blogging 86
  influencer outreach 86
  PR, campaigns 87
  press, releasing 87
Backlink, types
  directories 79
  editorial 78
  forum/comment 79
  natural 78
  outreach 78
  partnerships 78
  self-create 78
  social media 78
bad strategy 115
bad strategy, framework
  Coherent, actions 116
  Diagnosis 116
  guiding policy 116
Bing 110
Bing SEO 174
Brand Authority 88
Brand Authority, steps

leaders, engaging 89
niche, defining 89
personal brand 89
personal, branding 89
relevant groups, conversions 89
valuable content 89
Brand Authority, strategies
community, engaging 88
influencers, collaborating 88
multimedia, utilizing 88
outreach, leverage 88
user-generate content, promoting 88
valuable content 88

C

Competitor Analysis 138, 139
content audit, actions
action, required 136
Clicks/Impressions 136
comments/feedback 136
CTR 136
Keyword 136
method, indicating 136
rankings 136
relevance, maintaining 136
URL 136
content audit, steps
content, planning 138
content, prioritize 138
content quality, relevance 138
data performance, analyzing 137
gaps, identifying 138
content calendar 140, 141
Content, inventory 135
Content Strategy 129
Content Strategy, steps
audience 130
content audit 130
content, distributing 131, 132
content plan 131
content, reporting 132
goals, defining 130
tone voice, defining 131
Content, types
blog posts 134
calculation 134
case studies 135
category 134
E-books 135
FAQ, sections 134
how-to guides 134
infographics 135
newsletters 135
SEO 134
videos 134
webinars 135
Core Web Vitals, actions
image, optimizing 151
render-block, minimizing 151
resources, prioritizing 151
server response time 151
Core Web Vitals, key reasons
conversion rates, enhancing 148
crawling 148
mobile, experience 148
signals, ranking 147
user metrics, engaging 148
Core Web Vitals, steps 151
Core Web Vitals, tools
GTmetrix 149
Pingdom 149
Real User Monitoring (RUM) 149
WebPageTest 149

D

Data-Driven, copywriting 71, 72
Data Visualization, practices
audience, visualizing 196
chart data, choosing 194
Declutter 195
Storytelling 195
test, visualizing 196
Duplicate Content 28
Duplicate Content, issues 29
Duplicate Content, types
External 28
internal 28

E

E-E-A-T 69
E-E-A-T, aspects
authoritativeness 69
experience 69
expertise 69
Trustworthiness 70

G

GBP, platforms 109
GBP Reviews, implementing 106
GBP Reviews, managing 106, 107
GBP, strategies
consistent, information 110
content fresh, keeping 110
keyword, optimizing 110
platform-specific, utilizing 110
reviews, engaging 110
user interaction, encouraging 110
Generative AI 177
good strategy 114, 115
good strategy, components
Coherent, actions 115
Diagnosis 115
policy, guiding 115
Google, aspects
BERT 7
EAT 7
EEAT 7
Hummingbird 7
Mobilegeddon 7
Panda 7
Penguin 7
RankBrain 7
Google Business Profile (GBP) 102, 103
Google Business Profile, reasons
customer insights, comprehending 105
SEO, enhancing 105
Trust Credibility, building 105
Google Business Profile, steps 103, 104
Google, history 6
Google Index, process 20, 21
Google Index, steps
crawle 22
discovering 22
HTTP, handling 22
post-rendering 23
Google, notable features
Ads 8
image, results 8
initial query 8
Knowledge Graph 8
Local Pack 8
Snippets 8
Google Search Console (GSC) 17
Grouping Keyword 43, 44
GSC, setting up 17-19

H

Human-AI Collaboration 179
Human-AI Collaboration, ways 179, 180

I

identifying keyword 40
identifying keyword, strategies
  competitors 40
  drill down 40
  geographical variations 41
  Google, trends 40
  keyword list, finalizing 41
  keyword, planner 40
  keyword tools, exploring 41
  match, keywords 41
  online forums 41
  stages, intention 41
  start with what 40
  team client 41
Indexation, configuring 31
Indexation Puzzle, preventing 32
Internal Linking 75, 76
Internal Linking, impact 77
Internal Linking, strategies
  Anchor Text, utilizing 76
  breadcrumb navigation, incorporating 77
  content silos, implementing 77
  high-priority, prioritizing 76
  internal links, maintaining 77
  link quantity, balancing 76
  link value, optimizing 77
  logical site structure 76

K

Keyword Density/Intent, comparing 58-60
Keyword Research 35
Keyword Research, categorizing 42, 43
Keyword Research, goals
  relevant content 35
  reporting 35
  search engines, enhancing 35
  SEO, optimizing 35
Keyword Research, opportunities
  intent, searches 47
  lightweight, running 46
  platform-specific trends 46
Keyword Research, steps 35-37
Keyword Research, strategy
  business, model 39
  client, knowing 39
  field, operation 39
  persona, audience 39
  product, services 39
  purpose 39
  SEO Tools, existing 39
  USPs 39
Keyword Research, types
  Geographically Target 38
  Informational 37
  Long-Tail 37
  Navigational 37
  Short-Tail 37
  Transactional 37

L

Large Language Models (LLMs) 171
Lean Startup 124, 125
Link Building, case studies 91
Link Building, dashboard
  growth over time 93
  rank, improving 93
  referral, traffic 93
  score, authority 93
Link Building, key points
  link, diversity 92
  page, authority 92
  quantity/quality 92
  referral, traffic 92
  search engine, ranking 92

Link Building, purposes
guides, strategy 92
investment, justifies 92
transparency, enhancing 92
LLMs, aspects
ChatGPT 171
ELIZA 171
LLMs, challenges 172
LLMs, future trends 172, 173
Local Search Engine Optimization (Local SEO) 96, 97
Local SEO 175
Local SEO, advantages 176
Local SEO, aspects
advertise, strategy 176
index 175
keywords, visitors 176
Local SEO, importance 98, 99
Local SEO, key differences
geographical, targeting 97
local, keywords 97
profile, optimizing 97
Local SEO, key points
conversion rate 111
customer, reviews 111
profile, insights 111
search, visibility 111
website, traffic 111
Local SEO Keywords 99
Local SEO Keywords, key aspects
Geo-Targeted Phrases 99
Local Intent 99
Local SEO Rankings 100
Local SEO Rankings, ways
geographical, factors 100
local link, building 100
Map Pack, ranking 100
profile, listings 100
Local SEO, tools
BrightLocal 112
GBPI 112
Google Analytics 111
Localfalcon 112
Uberall 112
Local SEO, ways 108
Local Web Page, optimizing 101, 102

M

Map Pack 97, 98
Metatags 30
Metatags, optimizing 56-58

N

NAP 109
Non-SMART/SMART Goals, comparing 117

O

Objectives and Key Results (OKRs) 117
OKRs, steps 118

P

PageSpeed, issues 150
Prompt Engineering 177, 178

Q

Quality Content 55
Quality Content, roles
algorithm development 55
E-E-A-T 55
SEO Strategies, impact 56
SQR, optimizing 55

R

Real-Life Ranking Signals 181
Real-Life Ranking Signals, impact
real-life, visits 182
website, usage 181
REBUS Framework 165
REBUS Framework, issues 166, 167
REBUS Framework, parts
business, value 166
reasons 165
solution 166
stakeholder, configuring 166
Robots.txt 25-27
Robots.txt With Crawl Budget, optimizing 27

S

SAAS, parts
  climax 68
  Exposition 68
  fall action 69
  resolution 69
  rising action 68
SAAS, steps
  audience 67
  call-to-action, directing 67
  crafting 67
  engagement, ensuring 67
  relatable elements, emphasizing 67
  seamless, integrating 67
  tailoring 67
Search Engine Optimization (SEO) 1
Search Quality Rater 71
Search Quality Rater, points
  content creator 71
  content, maintenance 71
  E-E-A-T 71
  high quality main content 71
  page purpose 71
SEA/SEO, comparing 49
SEA, strategy 50
SEO, advantages
  Ever-Evolve, challenges 6
  High Intent 5
  Long-Term Results 5
  market, efforts 5
  Measurable 6
  Organic Traffic 4
  Trust, credibility 5
  user experience, enhancing 6
SEO, architectures 66, 67
SEO, equipment
  diversification 120
  market, developing 120
  market penetration 120
  product, developing 120
SEO, fields
  Content SEO 2
  Off-page SEO 3
  Technical SEO 2
SEO Google, tools
  Chrome DevTools 149
  network panel 149
  PageSpeed Insights 148
  UX, report 149
SEO Industry 180
SEO Industry Data, analyzing 180
SEO Market, analyzing 124
SEO, optimizing 3, 4
SEO, rank factors
  backlinks 10
  content, freshness 10
  high quality, content 10
  internal links 10
  mobile-friendliness 11
  On-page, optimizing 11
  search intent 10
  trust, authority 11
  website load, speed 11
  website, security 11
SEO Reporting 187-189
SEO Reporting, impact
  Realness Executive 192
  strategy central 192
  value, demonstration 193, 194
SEO Reporting, importance 185-187
SEO Reporting, tools
  Google Analytics 190
  Google Looker Studio 191
  Google Search Console 190
  Power Trio 190
SEO Report, structures
  Pyramid Communication 197
  Secret Weapon 197
SEO Return, compounding 12, 13
SEO, scenario 11
SEO Strategy Resources, types
  business resources 122
  content resources 122
  technical resources 122

SEO Strategy, topics
  competitive, analysis 122
  customer-centric, content 122
  trend, adaptation 122
SEO, techniques
  articles, length 64
  Bullet Points 64
  headlines/subheadings 63, 64
  Long-Tail Keywords 64
SEO With ROI, calculating 13, 14
SERP 46
SERP, strategy 47, 48
sitemap.xml 23, 24
sitemap.xml, content
  allow/disallow, directives 25
  sitemap, reference 25
  user-agent, declaring 25
Stakeholder Management 125
Stakeholder Management, categories
  operational profiles 127
  strategic profiles 127
Stakeholder Management, ways
  content, creating 126
  market manager 126
  senior, managing 127
  UX/UI, designing 127
  web, developing 126
Stakeholders, steps
  collaborative tools 142
  content creation, workflow 142
  editorial, guidelines 142
  feedback, iterating 143
  multi-channel, distributing 142
  performance, tracking 143
  publication, scheduling 142
  SEO, optimizing 142
status codes 19
status codes, key points
  200 OK 19
  301 Move Permanently 19
  404 Not Found 19
  503 Service 20
Structured Data 144, 145
Structured Data, types 145
SurferSEO 73
SurferSEO, key features 73
SWOT Analysis 121

T

Technical SEO Audit 157
Technical SEO Audit, parts 158, 159
Technical SEO Audit, types
  Business-Proof 160, 161
  Savvy SEO 161
Technical SEO Audit, ways 163, 164
Technical SEO, process 164, 165
TikTok 173
TikTok, architectures
  content, optimizing 173
  cross-promotion 174
  metrics, engaging 174
  performance, analyzing 174
  SEO-Friendly, content 173
  trends, participating 173
  user profiles, optimizing 173
TikTok, structures 174
topic cluster 61
topic cluster, benefits 62
topic cluster, structure 61

U

URL inspection 19

W

Website Migration 152, 153
Website Migration, steps 154, 155

Y

YouTube SEO 182, 183

Z

Zero-Click Searches 169, 170